T

TH

EUNUCHUS

THE CHARACTERS OF *THE EUNUCH*
Woodcut from *Terentius Comico Carmine*, Johann Grüninger, Strasbourg, 1503,
in the Founders' Library, University of Wales, Lampeter
(The lines indicate the relationships between the characters.)

TERENCE
THE EUNUCH

Edited with translation and commentary by

A. J. Brothers

Aris & Phillips Ltd – Warminster – England

ISBNs   0 85668 513 5   limp
             0 85668 512 7   cloth

British Library Cataloguing-in-Publication Data
A catalogue record of this book is available from the British Library

Printed and published in England by Aris & Phillips Ltd, Warminster, Wiltshire BA12 8PQ

FOR JOE AND TIM

Contents

Preface

When I began work on this edition of Terence's *The Eunuch* some years ago, no new full-scale edition of the play had appeared in Britain for over 100 years. The publication in 1999 of John Barsby's Cambridge edition changed that situation, and it will be apparent – even though this edition is somewhat different in its approach – how much, particularly in the commentary, I have benefited from the scholarship and acute judgement of his work. *The Eunuch* deserves a wide audience; it is to be hoped that this *desideratum* has now been achieved.

This is the second of Terence's plays which I have edited for Aris and Phillips, following on from *The Self-Tormentor* of 1988. Since I have found it all but impossible to re-write from scratch the general material I wrote then, Sections I-IV and VII of the Introduction to *The Eunuch* have been updated and adapted from the earlier work.

I am most grateful to Mr Adrian Phillips of Aris and Phillips Ltd for his stoical acceptance of the over-long delay in the completion of this edition, and I am greatly indebted to Aris and Phillips' Editorial Adviser, Professor M. M. Willcock, whose sharp eyes have removed many imperfections, and whose helpful suggestions and keen observations have improved the draft in so many ways. I record my thanks to several friends for their assistance over various matters, especially Mr Ian Barton, Dr Doug Lee, Professor Robert Maltby and Dr Emma Stafford; and I must make particular mention of Dr Demetrios Beroutsos, whose constant supply of information from the rich resources of Oxford has helped me immensely when pressure of work at my home University has kept me in West Wales. I am also grateful to the authorities of University of Wales, Lampeter for allowing me to reproduce the illustration which I have used as a frontispiece, and for granting me a term of study leave at an early stage in the preparation of the work. Finally, I could not have done without the help of Ms Bethan Ifans, who typed the whole work except the commentary with the greatest care and accuracy.

This book is dedicated to two very special people - to a staunch friend who is always there in good times and in bad, and to a splendid godson of whom I am so justly proud.

A. J. Brothers

Introduction

I   GREEK NEW COMEDY[1]

Terence's comedies are adaptations into Latin of Greek plays of the type known as New Comedy. Greek Comedy is conventionally divided into three periods called Old, Middle and New, though there was gradual and continuous development of the genre throughout. Old Comedy (to which most of Aristophanes' eleven surviving comedies belong) is the name for the type of comic drama produced at Athens down to about 400 BC, and Middle Comedy (of which Aristophanes' last two plays are our only examples) for that produced for about the first 75 years of the fourth century. New Comedy is "the name we give ... to the Greek plays (other than tragedies) written in the period following the death of Alexander the Great"[2] (323 BC).

By the New Comedy period Athens was no longer great and influential, but a city of comparatively little independent political importance in the kingdoms of Alexander's successors, and the old democratic freedom of speech which is such a feature of much of Aristophanes had gone forever. Accordingly, comedy became less and less concerned with satirical comment on prominent figures in public life and criticism of important topics of the moment, and more and more concerned with the less obviously appealing but much safer problems continually but timelessly raised in the fictional lives of ordinary people. New Comedy also dispensed with the scurrility and obscenity which had been features of Old Comedy, and the chorus, which had also featured prominently, was reduced to a role of virtual insignificance. Unfortunately, because of the absence of any texts worth speaking of between Aristophanes' last play, *Wealth* (Πλοῦτος, *Ploutos*) (388 BC), and our earliest datable example of New Comedy (317 BC), we know little about the rate of these changes or about the stages by which they occurred.

Until the beginning of this century our knowledge of New Comedy was almost exclusively derived from brief quotations preserved out of context by ancient grammarians and commentators, and from the Latin adaptations made by Plautus and Terence of lost originals from the period. But this situation began to change radically with the first substantial discovery of papyrus texts in 1905, and the discoveries have continued in fits and starts since.[3] The result has been one virtually

---

1   Our knowledge of New Comedy has been revolutionized by the discoveries of the last thirty or forty years, and older works on the subject are best avoided. The best short introduction is Sandbach (1977) chs 4 and 5.

2   Sandbach (1977) 55.

3   Gomme and Sandbach 3-4.

complete play, Menander's *The Bad-Tempered Man*[4] (Δύσκολος, *Dyskolos*), substantial portions of half a dozen others (particularly Menander's *The Girl from Samos* (Σαμία, *Samia*), where the gaps in our text do not prevent an appreciation of the play as a whole), and passages of a reasonable length from yet more. We can now form a first-hand, rather than a second-hand, impression of what New Comedy was like.

None of the really big discoveries so far made come from comedies which Plautus and Terence adapted.[5] But all of the major ones do at least come from the pen of the same writer of New Comedy as provided models for four of Terence's six plays - Menander. Of over 70 comic dramatists of whom we have evidence in this period, Menander is by far the most famous. An Athenian who lived from *c.* 342 to *c.* 291 BC, he began his dramatic career in 321, and wrote, according to one account, 108 plays altogether. During his lifetime his reputation did not stand all that high, with eight first prizes in dramatic competition - a respectable, but not a spectacular, record. Later in antiquity, however, he was regarded with an admiration which almost amounted to veneration, being particularly renowned for his excellence in character-drawing, his good plots and his mastery of language. Thus the learned scholar Aristophanes of Byzantium could say: "O Menander, o life, which of you imitated the other?", while Plutarch asked why any educated man would go to the theatre except to see Menander.[6]

Of the other writers of New Comedy we know much less than we do of Menander, and we possess few substantial passages from their works. Mention need only be made of one other, if only because he provided the originals for the other two of Terence's plays. He is Apollodorus of Carystus, a town on the island of

---

4   The English titles of Men.'s plays often exist in different versions. For instance, Miller prefers *Old Cantankerous* to *The Bad-Tempered Man*. With that one exception, I have adopted the English titles found in her Penguin translation.

5   The largest is a fragment of Men.'s *The Double Deceiver* (Δὶς 'Εξαπατῶν, *Dis Exapaton*) corresponding to Plautus' *The Two Bacchises* (*Bacchides*) 494-562. It contains 112 lines, about half of which are too incomplete to be intelligible, and is the first passage of any length where a real comparison of the Latin adaptation with its original is possible. It reveals considerable changes made by Plautus in his version, and serves as a warning of the perils of working back from adaptation to model. Text and translation, Arnott (1979) 140-65, Barsby (1986) 191-5; translation (with Plautus), Miller 171-81; comparison with Plautus, Sandbach (1977) 128-34, Barsby (1986), 139-45.

6   Körte II 7 (*testimonium* 32) and 9 (*testimonium* 41) respectively; the latter = Plutarch, *Moralia* 854B. Ter., for all his brilliance, was apostrophized by Caesar as only "half-sized Menander" (*dimidiate Menander*) (Suetonius, *Life of Terence* 7).

Euboea.[7] We are told he wrote 47 plays and won five victories; he probably became an Athenian citizen, and produced his first play about 285 BC.

One of the more important aspects of New Comedy for the student of Terence is the nature of the plays themselves. In form[8] these had five acts separated by song-and-dance routines performed by a chorus which otherwise took no part in the action of the play; the words it sang do not appear in our texts, the place for the songs merely being indicated by the presence of the Greek word meaning "[a performance] of the chorus" (χοροῦ, chorou) at the appropriate points. The number of speaking actors was probably limited to three, though some small parts could be taken by additional players.[9] The action was preceded (or interrupted early on, after one or two scenes) by an explanatory prologue which set the scene, introduced some of the principal characters, filled in some of the background to the plot and sometimes hinted at its outcome; the prologue-speaker was often some kind of divine or semi-divine figure who took no other part in the action, but whose privileged position enabled him (or her) to see the plot, and the misunderstandings and complications it usually involved, from the viewpoint of all the different characters at once.[10] As anyone who reads Roman comedy will quickly see, the chief alteration made to this form by Plautus and Terence in their adaptations is that they both dispensed with the chorus;[11] and, though Plautus sometimes retained the prologue in something like its New Comedy form, Terence substituted a prologue of a very different kind.[12]

As significant as the form of the plays is their content. They were normally set in Athens or one of the townships of Attica, and the scene usually represented a street backed by houses.[13] The action revolved around the fortunes of one or more

---

7   So called to distinguish him from another Apollodorus who wrote New Comedies, but came from Gela in Sicily.

8   With only one complete play, it is clearly impossible to be dogmatic about the form of New Comedy. But the general picture given by that play, on which my summary is based, has not been contradicted by any of the other texts which have been found.

9   This point has been the subject of some discussion; cf. Sandbach (1977) 78-80. For the problem as it applies to *The Bad-Tempered Man*, see Handley, E. W. (ed.) (1965), *The Dyskolos of Menander* (London) 25-30, Gomme and Sandbach 16-19, Ireland 5-6.

10   In the presence of the divine prologue, as in other features of New Comedy such as the monologue, it is usual to see the influence of Greek tragedy, especially Euripides, at work. A different type of prologue is sometimes found. In Men.'s *The Girl from Samos*, for example, the prologue (1-56) is spoken by one of the principal characters in the play, Moschion (Gomme and Sandbach 544-51, Miller 55-6). Whether Men.'s *The Eunuch* had a divine prologue has been much debated; see pp. 25–6 below.

11   Traces of the Greek chorus are held by some still to be present at places in Plautus, e.g. the flute player in *Pseudolus* (573-3a) and the chorus of fishermen in *The Rope* (*Rudens*) (290-305). A much less likely instance is to be found at Ter. *Hau.* 168-72.

12   Cf. Ter. *An.* 5-7, *Ad.* 22-4, and see further p. 16.

13   There are exceptions. For example, the original of Plautus' *The Rope* is set on the coast of Africa, with a cottage and a temple, while his *The Prisoners* (*Captivi*) is set in

middle-class families, with a love-affair almost invariably at the centre of the plot. All the characters were fictional, and the dialogue was almost entirely free of topical references except of the most innocent and incidental kind. In the plays stock motifs are frequently repeated, the same proper names for characters crop up again and again, and the characters themselves are generally variations on a number of stock 'types'. Prominent is the often impecunious free-born young man, around the difficulties of whose love-affair the plot revolves, and he may be assisted by a friend of similar age and class. In a society where marriages are arranged and free-born young men and women do not mix freely before they marry, the object of his affections is often a young girl who is supposedly a slave, or else a courtesan (ἑταίρα, *hetaira*) - who may be either money-grabbing and unscrupulous, or more kindly, with a genuine affection for him.[14] The young girl, sometimes already pregnant by the young man, is often during the course of the play discovered - through the not-uncommon motif of a 'recognition scene' - to be of free birth (having been exposed as a baby or captured by pirates at an early age), and the required happy ending is assured. In the case of the courtesan, if she is the unscrupulous type, she may be disposed of by parental decree and a more acceptable substitute provided to be the young man's wife, whereas, if she is kindly, the amorous attachment may be allowed to continue.[15] The young man's father usually opposes his son's affair unless and until the way is cleared for marriage, and is frequently represented as ill-tempered, disapproving, and mean with his considerable amount of money; he, too, often has a peer in the form of an elderly neighbour. But the son generally has an ally in the form of one of his father's slaves, who has a particular attachment to his young master and who shows great ingenuity in furthering the romance with the young girl or securing money (often from the unwitting father himself) to satisfy the expensive tastes of the courtesan; as a contrast to this smart city slave there is sometimes also a rather stupid but more conventionally loyal slave, often from the family's country estate. And so the list continues, with boastful soldiers who are often the young man's rivals in love, cooks continually talking about food, hard-bitten slave dealers or brothel keepers who have the young heroine in their clutches, parasites and flatterers, mothers who attempt a

---

Aetolia; Men.'s *The Bad-Tempered Man*, set in the country, requires two farmhouses and a shrine.

14   For the unscrupulous courtesan, see Bacchis in Ter.'s *Hau.*, and for the kindly one, Thais in Ter.'s *Eu.*, and, in a different situation, Chrysis in Men.'s *The Girl from Samos*. See also pp. 31–2.

15   See Plut. *Mor.* 712C: "Affairs with *hetairai*, if the women are headstrong and shameless, are cut short by some sort of chastening experience or repentance on the part of the young men, whereas, in the case of nice girls who reciprocate the love, either a legitimate father is found for them, or else additional time is given for the romance." The endings of Ter.'s *Hau.* and *Eu.* respectively point the contrast.

reconciliation between father and son, elderly family nurses who prove critical in the recognition scene, and so on.

It might be thought that such plays, with stock characters, frequently recurring motifs and situations, and a prologue which often hinted at what the ending would be, might be repetitious, dull and boring; but that, as Sandbach says,[16] is to misunderstand the nature of Greek art. What mattered to a Greek audience was not the playwright's destination (they knew anyway, since they were watching a comedy, that everyone would live happily ever after), but how he got there; the interest would be in the variations on the themes which he introduced on the journey.[17] Even leaving aside the plays of Plautus and Terence, where the possible presence of alterations makes judgement difficult, there is in what remains of New Comedy itself ample evidence of the variety and novelty, often of a most subtle kind, which a dramatist of the calibre of Menander could impart to character and to situation. Perhaps some writers of New Comedy did indeed produce dreary and predictable drama; but this would only serve to show how correct was antiquity's opinion of Menander's genius.

II   COMEDY AT ROME

Terence's adaptations of Greek New Comedy are known by the technical name (*fabulae*) *palliatae* "Greek-cloak plays", *palliatae* being coined from *pallium* "Greek cloak", and typifying the Greek setting and dress taken over with the originals. But Terence was not the first Latin writer to produce this type of play; for a proper picture of comedy at Rome, we need to look at his predecessors in the genre, and at the precursors of that genre in Italy.

The classic ancient account of the growth of drama (including comedy) at Rome is given by Livy (7.2.3-13), but it is generally accepted that this forms part of a fairly late tradition based on Greek antiquarian models, and is not to be trusted. However, Livy does mention in that account certain native forms which are at least akin to comic drama, and which probably antedate the production of the first *palliatae* and prepared the ground for the acceptance of that type of play.[18]

Among the most significant of these are Atellan farces (*fabulae*) *Atellanae*),[19] which were later included with other forms of entertainment as tail-pieces (*exodia*)

---

16   (1977) 62.

17   Whether the majority of a Roman audience, watching a Latin adaptation of one of these plays, would feel the same is another matter.

18   That is not to say that they are in any sense ancestors of drama proper at Rome, though the ancients certainly felt that they were, and they certainly coexisted with it. Much of our evidence for these native forms is late. See further Beare ch. II.

19   Beare ch. XVI.

after more substantial dramatic performances. These took their name from Atella, one of the Oscan towns of Campania where they first appeared in Italy, having perhaps developed from the Doric farces of the Greek colonies of the south. They achieved popularity early at Rome, where performances were in the hands of amateurs; later, however, they attained literary form.[20] We hear of two writers, L. Pomponius Bononiensis "of Bononia (Bologna)" (*fl. c.* 100-85 BC) and Novius (*fl. c.* 95-80 BC); surviving fragments of their work illustrate the coarseness of the genre. The plays seem to have been farcical masked performances, mainly illustrating provincial life, with stock characters such as Maccus ("the fool"), Pappus ("greybeard"), Bucco ("fat-cheeks") and Manducus ("champ-jaws").

There is another early form of dramatic expression, not mentioned in Livy's account - mime.[21] Like Atellan farce, this probably became widespread in southern Italy because of Greek influence, and this, too, later achieved literary form. Macrobius[22] preserves several anecdotes about its two chief writers, D. Laberius (*c.* 115-43 BC) and his contemporary Publilius Syrus, together with short passages of their work. We hear of troupes of mime actors (*mimi*) performing mimes, which soon rivalled Atellan farces in popularity as tail-pieces.

It was into a Rome where, according to most scholars, these forms of drama were already known that adaptations of Greek plays were introduced in 240 BC. That is the date of the first *palliata* (and of the first tragedy) of L. Livius Andronicus (*c.* 284-*c.* 204 BC), a Greek from Tarentum taken to Rome as a captive in 272 BC and subsequently freed.[23] It is generally assumed that the timing of this innovation was connected with the desire for a particularly memorable festival to celebrate the end of the First Punic War the previous year. After 240 BC Livius, who was also renowned for his Latin version of Homer's *Odyssey*, wrote other such plays, but we know the names of only three of his *palliatae*, and possess only about half a dozen lines, most of them incomplete.

Rome's second dramatist, Cn. Naevius (before 260-*c.* 200 BC), perhaps Campanian by birth, produced his first plays in 235 BC.[24] He too adapted both tragedies and comedies for the Roman stage, and also wrote the first native drama on Roman mythical or historical themes, and an epic poem on the First Punic War in which he had fought. We know the names of 35 of his *palliatae* and a number of short fragments survive. Naevius is said to have run into trouble as a result of attacks on prominent Romans - particularly the Metelli - which he included in his

---

20   Beare ch. XVII.
21   Beare ch. XVIII.
22   2.7.
23   Date: Cic. *Brut.* 72, *Sen.* 50, *Tusc.* 1.3; Gel. 17.21.42. A comedy and a tragedy:
      Cassiodorus' *Chronica*, though under the year 239 BC.
24   Gel. 17.21.45.

plays;[25] these led to imprisonment and later to exile. We are told he died in exile at Utica in North Africa.

The lessons of Naevius' punishment, if true, were not lost on the next dramatist, T. Maccius Plautus (*c.* 254-*c.* 184 BC),[26] whose plays contain only innocent contemporary allusions, one of which is actually to Naevius' imprisonment;[27] he wrote only *palliatae*, and was the first Roman writer so to specialize. Besides fragments, we possess twenty complete plays of his and an incomplete twenty-first. These are the 21 thought by the antiquarian M. Terentius Varro (116-27 BC) to be undoubtedly Plautine,[28] though he also ascribed others to him on grounds of style, and some plays not in Varro's list are said elsewhere to be by Plautus.[29]

Plautus took his models from Greek New Comedy,[30] using plays - where we know enough to say so - by Menander, Diphilus and Philemon among others; his choice shows considerable variety, embracing mythological burlesque, sentimental tragi-comedy, farce and domestic comedy. As far as we can tell without possessing his originals, he treated them with considerable freedom, sometimes seemingly almost as raw material, living from scene to scene and on occasion having little regard for the play as a whole. His plays contain frequent Roman puns and allusions, crudities and somewhat laboured clowning; slave roles are expanded, existing scenes lengthened and even occasionally new scenes inserted, causing inconsistencies and hold-ups in the action unthinkable in the Greek original. In this, his approach is very different from the one later adopted by Terence, who kept more closely to the spirit, if not the letter, of the Greek plays.

Plautus also differed from Terence in that, as if to compensate for his removal of the chorus, he included in many of his plays elaborate sung lyric passages, making the plays seem, as has often been suggested,[31] more like operas or musicals; there is evidence, necessarily small, that in this he was following Livius and Naevius, but, except for some short passages, Terence did not imitate him.[32]

---

25   But see Mattingly, H. B. (1960), 'Naevius and the Metelli', *Historia* 9, 414-39.

26   There is some doubt whether Plautus' gentile name (*nomen*) was Maccius or Maccus; but as Maccius is a known gentile name and Maccus was a character in Atellan farces, the former seems more likely, with the latter being a pun on the correct version. But see Gratwick, A. S. (1973), 'TITVS MACCIVS PLAVTVS', *CQ* ns 23, 78-84.

27   *The Swaggering Soldier* (*Miles Gloriosus*) 210-12.

28   This so-called 'Varronian recension' is dealt with at some length in Gel. 3.3.

29   E.g. Ter. mentions Plautus' *The Toady* (*Colax*) (*Eu.* 25 and n.) and *Joined in Death* (*Commorientes*) (*Ad.* 7), though neither appears in Varro's list.

30   It is possible that one or two may have been from Middle Comedy.

31   E.g. by Sandbach (1977) 120-1.

32   Ter. seems to experiment with such lyrics in his first play (*An.* 481-5, 625-38), then to give up; but he tries again in his last (*Ad.* 610-17).

The great Q. Ennius (239-169 BC), famous for his tragedies and the *Annals*, his epic poem on Rome's history, seems to have had little taste for comedy, since we only possess a very few fragments from the small number of *palliatae* he wrote, and the next comic poet of note is Caecilius Statius (*c*. 230-168 BC). Like Plautus, Caecilius wrote only *palliatae*, and, like Terence, he had difficulty at the start of his career;[33] he may also have begun a movement, followed by Terence and excessively vigorously advocated by Terence's critics,[34] towards greater faithfulness to the spirit of the Greek originals by cutting down on the puns, topical references etc. which are so typical of Plautus. We know the titles of over 40 of his comedies, and are fortunate to have preserved a comparison of three passages from his *The Necklace* (*Plocium*) with the relevant sections of its original by Menander of the same name (Πλόκιον).[35] Caecilius' successor was Terence, and after Terence we only hear of one other composer of *palliatae*, Sextus Turpilius (*c*. 180-103 BC).

About the time of Terence, another type of comedy arose at Rome, its plays known as (*fabulae*) *togatae* ("toga plays" from *toga*, the typical Roman dress, because their setting was purely Italian) or *tabernariae* (from *taberna*, a poor man's house, because they mainly portrayed lower-class life).[36] The theory that the emergence of *togatae* was a reaction against the increasingly Greek tone of *palliatae* is now largely discredited,[37] if only because both types existed side by side for over half a century; they are now seen as complementary, being parallel developments from the Romanized Greek plays of Plautus. Some 70 titles and about 600 lines have survived, the work of three dramatists, Titinius (perhaps Terence's contemporary), L. Afranius (born *c*. 150 BC, the most important of the three) and T. Quinctius Atta (died 77 BC); however, we cannot reconstruct a single plot. The Italian flavour of *togatae* is seen in the prominence of women, reflecting their higher status in Roman society, the absence of the clever slave, and the appearance of certain themes, such as paederasty, not found in Greek New Comedy. In one fragment Afranius expresses his indebtedness to Menander, and in another his admiration for Terence; these sentiments, coupled with his use of Greek proper names, may indicate the inability of the writers of *togatae* to break free from the influence of *palliatae*.

No more *palliatae* were written after the death of Turpilius, and no more *togatae* after that of Quinctius Atta, but the age of the theatre was not yet over. Literary Atellan farces were being written in Sulla's day, and literary mimes in Caesar's; and the age of Cicero was in many ways the golden age of Roman drama, when the audience knew its 'classics' and comic actors like the great Roscius could

---

33   Ter. *Hec.* 14-27.
34   See p. 20.
35   Gel. 2.23.
36   Duckworth 68-70; Beare ch. XV.
37   Duckworth 69; Beare 129.

make fortunes in their profession. References by writers like Quintilian[38] have been held to indicate that *palliatae* were occasionally revived under the early empire, but it was really only Atellan farces and mimes, and by the end of the first century AD only the latter (with the pantomime), which remained in vogue as regular entertainment. However, as theatre-goers' attentions were attracted elsewhere, a reading public arose for the more weighty drama, particularly in the so-called 'archaising age' of the second century AD, while during the next two centuries after that reading copies of the old dramatists continued to be made, especially for use in schools; it is significant that our earliest MSS of Plautus and Terence, and Donatus' commentaries on the latter's plays, all date from the fourth century AD.

PRODUCTION

Terence's plays were produced[39] at public festivals or 'games' (*ludi*), either regular ones of a religious character,[40] or ones arranged for special occasions such as victories or funerals. They were organised by magistrates, usually the aediles,[41] and they or other prominent figures would often augment the money given to them by the state for the purpose, doubtless hoping to further their political careers thereby. The magistrates would negotiate for plays with the leader of the company of actors (*dux* - or *dominus* - *gregis*), who would himself negotiate with the author, and also make all other arrangements, about costumes, masks[42] etc., necessary for the production. The company leader was a freedman, and in charge of the all-male company, whose actors were not necessarily, as is sometimes said, slaves.[43]

Theatres in Terence's day were temporary wooden structures erected for the occasion; the first permanent stone theatre in Rome was that of Pompey in 55 BC.[44] Unfortunately we know little about the design of these early structures (though doubtless they were fairly simple) and so it is impossible to be sure how Terence's plays were originally staged; what ancient writers say about production is often confused and sometimes misleading. It is of little help to look at later permanent theatres, since they were built with the design of Greek theatres very much in mind;

---

38   *Inst.* 11.3.178-82; but the reference could equally well be to *togatae*.

39   For all matters connected with production and staging in the Roman theatre, see Beare chs XX-XXIV (and appendices A-C, E-I); Duckworth 73-98.

40   *Eu.* was produced at the Megalensian Games; see the production notice.

41   See *Eu.* 20 and the production notice.

42   The question of whether masks were worn in Ter.'s day is much disputed, and a clear answer seems impossible. See Sandbach 111-12; Beare 192-4, 303-9; Duckworth 92-4.

43   See Beare 166-7; Duckworth 75-6.

44   Earlier attempts to build permanent theatres at Rome were stopped by the Senate as guardian of public morals; cf. Livy *Ep.* 48, referring to an incident in 151 BC.

the only certain clues are almost casual hints in the plays themselves, which, however, contain nothing like our modern stage directions.[45]

It seems that in early theatres the wooden stage was wide and shallow,[46] as befitted the 'normal' setting of a street; this arrangement facilitated the activities of the 'running slave' (*servus currens*),[47] and made more plausible the frequent (and often interrelated) stage-devices of eavesdropping,[48] asides[49] and failure to notice another character's presence.[50] Behind the stage stood the actors' accommodation, the front of which, containing three sets of doors representing the 'normal' three houses fronting the street,[51] formed the back-scene; the building was presumably a flimsy wood-and-canvas construction, but the doors were probably stout and heavy.[52] There were also two entrances from the 'wings', that to the spectators' left conventionally leading to the country and / or the harbour, that to their right to the centre of town.[53] There was probably little or no attempt to have realistic scenery, and there was no curtain; the only other feature was an altar on stage.[54] In the earliest times spectators may have stood or sat on the ground, but by Plautus' day there were benches;[55] the spectators' area must have been fairly open, since it could easily be invaded by people expecting rival attractions.[56] The audience, admitted free, was very mixed; there is evidence that the less attentive and intelligent had to

---

45   Phrases in the dialogue such as "But here's the woman herself, coming outside" (*Eu.* 79) and "But who's that coming this way?" (*Eu.* 228) are probably pointers for the audience, not stage directions; but they could be both.

46   When seen by the spectators. It is usually described as "long and narrow", presumably from the actors' point of view.

47   This stock character appealed to Ter. (e.g. Davos, *An.* 338-45; Geta, *Ph.* 179-96, 841-52; Geta, *Ad.* 299-321); he does not appear in *Eu.*, but is mentioned in a list of stock characters and situations given in the prologue (36).

48   E.g. Parmeno listening to Gnatho, *Eu* 232-66; Antipho listening to Chaerea, *Eu.* 549-56.

49   E.g. Parmeno at *Eu.* 254, 265, 418-19, 457-8, 459-60; Gnatho at *Eu.* 409-10, 422, 782.

50   E.g. Gnatho at *Eu.* 232-66.

51   All three are not always needed; *Eu.* requires two, representing the houses of Thais, and of the father of Phaedria and Chaerea.

52   In some plays the doors have to stand a lot of knocking, and opening them made a considerable noise; cf. *Eu.* 1029 and n.

53   The evidence is discussed by Duckworth 85-8.

54   Duckworth 83-4. The altar features prominently as a place of refuge in Plautus' *The Ghost (Mostellaria)* (1094-1145) and *The Rope* (688-880), and in Ter. *An.* 726-7 leafy branches are taken from it to protect a new-born baby which is to be placed on the ground; it is not mentioned in *Eu.*

55   Beare 171-2, 241-7.

56   Ter. *Hec.* 1-5, 33-6. For the correct interpretation of the second of these passages, which proves that theatres could also be used for other forms of entertainment, see Sandbach, F. H. (1982), 'How Terence's Hecyra failed', *CQ* ns 32, 134-5.

have tricky points spelled out carefully,[57] but, equally, a play with many twists and turns in a fast-moving plot needs concentration and a quick mind if it is to be properly appreciated.

III   THE LIFE AND WORKS OF TERENCE

A brief summary of Terence's life and career would run as follows. Born in Africa some time in the first quarter of the second century BC, he became a slave at Rome but attained his freedom. Under the name Publius Terentius Afer, he embarked - some said at a precociously early age - on a career as a writer of *palliatae*; in this career he enjoyed the support - according to some the active creative assistance - of a number of highly-placed Romans interested in Greek literature and culture. This fact, and certain aspects of his handling of his Greek originals, led to attacks on his methods by at least one other comic dramatist, against which he vigorously defended himself in the prologues of his plays. After a short, but by no means uniformly successful, career of no more than seven or eight years, during which he wrote just six plays, he died early in the 150s BC; the circumstances of his death were unknown.

Our principal sources for the details of this are three: Suetonius' *Life of Terence* (*Vita Terenti*),[58] what Terence himself says in his prologues, and the production notices (*didascaliae*) of his plays.[59] Unfortunately the first two of these must be handled carefully. As far as the *Life* is concerned, ancient biography is notoriously anecdotal, and much of what this one contains could, on a sceptical view, be held to be little more than fabrication based on vague hints found in the prologues and elsewhere;[60] moreover, Suetonius himself admits that there is little agreement about some of what he says.[61] As for the prologues, much of the material

---

57   E.g. the difference between Jupiter-disguised-as-Amphitruo and Amphitruo, and between Mercury-disguised-as-Sosia and Sosia (Plautus, *Amphitruo* 120-30, 142-7), and the fact that master and slave had exchanged dress (Plautus, *The Prisoners* 35-50).

58   One of the lives of poets from a biographical work on literary figures, *On Famous Men* (*De Viris Illustribus*) by C. Suetonius Tranquillus (c AD 70-c. AD 140), this has been preserved, perhaps in an abbreviated form, by being prefaced to Donatus' commentaries on Ter.'s plays; to it Don. has added a brief appendix of his own. Text: Don. I 3-10; translation: Radice 389-94.

59   These were probably compiled no later than the first century BC, and introduced into the MSS of Ter. at that time. The production notice of *An.* is not in our MSS, but can be reconstructed on the evidence of Don.

60   For this sceptical view, see Beare 91-4. Duckworth 56-9, though expressing doubt on some points, is more inclined to accept the broad outline of Suetonius' account.

61   E.g. whether Ter. came to Rome as a prisoner of war (*Life* 1), who his influential friends were (2; 4), and how he met his death (5).

in them which is relevant to Terence's career is given when he is defending himself against the attacks on his methods; since this defence will obviously be subject to special pleading, the information it contains will be suspect. Only with the production notices are we on surer ground, since their authenticity is undoubted; yet even here the record of the original productions has suffered from accretion of details about subsequent performances.[62]

According to the *Life* (5), Terence died while on a trip to Greece undertaken in his 25th year, shortly after his last plays were produced in 160 BC; he will therefore have been born *c.* 185 and have died *c.* 159 BC. Both these dates can be disputed, since some of our Suetonius MSS say '35th year', not '25th year', and the timing of his death could merely be an inference from the known date of the last plays. But such an inference is probably justified, given that Terence had produced six plays in the previous seven years and that after 160 BC no more appeared; and the MS reading '25th' certainly gives more weight than '35th' to the jibe of Terence's principal critic that he was a young upstart.[63]

Terence is said (*Life* 1) to have been born at Carthage in North Africa and to have subsequently become a slave at Rome of the senator Terentius Lucanus, who educated him and gave him his freedom. The senator's name provides circumstantial detail, so this may well be true; but the sceptical view holds that it could equally well be guesswork based on Terence's full Latin name, Publius Terentius Afer.[64] Afer is a good Roman surname (*cognomen*), but it also means 'African'; and, so the argument runs, since a freed slave customarily took his erstwhile master's gentile name (*nomen*), what could be more tempting to a biographer searching for material than to suggest that this Afer should have been African and slave to a Terentius?[65] Moreover, Terence's renowned skill with the Latin language might militate against the idea of foreign birth. On the other hand, as Sandbach says when drawing a comparison with the modern world: "Men who have won literary fame in languages not their own are not common ... but some can be named."[66]

The *Life* (3) tells how, when Terence presented his first play, *The Girl from Andros* (*Andria*), to the aediles for consideration, they told him to read it first to Caecilius, who was then doyen of Roman comic poets. This he did, at first, because

---

62   In the MSS the production notice of *Eu.* preserves traces of a performance some thirteen years after Ter.'s death; see commentary on production notice 1, 3 and 5.

63   See Ter. *Hau.* 23.

64   See Beare 93; Sandbach (1977) 135.

65   The same reason is given for the gentile name of the first Roman playwright, L. Livius Andronicus, who is said to have been freed by his master M. Livius Salinator. Such anecdotes have a habit of recurring in Roman bibliography, and this is not the only one connected with Ter. which finds a parallel elsewhere.

66   *Loc. cit.* in n. 64 above. In English literature, Joseph Conrad and Tom Stoppard come to mind.

of his shabby appearance, seated on a stool beside Caecilius as he reclined at dinner; but when he had read a few lines he was asked to join the meal, after which he read out the rest of the play, which was much admired. This time the disbelief of the sceptics does seem correct, since there is considerable difficulty with the story. Firstly, the anecdotal connection of a comic poet with his immediate predecessor is suspiciously neat; we are reminded of a tale connecting two of the great tragic poets of Rome, Pacuvius and Accius.[67] More seriously, there are chronological difficulties. According to Jerome's *Chronicle*, Caecilius died the year after Ennius, that is in 168 BC, when Terence was probably only 17; and why, if Caecilius so admired *The Girl from Andros*, was it not produced until 166 BC?[68] But the story is nevertheless additional testimony to Terence's youth when he embarked upon his dramatic career.

About the details of that career there is now general agreement among scholars, based on the evidence of the production notices, though some individual points are still disputed.[69] The following is the accepted picture:

Date	Title	Greek original	Occasion of production
166 BC	*The Girl from Andros* *Andria (An.)*	Menander, Ἀνδρία, *Andria*	Megalensian Games, April
165 BC	*The Mother-in-Law* *Hecyra (Hec.)* (a failure)	Apollodorus of Carystus, Ἑκυρά, *Hekyra*	Megalensian Games, April
163 BC	*The Self-Tormentor* *Heautontimorumenos* *(Hau.)*	Menander, Ἑαυτὸν τιμωρούμενος, *Heauton timoroumenos*	Megalensian Games, April
161 BC	*The Eunuch* *Eunuchus (Eu.)*	Menander, Εὐνοῦχος, *Eunouchos*	Megalensian Games, April
161 BC	*Phormio* *Phormio (Ph.)*	Apollodorus of Carystus, Ἐπιδικαζόμενος, *Epidikazomenos* *(The Claimant at Law)*	Roman Games, September

---

67   Gel. 13.2.

68   Flickinger, R. C. (1927), 'The prologues of Terence', *PhQ* 6, 237-8 believes that the delay was partly due to the removal of Caecilius' backing when he died soon after the play had been read to him.

69   See Arnott (1975) 47 and 60, n. 78.

160 BC	*Hecyra* (a second failure)		Funeral Games for L. Aemilius Paullus
160 BC	*The Brothers* *Adelphi (Ad.)*	Menander, Ἀδελφοὶ β, *Adelphoi* B[70]	Funeral Games for L. Aemilius Paullus
160 BC	*Hecyra* (third, and successful, production)		Roman Games, September (?)

The chief dispute here is over the relative positions of our play and *The Self-Tormentor*. The production notices tell us that the former was "written second" (*facta II*), the latter "written third" (*facta III*),[71] but the dates given in the same production notices are at variance with this. Some have therefore posited an unsuccessful production of *The Eunuch* in 165 or 164 BC,[72] but this idea sits badly beside evidence that the play was an unprecedented success in 161.[73] Alternatively it could be that *The Eunuch* was written second but produced third,[74] but a two-year delay before production again seems unlikely.

This list exhibits certain interesting features: the slow start to Terence's career, possibly implying difficulty in getting himself established and accepted, his problems with *The Mother-in-Law*, his fondness for Menander, and his predilection for retaining the titles of his Greek originals. The first point may have been due as much to opposition from rivals as to Terence's own abilities; the problems with *The Mother-in-Law* are explained more fully in the two prologues to that play (1-5, 21-38). Over the final two points, Terence stands out in contrast to Plautus. Perhaps as few as four of Plautus' 21 plays are from originals by Menander,[75] as opposed to

---

70   Men. wrote two plays with this title, conventionally known as Ἀδελφοί (*Adelphoi*) A and B. The former was the original for Plautus' *Stichus*, the latter for Ter.'s *The Brothers (Adelphi)*. See Körte II 14-19.

71   The first unsuccessful production of *Hec.* is discounted in the numbering given by the production notices; the play is placed fifth.

72   E.g. Duckworth 60 and n. 51; Radice 159 and 395.

73   *Life* 3; see also p. 27.

74   E.g. Thierfelder, A. (ed.) (1981), *Terenz, Heautontimorumenos: Einer straft sich selbst* (Stuttgart) 146-7. Don. I 267 says "it was produced third" (*edita tertium est*).

75   *The Two Bacchises, The Tale of a Trunk (Cistellaria)* and *Stichus* are certainly adaptations of plays by Men., and the original of *The Pot of Gold (Aulularia)* may also have been his; see Gomme and Sandbach 4-8. There may be more, since the originals of several of Plautus' plays are unknown.

Terence's four out of six; and, while Terence only changed the title of one play,[76] Plautus not infrequently adopted Latin titles.[77] Does this reflect a desire by Terence to preserve the spirit and atmosphere of his originals, as opposed to Plautus' rather less obvious concern for faithfulness to the spirit of his models?

It was believed in antiquity that Terence was encouraged in his career by some famous and noble Romans.[78] The favourite candidates for this role were P. Cornelius Scipio Aemilianus (Africanus Minor, 185/4-129 BC), C. Laelius and L. Furius Philus, the leading lights of the so-called 'Scipionic Circle';[79] some even went so far as to say that Scipio and Laelius had actually written at least part of what was passed off as Terence's work. In the *Life* (4), for instance, Laelius is said, on the testimony of the biographer C. Cornelius Nepos (*c.* 99-*c.* 24 BC), to have written a passage which included *Hau.* 723. This tradition of actual help persisted, though the careful words of Cicero[80] and Quintilian[81] seem to cast doubts on its reliability. It was probably mere gossip, the inevitable consequence of Terence's known friendship with these highly-placed Romans. But of the fact that Terence did enjoy the friendship of the great (as opposed to being a front for their creative activity), there seems little doubt; the very fact that, when he mentions the accusation of receiving help in two of his prologues, he makes evasive replies instead of denying it (*Hau.* 22-6; *Ad.* 15-21) is tantamount to proof. Moreover, the involvement of the Scipionic Circle is rendered highly likely by the fact that two of Terence's plays were put on at the funeral games for Scipio's father, L. Aemilius Paullus.[82]

---

76   *Ph.*, given the name of a character in the plot - see *Ph.* 24-9. As well as the reason given there, Ter. may have felt that the title Ἐπιδικαζόμενος (*Epidikazomenos*), *The Claimant at Law*, describing a particular Greek legal process, was too obscure.

77   E.g. *Captivi* (*The Prisoners*), *Mercator* (*The Merchant*), *Miles Gloriosus* (*The Swaggering Soldier*), *Rudens* (*The Rope*), all employing good honest Latin words.

78   *Life* 2; 4. Suggestions there that it was Ter.'s physical attractions which appealed to his patrons can be dismissed as pure scandal-mongering.

79   "A philosophic and literary coterie of mid-second-century philhellenes known as the 'Scipionic Circle' sought ... to promote the study of Greek at Rome and to develop the Latin language and literature" (Carney, T. F. (ed.) (1963), *P. Terenti Afri Hecyra* (Salisbury, Rhodesia) 6); but see Strasburger, H. (1966), 'Der 'Scipionenkreis' ', *Hermes* 94, 60-72. Some ancient writers found the relative ages of Ter. and Scipio a problem, and other possibilities were suggested; particularly attractive is the learned C. Sulpicius Gallus, consul in the year *An.* was produced (*Life* 4). It is not impossible that Sulpicius started Ter. off, and the Scipionic Circle took him up later.

80   *Att.* 7.3.10: "Terence, whose plays ... were thought to be written by C. Laelius." In *Amic.* 89 Cicero pictures Laelius calling Ter. his "intimate friend" (*familiaris*).

81   *Inst.* 10.1.99: "though the writings of Terence are ascribed to Scipio Africanus."

82   Scipio was adopted into the family of the Scipiones, and his *cognomen* Aemilianus reveals his origin as an Aemilius.

The only point of agreement about Terence's death[83] is that he was journeying abroad at the time, probably to Greece. There is no agreement about the reason for his journey (to escape talk that he was not the real author of his plays, or to study Greek customs and character), the place of his death (at sea, in Arcadia or on Leucadia) or the cause (shipwreck, disease or grief at the loss of his baggage, including plays, sent on home ahead). Some authorities mentioned the year 159 BC; this could be correct, or merely a date chosen as the year after his last plays were known to have appeared. Clearly Terence's end was largely a mystery, and therefore the subject of much guesswork.

IV   TERENCE AND HIS CRITICS

As already mentioned, throughout his career Terence was attacked on several counts; therefore, though he dispensed with the explanatory prologues of his Greek originals,[84] he chose to substitute 'literary' or 'polemical' ones,[85] in which to reply to the criticisms of his work.[86] These prologues therefore provide a unique insight into the specialized debate about dramatic aims and methods which was going on at the time.[87] They are, however, partisan and biased; not only do we not know whether Terence is making an honest defence against the charges laid against him, but we do not even know whether he is fairly representing what those charges were. We are in the position of people able to read a defence lawyer's speech, but not able to read the speech for the prosecution and not knowing exactly on what charge the defendant is arraigned.

Terence sometimes refers to critics in the plural, calling them "spiteful individuals" (*malevoli, Hau.* 16), "those spiteful characters" (*isti malevoli, Ad.* 15), "enemies" (*advorsarii, Ad.* 2), or simply "those people" (*isti* or *illi, An.* 15, 21; *Ad.* 17); at other times he singles out one man, whom he calls "a spiteful old poet" (*malevolus vetus poeta, An.* 6-7; *Hau.* 22), "an old poet" (*poeta vetus, Ph.* 1, 13), or simply "that chap" (*is, Eu.* 16; *Ph.* 17; *ille, Hau.* 30, 33; *Ph.* 19, 23). Ancient commentators say that this individual critic was the dramatist Luscius Lanuvinus "of

---

83   *Life* 5.

84   *Ad.* 22-4.

85   *An.* 5-7.

86   The two prologues to *Hec.* (for the second and third productions) are rather different from the rest, being 'literary' but not 'polemical'. They are not concerned with replying to attacks, but solely with securing a hearing for the play.

87   Although not the point at present under discussion, it is interesting to speculate how many of the audience would really be interested in this esoteric squabble, and what effect these specialist prologues had on their mood and receptivity as they prepared to watch the plays. Ter. clearly felt the defence of his reputation important enough to risk boring at least some of them. See also n. 135.

Lanuvium"; the plurality of critics were probably the lesser associates of this one real opponent. Unfortunately, apart from what is said in Terence's prologues and in Donatus' commentary, we know only one fact about Luscius which is independent of the context of this debate - he appears ninth in a canon ranking ten writers of *palliatae*, compiled by Volcacius Sedigitus *c.* 100 BC.[88]

As for Terence and Donatus, Terence tells us (*Eu.* 7-13) that Luscius "by accurate translation and poor composition has produced bad Latin plays out of good Greek ones", that he produced a version of Menander's *The Phantom* (Φάσμα, *Phasma*) and that in *The Treasure* (Θησαυρός, *Thesaurus*)[89] he made the defendant in a dispute over ownership of some gold speak before the plaintiff; commenting on the passage, Donatus gives the plots of Menander's *The Phantom* and Luscius' *The Treasure*.[90] In *Ph.* 6-8 Terence implies that Luscius depicted a youngster crazed (by love?) and seeing a doe chased by hounds and begging his help; Donatus merely adds that such scenes are more appropriate in tragedy.[91] Lastly, at *Hau.* 30-2 Terence criticizes Luscius for a scene of "a crowd making way for a slave running down the street". He also more than once threatens to expose more of Luscius' faults if his attacks do not stop.[92] In this meagre supply of information, much of it probably distorted as part of Terence's counter-attack, it is, as Duckworth says,[93] the comment that Luscius is an accurate translator but a poor writer that is the most enlightening in connection with the quarrel between the two men.

Before turning to the central issue, it is best to deal first with two other charges made by Luscius. The first (*Hau.* 22-6; *Ad.* 15-21) is that Terence had embarked on his career without adequate preparation (and, by implication, when too young) and had received help from his influential friends. Luscius believes, or tries to make out, that the only explanation for this sudden new arrival on the dramatic scene must be that Terence's work was not really his. We have seen that Terence was very young at the start of his career, and that he did have friends in high places; we have also seen that such friendships, coupled with his youth, would inevitably bring accusations of collaboration. Terence's defence is no defence at all, but evasion, probably because of the embarrassing position in which he found himself. In *The Self-Tormentor* he tells the audience to decide, and in *The Brothers* he says that

---

88 Gel. 15.24, where it is said to come from Volcacius' *On Poets (De Poetis)*. This famous list (which places Caecilius first, Plautus second, Naevius third, Ter. sixth, Turpilius seventh and Ennius last) is not as useful as it may seem, since we know nothing of the criteria used in compiling it. Cf. Suetonius, *Life* 7.

89 It is implied, though not explicitly stated, that this play was also by Menander; cf. 10-13n.; Körte II 77-8.

90 I 272-3. The description of *The Treasure* contains our only fragment of Luscius' work; see 10-13n.

91 II 352.

92 *Eu.* 16-19; *An.* 22-3; *Hau.* 33-4.

93 65.

while his critics regard it as "a reproach" (*maledictum*), he considers it "the greatest compliment" (*laudem ... maxumam*) to find favour with such men; and he counters the implication of immaturity by calling Luscius old.

The second 'minor' charge (*Ph.* 4-5) is that Terence's plays were slight in content and stylistically thin.[94] It is at once the easiest and the hardest to assess - easiest because we can read Terence for ourselves, hardest because such judgements are necessarily subjective. It is also the cleverest from Luscius' point of view, because its subjectivity makes it as difficult to disprove as to prove. P. Fabia[95] considers Terence guilty, and the charge "une accusation fondée". He does this by comparing Terence with Plautus and by referring to some ancient opinions, particularly the famous ones of Cicero and Caesar.[96] Cicero says of Terence "you make Menander known among us with quietened utterance" (*Menandrum in medium nobis sedatis vocibus effers*), and Caesar says "would that vigour had been combined with your smooth writing" (*lenibus atque utinam scriptis adiuncta foret vis*); but what these statements mean is much discussed and much disputed.[97] Decision is, of course, impossible. It was perhaps because of this that Terence did not even try to reply; instead he launched into the attack on Luscius' scene of the mad youngster, already mentioned.

Luscius' most important charges refer to Terence's treatment of his originals. In the first two prologues (*An.* 16; *Hau.* 17) Terence, quoting his critics, uses the phrase "to mess about with, spoil plays" (*contaminare fabulas*) in describing what he is supposed to have done; in the prologue to *The Eunuch* (19-26) he says that, when Luscius saw the play during a preliminary performance before the aediles, he accused him of plagiarism (*furtum*). Concerning the first point Terence admits (*An.* 9-14) to transferring into his version of *The Girl from Andros* suitable elements from a similar play by Menander, *The Girl from Perinthos* (Περινθία, *Perinthia*); in answer to the second (*Eu.* 27-34) he agrees he transferred into his version of Menander's *The Eunuch* two characters from Menander's *The Toady* (Κόλαξ, *Kolax*), but denies that he has plagiarized the work of Roman writers, saying that he was unaware that Naevius and Plautus had already produced versions of *The Toady*. In addition, in the prologue to *The Brothers* (6-11) he says that he has incorporated into his version of Menander's play a scene from Diphilus' *Joined in Death* (Συναποθνήσκοντες, *Synapothneskontes*) which Plautus had omitted in his version of that play, also *Joined in Death* (*Commorientes*).

---

94   *Ph.* 5: *tenui esse oratione et scriptura levi.*
95   *Les Prologues de Térence* (Paris and Avignon, 1888) 252-61.
96   Quoted by Suetonius, *Life* 7.
97   See Duckworth 385-6, and the bibliography in 385 n. 4. It is worth noting that Ritschl's alteration of "utterance" (*vocibus*) in the Cicero passage to "emotions", "passions" (*motibus*) has been widely accepted, and that in the Caesar passage "vigour" (*vis*) can become "comic vigour" (*vis comica*) by altering the punctuation at the end of the line.

All this has led to immense debate from the time of Donatus onwards, to which justice cannot be done here.[98] Since Terence uses the verb *contaminare*, scholars have adopted the noun *contaminatio*[99] to describe what Terence is supposed to have done, and argued about what that is. Some have said that the word signifies only 'combination', referring to combining more than one original into one Latin play; but the prevalent opinion inclines to 'spoiling' - which is the normal and obvious meaning of the word.[100]

This approach seems to contain two faults. Firstly it overlooks the fact that *contaminare* appears in only the first two prologues and that thereafter attention switches to plagiarism (*The Eunuch*) or making use of scenes discarded by earlier Roman playwrights in their adaptations (*The Brothers*); secondly it seeks to limit *contaminatio* to one precise and identifiable procedure. To take the second point first, A.S. Gratwick has already pointed out[101] that *contaminatio* might have no such specific reference, but might be "merely the quotation of Luscius' abusive description of Terence's particular procedure". It could equally be that the word is not Luscius', but *Terence's*, description of what Luscius had accused him of doing, and a deliberately vague and evasive one at that. It would therefore be profitless to try to discover what the word referred to, since Terence was deliberately using it to cover all or any of Luscius' criticisms about his handling of his originals, with no precise reference in mind. As for the first point, we can now see why Terence only uses the word *contaminare* in the first two prologues: he was being purposely vague there, but, when Luscius charged him semi-publicly before the aediles with something definite and precise, plagiarism, he could no longer use his umbrella-word, but had to reply more directly.

But whatever the answer to that particular problem, Terence certainly sometimes altered his originals in adaptation, and sometimes used elements from more than one play. Twice (*An.* 18-21; *Hau.* 20-1) he claims he has precedents;

---

98   See, for example, Arnott (1975) 48-50; Beare 98-102, 310-13; Duckworth 63-4, 202-8; Sandbach (1977) 139-40; Chalmers, W. R. (1957), 'Contaminatio', *CR* ns 7, 12-14; Beare, W. (1959), 'Contaminatio', *CR* ns 9, 7-11, with bibliography; Kujore, O. (1974), 'A note on contaminatio in Terence', *CPh* 69, 39-42; further bibliography in Marti (1963), 23-7, Cupaiuolo (1984) 454-6.

99   The noun does not appear in Latin until used by Ulpian (died AD 228) in the *Digest*; but scholars have found it helpful to employ it when discussing the process Ter. uses the verb *contaminare* to describe.

100   As in the only other appearance of the word in Ter. (not in the so-called 'specialist literary' sense in a prologue, but in the body of a play) at *Eu.* 552. It is surely wrong to assume that a word always otherwise used in the sense of "sully" could have the neutral sense "combine" when used in Ter.'s prologues.

101   (1982) 117.

once (*An.* 18) he lists these as Naevius, Plautus and Ennius,[102] and adds that he prefers their "carelessness of approach" (*neglegentia*) to his critics' "incomprehensible exactitude" (*obscura diligentia*). Why then does Luscius criticize Terence for what others have done before? The answer may lie in a change of fashion and ideas, possibly linked to the emergence of *fabulae togatae*.[103] Since Plautus' day there had been a swing away from ready incorporation of Roman elements into adaptations of Greek plays; such elements could now find their outlet in *togatae*, and so some writers of *palliatae* advocated closer adherence to Greek originals. Foremost among these purists was Luscius, but he demanded faithfulness to the letter, as well as the spirit, of Greek plays, and was willing to use his theories in a campaign to oust a young rival. The rival, however, felt that Luscius was going too far; Terence believed in reflecting the spirit of originals, but felt that adherence to their letter was "incomprehensible exactitude" which produced bad plays. That is why he called Luscius an accurate translator but a poor writer, and why he criticized him for translating without alteration scenes more suitable for tragedy and scenes where defendants spoke before plaintiffs.

V   *THE EUNUCH* AND ITS RELATIONSHIP TO MENANDER[104]

In the prologue (19-20) Terence tells us that his play is an adaptation of Menander's play of the same name (Εὐνοῦχος, *Eunouchos*), but he adds (30-3) that he has introduced into his version two characters, a toadying sponger and a boastful soldier, from Menander's *The Toady* (Κόλαξ, *Kolax*). This is as far as he goes, and the reader gets the impression that he would not even have admitted that much, had not Luscius, at a preliminary performance of the play before the aediles, accused him of taking these two imported characters from existing Latin adaptations of *The Toady* instead of directly from Menander (19-26).[105] Naturally, Terence only defends

---

102   It might seem odd for Ter. to appeal to the precedent of Ennius, who had so little to do with *palliatae* (see p. 8); but Ter. could equally well be thinking of the way Ennius handled the originals of his tragedies.

103   See p. 8.

104   The matters discussed in this section are also referred to at the appropriate points in the commentary; in particular, more is said about the scenes involving the two characters from Men.'s *The Toady*. Ludwig (1959), with references to earlier literature, is invaluable in assessing the problems raised; useful summaries are provided in English by Webster (1960) 67-76 and (1974) 139-41, Ludwig (1968) 172-3, and Sandbach (1977) 142-5 and (1982) 547-8. See also Fabia's introduction and Barsby (1999) 17-18.

105   It is interesting that Luscius does not go on to attack Ter. for using two Men. plays to create only one of his own, since, according to some, this is exactly what is meant when Ter. uses the word *contaminare* in the prologues to *An.* and *Hau.* to describe the substance of his critic's attacks. Those who hold this view of *contaminare* must believe

himself on the specific point on which Luscius had attacked him; it certainly does not follow that introducing the sponger and the soldier is the only change that he has made - though the implication is that it is the largest and most obvious.

If we wish to try to establish the full extent of Terence's alterations to his (principal) original, we have some other aids. One of the most obvious is the commentary - extant for all of Terence's plays except *The Self-Tormentor* - of the fourth-century AD grammarian Aelius Donatus, which - for all its imperfections - is on occasions extremely valuable;[106] there is also a later, less helpful commentary by Eugraphius.[107] There also exist a few fragments of Menander's *The Eunuch* (two of which are given by Donatus),[108] two mutilated pieces of papyrus containing portions of his *The Toady*, as well as a number of other, shorter fragments from that play,[109] and one or two other Menander fragments which, though not attributed to any particular play, have been claimed by some to belong either to *The Eunuch* or to *The Toady*; some, though not all, of these can with greater or lesser certainty be matched up with parts of Terence's text.[110] The other principal method of proceeding is, of course, to study Terence's play. Such things as seeming inconsistencies in the plot or characterization and obscurities or awkwardnesses in the staging may (or may not) indicate points at which Terence has departed from his original.[111] And, if one

---

that Luscius did not bother to mention it here because he regarded plagiarizing the works of earlier Latin writers as an even worse offence. It may indeed have been worse; but Luscius' failure to employ the word and / or to criticize the use of two Greek plays might be further evidence to support the view (see p. 19) that Ter. (or Luscius) was only using *contaminare* as a vague word to describe the handling of originals, without any specific or technical reference at all.

106   See Grant (1986) 60-96; he notes (60-1): "The commentary ... is not the work as Donatus originally composed it but a late compilation of scholia which were in the original commentary and of later non-Donatus notes." As it stands, it combines at least two versions. The original probably relied heavily on the earlier commentary of Aemilius Asper (late second century AD), which is now lost. The section on *Eu.* as it has come down to us is given in Don. I 263-497. On the quality of the commentary, see n. 120 below.

107   Eugraphius probably wrote his commentary in the late fifth or early sixth century AD. It is a work much inferior to that of Don., from which parts of it are drawn, and often merely paraphrases Ter.'s text; as with Don.'s commentary, it has two versions. The section on *Eu.* is given in Don. III i 87-150.

108   Körte II 66-9, Barsby (1999) 304-5.

109   Körte I 110-19, with xlvii-l, Arnott (1996) 151-203, Barsby (1999) 305-11. See also Gomme and Sandbach 419-33.

110   Problems of matching are discussed at the appropriate points in the commentary.

111   It would, however, be wrong to assume that every one of what we choose to regard as 'imperfections' of this type must automatically be the work of Ter.; it is at least possible that some of them may have been present in Men. too. On the other hand, because of the latter's great skill as a dramatist (particularly concerning characterization

accepts the probability of the theory that Menander never wrote a scene which contained more than three speaking actors,[112] then the five scenes from our play which do contain more will obviously need examination.

Any discussion must begin with the sponger and the soldier. In the play, the love-affair of the young Athenian Phaedria with the courtesan (*meretrix*) Thais is blighted by the presence of a rival in the form of the boastful soldier (*miles gloriosus*) Thraso, who has in tow a hanger-on, the toady (*colax*) or sponger (*parasitus*) Gnatho. Thais persuades Phaedria to give place to Thraso for a short period, in order that she may receive from the soldier the gift of a young girl. This girl, Pamphila, had been brought up with Thais on Rhodes, and Thais believes that she is close to establishing that she is actually a free-born Athenian whom she will shortly be able to reunite with her family in the shape of the girl's brother Chremes. In 232-91 Gnatho comes to Thais' house and, after delivering a speech about his own 'trade' (232-64), hands over Pamphila. Later, in two further long scenes (391-453, over half of which has little or nothing to do with the plot, and 454-506), Thraso, accompanied by Gnatho, comes to take Thais to supper at his house. The supper, which takes place off-stage, is a disaster, because Chremes arrives at Thais' invitation and Thraso assumes that he is another contender for Thais' favours like Phaedria. In 771-816 Thraso returns with Gnatho and an 'army' of servants to lay siege to Thais' house and recover Pamphila by force, but is thwarted when Chremes (who, like Thais, has got back before he arrives) claims that Pamphila is free-born. Nothing is heard of Thraso and Gnatho thereafter until the last three scenes of the play; they reappear at 1025 and, in an ending which has surprised many and upset - even shocked - not a few, Gnatho succeeds in persuading Phaedria to admit him among his circle of friends and to allow Thraso to continue in some favour with Thais.

There is another major strand to the plot.[113] Phaedria's brother Chaerea sees Pamphila being taken to Thais' house and falls madly in love with her. He takes up his servant Parmeno's (initially jocular) suggestion that, in order to get into Thais' house and be near Pamphila, he should change places with a eunuch whom Parmeno is taking to Thais as a present from Phaedria. Once in the house, Chaerea rapes Pamphila, and when she is later found to be free-born, he obtains his father's permission to marry her; at the same time Thais is taken under the father's protection. A third, less important, strand is dependent on the second, and concerns the revenge which Pythias, one of Thais' maids, takes on Parmeno for his part in

---

and over entrances and exits), it might be thought more likely that such problems arose in the process of Ter.'s adaptation.

112   See p. 3, and n. 9.

113   All Ter.'s plays except *Hec.* have a 'double' plot involving the love-affairs of two young men. For some useful remarks on such plots, see Levin; he points out that in *Hau.*, *Eu.*, *Ph.* and *Ad.*, one is a 'marriage-plot' (Chaerea and Pamphila in our play), the other a 'liaison-plot' (Phaedria and Thais) which cannot result in a marriage.

arranging Chaerea's escapade. With neither of these two strands do Thraso and Gnatho have anything but the most tenuous of connections.

It is clear, then, that the two characters which Terence imported from Menander's *The Toady* - associated as they are with only one of the two main strands of the plot, and being on stage in only seven scenes (just over 300 lines), parts of which (232-64, 395-433) have nothing to do with the play at all - can easily be isolated, and the way in which they have been integrated into the action can be reasonably well established.[114] But what does Terence mean by saying (32) that he has "transferred" them into *The Eunuch*? Do they form additional characters which were not there in Menander's *The Eunuch*, or do they replace similar characters - a rival and his henchman / slave - who did appear in that play? And if the latter, did those characters both appear and speak in Menander, were they mute characters, or did they never actually appear on stage at all? It is now generally agreed that a rival did exist in Menander's version of *The Eunuch*, and that he was probably a soldier;[115] and most would accept that he did feature as a speaking character in the play.[116] Whether that rival had an associate - at any rate one who had as prominent a role as Gnatho has - is more debatable.[117] In favour of the idea is the fact that Parmeno must see Pamphila being delivered to Thais' house in order to suggest to Chaerea that he should pose as the eunuch (and the audience should see it too), and that the girl is more likely to have been delivered by the rival's henchman or slave than by the rival himself; moreover, if the rival were a soldier, a sponger - customarily associated with the boastful soldier in this type of play - would be the natural person to do this. But this is not to say that this henchman / slave also appeared in the later scenes where Gnatho now appears, since, by application of the 'three-actor rule', Gnatho seems a most likely character to have been added by Terence in most of them.[118] It further follows that, if a Gnatho character was not present at the end of Menander's *The Eunuch*, the part of the deal with Phaedria

---

114 See the references in n. 104 above; also Gaiser 1064-5.

115 The rival / soldier is mentioned as early as 125, and his influence is felt throughout much of the action; soldiers are frequently the rivals of young men in this type of play. See Ludwig (1959) 26, Lloyd-Jones 283, Webster (1974) 139, Sandbach (1975) 201 and (1977) 142-3, Gratwick (1972) 31 (though expressing doubt that he was a soldier), Fabia 41. McLeish 57-9 believes that there was no rival in Men.'s play.

116 Fabia (41) disagrees, believing he was only mentioned and did not appear.

117 Sandbach (1975) 201 and (1977) 143 thinks he was "an additional character", adding at the latter place "except inasmuch as at his first entrance he replaces a slave who brought the 'heroine' to Thais' house as a gift from the rival"; cf. Ludwig (1959) 26. Webster (1974) 140.

118 391-453 contains only three speaking characters (Thraso and Gnatho, with asides by Parmeno) and 1025-30 contains two (Thraso and Gnatho, with Parmeno present but not speaking). The other scenes (454-506, 771-816, 1031-49, 1049-94) all contain more than three.

which involves Gnatho, and Gnatho's role in striking any deal at all, must either come from *The Toady* or be the work of Terence - even if the general tenor of the conclusion and the way it affects Thraso are genuinely from *The Eunuch*. In the last resort, however, since we know nothing of how either of Menander's two plays ended, any attempt to solve the vexed problem of how Terence's ending relates to (either of) Menander's must be no more than inference.[119]

A number of other changes, not connected with Thraso or Gnatho, have been identified or at least suggested, though not all of them command universal assent. Some of these are indicated by Donatus, though it is difficult to understand why he does not mention more. If he is able to comment on comparatively minor or individual points (I 329 on 289, I 382 on 507, I 472 on 971), and sometimes to quote the original Greek (I 278 on 46, I 416 on 689), why does he not, for instance, mention the Thraso / Gnatho alterations in much more detail than he does?[120] The most significant point he does mention (I 387 on 539) is that the character of Chaerea's friend Antipho was not in Menander. In Terence's play Antipho explains in a short monologue (539-45) that he has come in search of Chaerea, before his friend bursts out of Thais' house elated about his conquest of Pamphila, and describes to him his adventures inside (545-614); in Menander, says Donatus, Chaerea told the story in a longish monologue.[121] On smaller matters, Donatus says (I 477 on 1001) that Menander explained more clearly than Terence does about the father's previous hostility to Thais, and (I 382 on 507) that in Menander Chremes was a 'rustic' young man.[122]

One substantial alteration not mentioned by Donatus concerns Dorias. It seems highly likely that this second maid of Thais has been created out of the role of the first maid, Pythias.[123] At 500ff. Thais tells Pythias that, if Chremes arrives during her absence at Thraso's supper party, she should as a last resort bring him to her there; in fact at 538 Pythias tells Dorias to do this. When Dorias returns bringing Thais' jewelry with her, she delivers a monologue (615-28) about the quarrel which broke out over Chremes' presence at Thraso's, but does not actually take the jewelry inside until 726. In the interim she stands about awkwardly during a monologue by

---

119   See the introductory note to Act Five Scene Nine (pp. 207–8).

120   He does not mention the matter in his comments on the prologue, where he might be expected to, but does so at I 314 on 228 and quotes the prologue (26) there;   the problem is the same for his comments on the other plays. The answer presumably lies in the standard of his criticism and / or the condition in which his commentary has come down to us.

121   Webster (1974) 140 feels he did appear in Men., coming on at the end of Chaerea's monologue.

122   Don. mentions Chremes' 'rustic' characteristics in our play at I 385 on 531, I 428 on 745 and I 444 on 803. See Fabia 50, n. 3.

123   Webster (1960) 72-3 and (1974) 140 ("an unnecessary addition by Terence"), Ludwig (1959) 18, n. 1, Sandbach (1975) 201.

Phaedria (629-42) and takes only a very small part in the following two scenes (643-67, 668-726), both of which involve Pythias and the second of which contains four speaking characters. It seems likely that in Menander the Pythias character took Chremes to Thraso's herself, returned from there with the jewels and, after describing the quarrel, took them inside before Phaedria's monologue, returning after it to take part in the following two scenes. Moreover, if this suggestion of what happened in Menander is correct, it has the advantage of making Pythias absent at Thraso's during Chaerea's rape of Pamphila, whereas in Terence she has to be outside Thais' house at the time - not an impossible situation, but a dramatically less convenient one.[124] Similar "multiplication and thickening up"[125] by Terence should be seen in the creation - or more probably the elevation from mute to speaking status - of the roles of Sanga, the only one of the four named members of Thraso's 'army' who is given anything to say (776, 778-9, 816), and of Sophrona, the nurse summoned to confirm Pamphila's identity, who speaks only one word (913).[126]

The principal points mentioned so far - substitution of Thraso for the rival of Menander's play, expanding the role of the rival's henchman / slave in the form of Gnatho, creation of Antipho and Dorias, assigning a few words to Sanga and Sophrona - would all, if true, have a common purpose. Terence is injecting life and action into a play which he presumably felt did not contain enough of them for the tastes of his Roman - as opposed to the original Greek - audience. By increasing the number of speaking roles and by introducing the exaggerated characters of Thraso and Gnatho, he adds variety and movement, and above all creates more obvious humour, often of a fairly broad and farcical kind. This can be seen particularly clearly in the two passages concerning Gnatho (232-64) and Thraso and Gnatho (395-433) which seem to have nothing to do with the plot of the play.

A separate matter, and a controversial one, is whether there was a divine prologue in Menander's *The Eunuch*.[127] Those who hold that there was suppose that its removal has led Terence to transfer some of the expository material it contained into the body of his version of the play - principally into Act One Scene Two (81-206), where Thais explains to Phaedria her own and Pamphila's backgrounds, her relations with Thraso, her desire to get Pamphila from him, and, most importantly, the genuineness of the story she has told Phaedria about all this and the sincerity of her feelings for him. The extent of such alterations is, however, not agreed.[128]

---

124   In describing his escapade Chaerea says (581) that Thais had taken her maids with her to Thraso's, leaving only a few new girls behind. There is no mention of Pythias or, indeed, of Dorias, who must have been inside at the time (538).
125   Webster (1960) 73.
126   Sandbach (1975) 199.
127   See the introductory note to Act One Scene Two and 189ff. n.
128   E.g. Webster (1960) 70 and (1974) 139-40, Lefèvre (1969) - quoted in Gratwick's review (1972) 30 - and others feel that Ter. has made a number of alterations at various points throughout the scene. Brothers (1969) believes that changes are confined to the

Others believe that there was no divine prologue in Menander's play, and that there Thais gave the information herself, speaking in character, in a sort of "quasi-prologue", rather as Moschion does in a long monologue at the start of Menander's *The Girl from Samos*.[129] Thus, they argue, there is no reason why 81-206 should not be a reasonably faithful adaptation of Menander, with only such alterations as are required by the substitution of Thraso for the rival of his *The Eunuch*.

Lastly, it is worth remarking that we know that Terence has changed the names of a number of the characters; it is not unreasonable to suppose that he did so with them all.[130] The scholiast on a passage of Persius tells us that in Menander the Phaedria character was called Chairestratos, the slave Parmeno was Daos and Thais was Chrysis.[131] Donatus (I 472 on 971) says that in Menander the father was called Simon, whereas in Terence he is not named. One of the fragments of *The Toady* makes it clear that the toady in that play was called Strouthias, while Plutarch's citation of part of it adds that the soldier was Bias.[132] The name Gnathon ('Jaws', an obvious name for a greedy toady / sponger) occurs twice in one of the papyri which contain portions of that play;[133] opinion is divided on whether Strouthias and Gnathon are one and the same or two different characters.[134]

---

end (189-206). Another point in favour of the existence of a divine prologue in Men. (not so often mentioned) is that in Ter. the whole Chaerea story, and indeed his very existence, comes as a complete surprise at 289; but perhaps Men., too, wanted the element of surprise.

129   E.g. Lowe (1983) 441-2, who says (441): "A divine prologue could ... have given no information which Thais could not. ...: If ... there seems no place for a divine prologue and no positive reason for one, it must be regarded as probable that none existed." For Moschion in *The Girl from Samos*, see Miller 55: "The play has no need of a divine prologue, because Moschion can tell us all the necessary facts." Cf. Lowe (1981) 9, and see n. 10 above.

130   Barton says (33): "Terence too regularly changes the names provided in his source plays."

131   Schol. Pers. 5.161. In Persius, 5.161-75 is stoic moralizing based on Chairestratos' indecision at the start of Men.'s play; but there are verbal echoes of Ter.'s version, principally the use of the words "So what am I to do?" (*quid(nam) igitur faciam?*, 172) with which the Roman play opens (46).

132   Körte I 118, fr. 2; Plut. *Mor.* 57A.

133   Körte I 114, ll. 68 and 69.

134   For example, Körte (I xlix) is against the identity; Gomme and Sandbach (421-2) think "the balance of probability" favours it, citing, as do others, a possible parallel in the adoption by Curculio of the name Summanus in order to trick a pimp and a soldier client of his (Pl. *Cur.* 43). See also Arnott (1996) 157-8.

VI   THE EUNUCH AS A ROMAN COMEDY

Many, perhaps most, of Terence's audience would have known little (and probably cared less) about Menander. They would have been completely unaware of the sort of problems discussed in the previous section, except for what they were told in the prologue - and that, as we have seen, is only comparatively little, confined to the major alteration.[135] What would have concerned them much more would be what entertainment they would get from the play as it stood, and we do well to remember this fact when studying it today.[136]

The Eunuch was a great success when first performed; we are told that it was put on twice in the same day and won a prize of 8,000 sesterces, an amount which no comedy by any poet had been awarded before.[137] This success must have been largely due to the fact that it is the most Plautine of Terence's plays. The presence of larger-than-life characters (particularly Thraso and Gnatho), and the farcical and exaggerated humour and the vigorous action - such as the siege of Thais' house (771-816) - which they bring into the play, all contribute to making it what we, depending on our sense of humour, would call the 'funniest' of his comedies, and one can easily imagine that the Roman audience would have felt the same. Further, the play has more speaking characters than any other by Terence (or, for that matter, by Plautus), and this too may well have contributed to its success.

As has been seen, the play has a double plot,[138] concerned with the love-affairs of the two brothers Phaedria and Chaerea; but, as its title makes clear, it is the story of the false eunuch Chaerea, rather than that of his brother, which is the chief focus of attention for most of the time. Although at the start we are presented with the problem of the relations between Phaedria and Thais, the emphasis soon shifts to the other brother when Phaedria departs for the country at 224. Thereafter, it is really only in the final scene (1049-94) that Phaedria's problem comes to the fore again - having been more or less dormant for over 800 lines - and finds its solution in the

---

135   It is easy to imagine that this section of Ter.'s audience, having little interest in what was told them in the prologue, would have virtually 'switched off' while it was being delivered; others would have listened to it with rapt attention. Ter. clearly felt that defending his reputation before the educated citizens of Rome was of paramount importance, even if the less well-informed among his audience might become bored. But, as he always feels it necessary to plead for a fair hearing for his plays, he was clearly taking something of a risk in not engaging the whole audience's attention right from the start.

136   Cf. Arnott (1975) 4: "research could be more profitably directed into what the comedies of Plautus and Terence have themselves to offer than into their uncertain relationships with lost sources."

137   Suetonius, *Life* 3. It is not specifically said that these statements refer to the first performance, but it is the obvious interpretation. See also Don.'s preface to *Eu.* I 266.

138   See n. 113 above.

arrangement made with Thraso. Significantly, Phaedria himself remains off-stage for some 400 lines after his departure, while the action concentrates on Chaerea's escapade. And when he returns (629), he becomes more connected with his brother's love-affair than with his own, as he is told of the rape and finds out from the real eunuch what Chaerea has done (643-717).[139] Admittedly, Chaerea too is absent for about half the length of time that Phaedria was earlier (615-839), but during his absence the discovery of the rape and of the identity of its perpetrator, first by Pythias and then by Thais (643-726; 817-39), means that his presence is still being felt. By contrast, from 225 to 628 Phaedria is not only out of sight, but largely out of mind as well.[140]

Thus in the first 600 lines or so the two main strands of the plot are not particularly closely interwoven, in the way in which they are from quite early on in, for example, *The Self-Tormentor* or *The Brothers*. The immediate points of contact between Phaedria's story and Chaerea's are Parmeno, who advises both brothers, the real eunuch Dorus, who is Phaedria's gift to Thais, and the fact that Pamphila is taken to Thais' house. But apart from that the two stories can hardly be said to depend on one another very much for their development or their outcome; Phaedria's story is put 'on hold', as it were, while Chaerea's pursues its own swift course. Neither brother assists the other in his love-affair in the way in which, for instance, Aeschinus helps his brother Ctesipho in *The Brothers*, and, indeed, it is not until the start of the final scene (1049) that the two of them even meet on stage at all. Towards the end of the play, however, the two stories do interact more: Phaedria's questioning of Dorus (691ff.) establishes the fact that it was Chaerea who carried out the rape; the father's panic-stricken rush into Thais' house (996) results not only in the betrothal of Chaerea and Pamphila (1036), but also in Thais receiving the old man's protection, which ensures the future of Phaedria's relationship with her and gives him the ascendancy over Thraso (1037-41); and in the final scene Chaerea advises his brother in his negotiations with Gnatho (1068, 1083). So, particularly in the last 100 lines, the two elements are skilfully brought together to round off the play.

Although their two stories are to a large extent independent of one another, by their presence in the same play the two brothers provide an effective and entertaining contrast of character and personality which is one of *The Eunuch*'s main points of interest; this is seen particularly, of course, in their approach to love. In the first place, the situations in which they find themselves are quite dissimilar,

---

139 The monologue which he delivers on his return (629-42) reminds the audience of his problem and further characterizes him by his inability to endure separation from Thais for the agreed period of two days. But there has been no change in his situation, nor any progress towards the resolution of his difficulties.

140 Gnatho talks of him as Thraso's rival at 437-45, and Parmeno presents his gifts to Thais at 461-85, but there is no development in his problem at either point.

because the two types of love-affair are very different: Phaedria's constitutes a 'liaison-plot',[141] since he is in love with the courtesan Thais whom he cannot ever expect to marry, while Chaerea's constitutes a 'marriage-plot' in which the discovery of Pamphila's identity clears the way for betrothal and marriage.

The reaction of Phaedria, the elder brother, to his relationship has been said "to look forward to the self-conscious and emotional love poetry of Propertius and Tibullus".[142] He is a total slave to his mistress, from whom he cannot escape, however much he may occasionally think he wants to. Despite his attempts to be firm with himself (46-9), he knows his own weakness (50-5), misery (71) and helplessness (72-3). As his slave Parmeno sees (178), he is easily outwitted by Thais' ploy of being prepared to give way to him (171-7), and, even though he cannot stand the thought of a rival, he is quickly persuaded by her request that he give place to Thraso for two days (185-6). But when it comes down to it, despite his supposed resolve (221-4), he cannot prevent himself from coming back before the time is up (629-41). He has been continually giving Thais presents, culminating in the Ethiopian slave-girl and the eunuch who feature in the play (163-9), and though it is nowhere specifically stated that the expense has been too much for him,[143] in the final scene he is eventually persuaded by Gnatho's argument that he has too little money to supply all Thais' wants himself and needs the resources of the wealthy and over-generous Thraso to enable his relationship to continue.[144] Overall, he cuts a rather sad figure; his complaints sound pathetic (91-4) and in his farewell to Thais as he leaves for the country he readily gives way to unmanly lovesick entreaty (191-6).

But it would be wrong to say that Phaedria is merely a pathetic figure. Granted, he is weak, indecisive and irresolute, but we are surely meant to see in his situation evidence of the helplessness of a man confronted with the power of love[145] - a helplessness which is stressed through Parmeno's remarks about the great change which has come over his young master since the relationship began (225-7). While naturally finding some of Phaedria's words and actions amusing, the audience - even

---

141 See n. 113 above.

142 Hunter 93; cf. Barsby (1999) 90, who says: "In many ways [Phaedria] foreshadows the 'elegiac' lover, as later developed in Catullus and Roman elegy."

143 Parmeno's comment (1000-1) that Phaedria's father has long wanted "to do something drastic" to Thais' household may perhaps indicate his annoyance at the cost of his son's affair (especially as Don. I 477 tells us that his hostility was more fully explained in Men.); but this is far from certain.

144 One of the several 'unsatisfactory' features of the ending of the play has been held to be the fact that the possessive and jealous Phaedria is after all willing to share Thais' favours with Thraso. Whether the financial argument is enough to explain this is a matter of opinion. See pp. 207-8.

145 Thais herself refers to the power of love (881). Admittedly she is there talking in the context, not of Phaedria's love for her, but of the passion which led Chaerea to rape Pamphila; but it is hard to believe she does not have Phaedria in mind as well.

those who had not been through the same sort of thing themselves - would still realize that the young man was someone to feel for, not simply deride and mock. And it must be admitted that, when not directly concerned with his own affairs, Phaedria reverts to his old self (cf. Parmeno's description of him at 226-7) and shows resolution and determination, as in his reaction to Pythias' story of the rape - that she must be either drunk or mad (655-7) - and in his vigorous, clever, sometimes abusive and violent, interrogation of Dorus (691-717).

Chaerea is quite different. He is the younger brother,[146] gregarious and popular (539-41), confident, eager, impulsive and opportunistic. He fancies himself as a real ladies' man and a connoisseur of feminine beauty (296-7, 360-1, 565-6) and falls in love at first sight (307, 568). Despite his initial unhappiness at having been delayed and losing track of Pamphila (292-3), he is really more angry (302-3, 323) than depressed. He is as quick to take up Parmeno's suggestion that he change places with the eunuch (376-81), as he is later to seize the opportunity of finding himself alone with Pamphila (604-6); he is as elated at his own success with Pamphila (549-56), as he is later overjoyed that he can marry her (1031-6); he is as happy for his brother's good fortune as he is for his own (1037-41); and he realizes that he has Parmeno, his father and Fortune to thank as well as his own daring, and prays to Jupiter that his family's happiness will last (1044-9). Earlier, when Parmeno objects that his suggestion had only been made in fun and that it would be wrong to carry it out, he has ready counter-arguments to hand (382-7) - as he later has for Thais (872-5) - and is quite prepared to shield his servant from any future blame (388-9) and to assume responsibility (390). He seems, from one point of view, a happy, likeable rascal.

But, of course, that is not the whole story. *The Eunuch* is the only extant play of this type, Greek or Roman, where a rape takes place during the action.[147] Chaerea glories in his act (549ff.), and even though Terence has him suppress the details in his account to Antipho (604), Pythias later mentions how he tore the girl's clothes and hair - and actually did this after the rape (645-6).[148] To make matters worse, Chaerea cannot claim the often-employed excuse that he acted when he was drunk at a nocturnal festival, and he later pretends to Thais that what he has done is only "something small" (856). It seems a poor defence to say that he thought the girl was only a slave (858), that she was in the house of a courtesan and that, once

---

146   About eighteen years old; cf. 290n.
147   It is not uncommon for a rape to have occurred before the action opens, as in, for example, *An.*, *Hec.* and *Ad.*, and in Men.'s *The Girl from Samos* and *The Arbitration*. Sometimes, as in *An.* and *Ad.*, the girl concerned gives birth behind the scenes during the course of the play.
148   The clothes are also mentioned by Thais at 820. There is a description of torn clothes and the girl tearing her own hair in her distress in Men.'s *The Arbitration* (488-91); but again, the rape had taken place before the action opens.

she was found to be free-born, he was absolutely determined to marry her (888).[149]
All this has proved too much for modern taste, just as it did for Donatus, who in
several notes tries hard to excuse Chaerea on the grounds of his ignorance of the
girl's identity, the power of love or his youth.[150] But for us such excuses carry little
weight.

For ancient audiences, however, things were different. In Greek New Comedy,
certainly, rape was regarded as an acceptable ingredient of the plot, since in society
"although rape was regarded as a disgraceful act, it was by no means an
unpardonable or unthinkable one".[151] Thus "young men who ravish girls in comedy
remain secure in the possession of the audience's sympathy ... It is clear that, by a
certain intelligible, if not modern, scale of values, the violation of a respectable girl
is less shocking than her consent to seduction."[152] As for Roman audiences, even
though their attitude to real rape may have been very different, they were
presumably content to accept its occurrence in drama as an aspect of the society in
which that drama was set. But that still leaves the question of the attitude, in both
societies, to the rape taking place during the course of the play rather than before -
sometimes long before - the action begins. We know of no parallel; ancient
audiences may have done. But whether they did or not, it is clear that the whole
matter would have upset them less than it does us.

Thais presents yet another picture of love. She is a professional courtesan who
makes her living from the men who buy her favours, numbering the deceased friend
of 119-20 and Thraso among her lovers as well as Phaedria - and doubtless there
were more. She is sometimes depicted as scheming and calculating (67-70) and
greedy for money and presents (79-80, where Parmeno calls her "that blight on our
estate", 163-9, 1075) - the type whose gracious public image contrasts with their
sordid life at home (934-40). In this she conforms to the conventional picture of the
courtesan exhibited, for example, by Bacchis in *The Self-Tormentor*.[153] But she is
not in fact a character after this stereotype, but has a kindlier, more genuine side to

---

149 At the time of the rape Chaerea may have been hoping to have Pamphila as his mistress
     in a Phaedria / Thais type of relationship, and he perhaps hints at this at 613-4. But the
     matter is not pursued; dramatically, it does not have to be, since any such intention is
     overtaken by events.

150 See Hunter 94: "it is hardly possible for the modern reader to find the subsequent
     delight which Chaerea expresses in his achievement anything but repulsive." He lists
     the relevant Don. notes at 167, n. 20. Philippides attempts to defend Ter.'s treatment of
     the incident by pointing to several verbal echoes of marriage ritual employed by
     Chaerea in his account (see 592n.); but such details hardly cancel out the overall feeling
     of disquiet about the whole episode.

151 Gomme and Sandbach 33.

152 Griffin, J. (1985), *Latin Poets and Roman Life* (London) 126-7.

153 See particularly *Hau.* 227, where Bacchis is described as "grand and grasping, full of
     airs and graces, extravagant, and high and mighty".

her nature.[154] She is what Donatus (I 309 on 198) terms a "kindly / honest courtesan" (*bona meretrix*), a variation on the type, seen not only in Terence (Bacchis in *The Mother-in-Law*) but also earlier in Menander (Chrysis in *The Girl from Samos*, Habrotonon in *The Arbitration* ('Επιτρέποντες, *Epitrepontes*)).[155] She confesses to her genuine affection for Phaedria, not only to his face (95-7) but also, more importantly, when she is alone (199-201); her concern for Pamphila's future seems genuine enough, even if combined with self-interest (145-9, 201-2, 868-71); and she is prepared to accept Chaerea's arguments and to forgive him for what he has done (876-81). But the self-interest just mentioned is always there, and it would be unwise to see Thais' kindly actions in a totally altruistic light. She is a foreigner (107), and, though not without means,[156] she is alone in the world (147-8). Her chief object is therefore to acquire friends (149) and a protector or patron at Athens (770), and it is in this light that we must see not only her plans for Pamphila, but also her treatment of Chaerea. It is a neat and unexpected twist to the plot that through the rape of Pamphila - the very thing which she thought had destroyed her plans (827-8, 867-71) - and the girl's betrothal to Chaerea, she finds that patron not in Chremes as she had expected, but in Chaerea's father (1039-40). One last point has to be mentioned - that, as with Phaedria so too with Thais, the conclusion of the play has seemed to some to conflict with the earlier picture; they have found it strange that the independent-minded and professional courtesan's affairs should be arranged between Phaedria, Thraso and Gnatho, without her wishes being consulted in any way, without her consent and behind her back.[157]

Like Thais, the slave Parmeno is also not quite the character we or the audience would most readily have expected. He is not the typical 'cunning slave' (*servus callidus*) often found in this type of comedy, a figure who was a great favourite with Plautus and of whom Syrus in *The Self-Tormentor* provides a good example in Terence. This cunning slave is a highly successful operator whose inventive machinations on behalf of his master's son often provide the mainspring of the

---

154   It therefore becomes necessary to explain the presence of the examples of the conventional characterization in the play. Parmeno's comments (67-70, 79-80, 934-40 - the majority of those given) can be explained as those of a fairly undiscerning slave who sees everything in black and white - in this case black; Phaedria's remarks at 163-9 as spoken at a time of emotion, frustration and disappointment; Gnatho's at 1075 as designed to encourage Phaedria to accept his proposals.

155   See p. 4, and n. 14. My earlier contention (Brothers (1969) 316 and n. 4) that Don.'s comment at 198 must mean that the depiction of Thais as kindly is a Terentian innovation / alteration is wrong. It may mean this, but it does not have to.

156   She has been left some property by the friend who brought her to Athens (120), and runs a considerable establishment - as maids she has, besides Pythias and Dorias, the unspecified number who accompany her to Thraso's (506, 581), and the few new ones who are left behind to look after Pamphila's needs (581-2).

157   See the introductory note to Act Five Scene Nine (pp. 207-8).

action. Parmeno, however, is not particularly successful,[158] but is an example of the 'bungling' slave, in much the same way that the kindly courtesan is a variant on the expected picture of that character-type. At first, with his advice to Phaedria (57-80), he seems likely to turn out in the expected way.[159] Later, however, far from leaping into action, he is aghast when his jocular suggestion that Chaerea should change places with the eunuch is taken seriously (378-9), is afraid that the adventure will prove "too hot to handle" (380) and a rod for his own back (381), and is finally reduced to extracting from Chaerea a promise that no blame will attach to him (388-9) and to uttering a feeble prayer for success (390). Later still, when he returns to see how Chaerea has fared (923), he is only too keen to take the credit for his original suggestion and makes exaggerated claims about the benefits it will bring the young man (929-40). Then, when Pythias tells him a pack of lies about Chaerea's impending punishment as an adulterer (943-58), he swallows the story hook, line and sinker and repeats it to the brothers' father; by now he is speechless and shaking with fear (977-8) and then more than once denies all responsibility for the escapade for which he was so recently claiming credit (980, 988). Pythias rubs salt into his wounds by explaining how she has duped him (1009-16),[160] and Parmeno, despite a feeble threat to get his own back (1019), is reduced to utter misery (1023-4), fearing the punishment with which the old man had threatened him (989-90) and which Pythias sees is in store for him (1021-2). However, he soon learns of the happy ending to both Chaerea's and Phaedria's troubles and of Chaerea's gratitude (1034-41), and we assume, as presumably he does, that the punishment will not be inflicted.[161] But his less-than-successful role is perhaps stressed by the fact that, when he leaves the stage at Chaerea's bidding to tell Phaedria the good news (1042), he does not reappear. His part in the play ends on a low note.

However, we cannot leave Parmeno without mentioning that he also has some endearing characteristics, particularly his loyalty to the two brothers. At 469-85 he does his best to fulfil Phaedria's instructions (214-5) to make his presents to Thais appear in as good a light as possible and to ingratiate his young master with the

---

158 Gratwick (1972) 30 n. 5 refers to "the dim Parmeno".

159 After centuries of assumption - from Horace and Persius to Fabia and Ludwig - that Parmeno's advice in the opening scene is both practical and consistent, it has recently been suggested that it is not, and that what he says foreshadows his later 'bungling' role. The arguments depend partly, but not wholly, on whether 50-6 are ascribed to Parmeno or Phaedria. See Barsby (1990), with references to other literature. He suggests (10) the "intriguing possibility" that the "bumblingly ambiguous Parmeno" could even be a Terentian innovation.

160 It is no doubt in order to point up the contrast between Parmeno and the cunning slave that Ter. has Pythias say that she had at first thought him "such a cunning, clever fellow" (1011), the word *callidus* actually being used.

161 Slaves, whether cunning or not, obtain forgiveness, however grudgingly given, by the end of these plays; they are, after all, comedies.

courtesan; he is consistently rude to and about Gnatho and Thraso (254, 265, 272, 288, 418-9, 430, 457-8, 464, 489-91, 494-5); and even when he is convinced that he is in desperate trouble, he tries to prevent Chaerea's punishment by revealing the young man's identity (961-2), and he realizes he must help him by telling his father, even if it means he will be punished himself (968-9). A bungler who is terrified of the old man he may be; but he is also, within his limited capabilities, a champion of his two younger masters.

Pythias is an engaging character who has an unusually large role in the play for a maid (or, more strictly, female slave, *ancilla*). She is on stage for over 300 lines (500-38, 643-754, 767-8, 817-922, 941-70, 1002-23),[162] and makes a considerable contribution to both the dialogue[163] and the action. She is forceful, lively, clever and ebullient, showing initiative and resource, especially in her revenge on Parmeno (910ff.), where her inventiveness and convincing play-acting fool the slave completely (943-70), and she gets great amusement from his gullibility and discomfiture (1002-23). Earlier, she uses all her charm on Chremes when she wants him to comply with Thais' instructions (531-7), and is sufficiently authoritative to tell Dorias to do what Thais had asked her to do herself (538). When the rape is discovered, her threats against the perpetrator, both before he has been unmasked and when she later confronts him, are violent (647-8, 859-60), and she is angry with Phaedria as the giver of the gift (651-2) and very scornful of his protestations that it was Dorus who went into Thais' house (680-2, 685-9). When Thais in turn finds out what has happened, she temporarily loses her self-assurance before her mistress' anger (817-33), but she quickly regains it when she spots the returning Chaerea, suggesting he should be arrested immediately and protesting at his impudent and self-confident manner (834-9). When Thais confronts Chaerea, she protests at his explanations (856-8), warns her mistress against trusting him (883, 896-900) and still strongly distrusts him herself (884, 901-4) and mocks him (908), even when Thais has come completely round. Thais herself has to restrain this spirited woman more than once (861, 884, 899). We feel that it is only when she has failed to ensure that Chaerea gets what she regards as his just deserts that she turns her attention to getting the revenge on Parmeno which she had threatened some time before (718-9).

Thraso, who is the only example of the 'swaggering soldier' (*miles gloriosus*) in Terence, is yet another character who is not quite what we expect. Unlike, for example, Pyrgopolynices in Plautus' *The Swaggering Soldier*, he does not continually boast of his military exploits.[164] Instead he prides himself on his ability

---

162 These lines represent the minimum for Pythias' presence on stage, since more than once there is doubt about the precise point at which she enters or leaves. See the introductory note to Act Three Scene Three, 754n., 767n., 941n.

163 Martin discusses how Ter. "lends emphasis to her character by according her a markedly distinctive manner of speaking" (139).

164 At 482-3 Parmeno tells Thais that Phaedria does not "talk of his battles and show you his scars ... like someone [Thraso] does", thus viewing Thraso as a soldier in the typical

to please others (395-6), especially his superiors (397-8, 401-7), and on his wit at other people's expense - such as the man in charge of the elephants (412-5) and the young man from Rhodes (419-26), where, as elsewhere,[165] his wit is coarse and crude. Moreover, his siege of Thais' house (771ff.), with a motley band of kitchen slaves as his 'troops', is all empty bombast[166] and, when Thais and Chremes stand up to him, he leaps at the chance (offered by Gnatho's advice, 811) to call it off immediately (814). And his desire to find favour with Thais is unmanly and pathetic in its intensity (391-2, 446, 455-7, 1053-5), while his jealousy knows no bounds (137ff., 615ff., 792ff.).

He is more typical of his type in his general dullness of intelligence.[167] He is noted, too, for his gullibility and his total inability to see when he is being mocked to his face - both characteristics being emphasized by the remarks, aside or spoken aloud, of others (especially Gnatho, 409-10, 428, 452-3, 782, 1089-91). And at the end of the play, even when he has been totally humiliated and been forced to crawl both unsuccessfully to Phaedria (1061ff.) and more successfully to Gnatho (1054ff.) to be allowed to retain a place in Thais' affections, he still thinks he has got what little he has got because of his great popularity with all and sundry (1091-2). All in all, he is an unattractive and undeserving character, and one more surprising feature of the ending of the play is the fact that he is permitted to retain a 'part-share' in Thais.[168] But the price he will pay is heavy. Not only will he put his wealth at the disposal of Thais (and, one suspects, of Phaedria and Chaerea too) for the foreseeable future (1073ff.), but he will also have to bear the cost of feeding and entertaining Gnatho whenever the toady chooses (1058-60).

The remaining major character in the play is Gnatho, the toady or sponger (*colax* or *parasitus*).[169] Spongers are professional 'hangers-on', whose main aim in life is to obtain free meals at the tables of those to whom they attach themselves; they earn their keep either by being the butt of jokes and being knocked about (cf.

---

mould. This may be an indication that the rival in Men.'s *The Eunuch*, whom Thraso replaces, had been a soldier of the conventional type.

165 Cf. his lecherous remark about the false eunuch Chaerea (479).

166 Cf. 785, where Thais says he is "a great big windbag".

167 Cf. Gnatho at 1079: "He's silly, stupid and slow, and spends his nights and days snoring away."

168 The 'obvious' ending would involve the total ousting of Phaedria's rival, and there may be indications in Ter.'s text that this is what did happen in Men.'s *The Eunuch* (see 1040n., 1063n.).

169 The words *colax* (κόλαξ, lit. "flatterer") and *parasitus* (παράσιτος, lit. "someone who eats alongside", i.e. at someone else's table, not his own) emphasise the two chief aspects of the character's way of life - his art of flattery and the use of it to obtain free meals. In the body of the play Gnatho is always termed a *parasitus* (228, 264, 347), as he is also in the prologue (26, 30), though on the latter occasion he is called a "*toadying* sponger" (*parasitus colax*).

244-5n.) or by their witty conversation and clever jokes. Gnatho, who adopts the
second approach, is the only example of the type in Ter., whose only other parasite,
the name-character in *Ph.*, is rather different.[170]

Gnatho explains his 'philosophy' of sponging (which is not as new and original
as he claims it is; see 247n.) in his speech at 232-64; his words characterize him as
arrogant, self-centred and self-satisfied, a man whose sole objective is to do well for
himself, regardless of the feelings and wishes of everybody else. He is seen putting
his philosophy into action principally in his conversation with Thraso in Act Three
Scene One (391-453), but also in the siege scene (771-816). Various aspects of his
unpleasant character are exhibited in his attitude to Parmeno (270-87, 477-8), his
snide remarks behind Thraso's back (409-10, 782) and his brokering of the final deal
with Phaedria (1067-85). He is thoroughly detestable, and the fact that he does so
well out of the arrangements agreed at the end is the most surprising of the several
surprising elements of that conclusion.

Enough has been said already to indicate that the end of the play strikes the
modern reader as peculiar - though we must always beware of assuming that Ter.'s
audience would have felt the same way as we do. As far as the characters in the
Phaedria / Thais half of the plot are concerned (and only they, since Chaerea's
problems have already been solved), none of them seems to get his or her just
deserts. They come out of things either with less than they wanted (Phaedria) or
with more than they deserve (Thraso and Gnatho) or with their future settled for
them above their heads (Thais). It is more than likely that at least some of these
strange features are the result of the import of Thraso and Gnatho from Men.'s *The
Toady*, and the consequent substitution of the ending of that play for the ending of
Men.'s *The Eunuch*. For fuller details, see the introductory note to Act Five Scene
Nine (pp. 207–8).

VII   THE TEXT[171]

The manuscripts of Terence - the number of which has been put as high as 650, with
more than 100 dating from the ninth to thirteenth centuries - are divided into two
main groups. In the first group there is just one representative, the codex Bembinus

---

170   Phormio belongs to the sub-type of professional 'fixer', who assists others in their
      schemes, and in these cases there is less stress on food and getting fed. On at least one
      occasion Gnatho seems to belong to this sub-type himself - see 434ff. n. The more
      normal 'hungry' parasite is more frequent in Plautus (e.g. Ergasilus in *The Prisoners*,
      Curculio in the play of that name, Peniculus in *The Brothers Menaechmus*
      (*Menaechmi*), Saturio in *The Persian* (*Persa*) and Gelasimus in *Stichus*.
171   The best short modern discussion is by M.D. Reeve in Reynolds (ed.), 412-20. The
      most detailed work, though one now superseded on some points, is Jachmann. For
      recent developments on Jachmann's work, see Grant (1973), (1975) and (1986).

(A). This has the distinction of being one of our earliest manuscripts of a Latin writer, dating from the late fourth or early fifth century AD, and it presents the plays in the order given in the production notices (*An., Eu., Hau., Ph., Hec., Ad.*). The second group, commonly known as 'Calliopian' because some of them bear witness to a recension by a certain Calliopius,[172] embraces the medieval manuscripts. It is itself divided into three sub-groups. Two of these, the large γ class and smaller δ class, go back to lost archetypes known as Γ and Δ respectively, which themselves in turn go back to a common lost archetype designated Σ. The third Calliopian class, which is by far the largest, is the so-called 'mixed' manuscripts, which appear to share, to differing extents, the characteristics now of γ, now of δ, and do not go directly back to either Γ or Δ; given the availability of manuscripts for copyists to consult in the middle ages and the frequent copying which must have been done, it is hardly surprising that such a mixed group should arise, though it is sometimes difficult to establish exactly what has happened to individual manuscripts in this area of the tradition.

The relationship of the lost Calliopian archetype Σ to A has been much discussed. It is now generally accepted that the presence of errors common to them both ensures that they both go back to a lost archetype of their own designated Φ, and are not, as Marouzeau holds,[173] independent of one another in separate descent from Terence. The associated matter of the date of Σ, and its relation to the date of A and of Φ, cannot be known with certainty, though there are some clues;[174] neither can the date of the division of Σ into the Γ and Δ traditions.

The division into the γ and δ classes is based upon three principal differences: omissions and errors common to one group and not the other; the order of the plays (in both cases different from that in A) - in δ an alphabetical sequence (*An., Ad., Eu., Ph.* (= *F.*), *Hau., Hec.*),[175] and in γ *An., Eu., Hau., Ad., Hec., Ph.*;[176] and thirdly the

---

172 "The identity of Calliopius and the extent of his influence on the tradition are problems that remain unsolved" (Grant (1975) 123, n. 1).

173 I 85ff.

174 For instance, since both A and the Calliopians contain the summaries (*periochae*) of the plays written by C. Sulpicius Apollinaris sometime in the middle of the second century AD, it has been supposed that Φ must be later than that date. But "such an embellishment would be apt to spread" (Reeve in Reynolds (ed.) 414, n. 18).

175 Grant (1975) 152 thinks that this alphabetical arrangement is "a secondary development within the δ branch", i.e. it may not have been a characteristic of Δ, but arose later.

176 Marouzeau I 81 gives the order in γ incorrectly. F. Leo (1883), 'Die Überlieferungsgeschichte der terenzischen Komödien und der Commentar des Donatus', *RhM* 38, 317-47 believes (319) that the order represents the four plays from Menander followed by the two from Apollodorus. Grant (1973) 102-3 finds this "not very convincing"; he suggests the ingenious alternative that the order derives from a "two-volume edition" based on the same chronological sequence as appears in A, but in

presence in some γ manuscripts of miniature illustrations at the head of scenes, depicting the characters featured. Jachmann showed that these illustrations are based upon reading of the text, and not, as was once thought, upon memories of actual performances (and therefore in origin antedating the demise of Terence in the theatres). The date the miniatures arose within the tradition is uncertain, as is their precise provenance.[177]

Although, as has been said, A and Σ contain a number of common errors, and although A has others which are not found in Σ, A is nevertheless in general superior. This is not necessarily because of its considerably greater age, but because the tradition of which it is the sole representative is, relatively speaking, purer and less subject to emendation and interpolation than that represented by Σ. The latter contains more such changes, many of them probably designed to make Terence easier to read in schools. As to the Σ manuscripts themselves, it had long been accepted that the δ class was superior to the γ class, but this is yet another of the traditional views about the transmission of Terence's text which has been seen not to have the force it was once believed to have.[178]

In the apparatus criticus of this edition the following manuscripts are cited:

1	A	Codex Bembinus (Vatican lat. 3226)	4th/5th cent.
2	δ manuscripts:		
	D	Codex Victorianus (Florence, Laur. XXXVIII 24)	10th cent.
		Lacking *Eu. periocha*.[179]	
	G	Codex Decurtatus (Vatican lat. 1640)	11th cent.
		Lacking *Eu.* 848-1021.	
	p	Codex Parisinus (Paris lat. 10304)	10th cent.
	L	Codex Lipsiensis (Leipzig 1 37)	10th cent.
		(L is classed by some as 'mixed'.)	
3	γ manuscripts:		
	P	Codex Parisinus (Paris lat. 7899) - illustrated	9th cent.
		Lacking *Eu. periocha*, 1-30, 643-51; 1-30 and 643-51 are supplied by later hands.[180]	
	C	Codex Vaticanus (Vatican lat. 3868) - illustrated	9th cent.
		Lacking *Eu. periocha*, 1-45; 1-45 are supplied by a later hand.[181]	
	F	Codex Ambrosianus (Milan, Ambr. H 75 inf.) - illustrated	10th cent.

---

the second volume of which the last three plays (*Ph.*, *Hec.*, *Ad.*) were re-arranged into alphabetical order.
177 Grant (1973) 100ff. feels that they were not directly designed for Γ.
178 See, for instance, Duckworth 438 and n. 2, and Reeve in Reynolds (ed.) 413.
179 Statements about omissions refer only to those in *Eu.*
180 '(P)' in the apparatus criticus.
181 '(C)' in the apparatus criticus.

Lacking *Eu.* 1-415, 424-36, 454-7; 416-23 are supplied
by a 15th-century hand.

E	Codex Riccardianus (Florence, Ricc. 528)	11th cent.
	Lacking *Eu. periocha.*	
η	Codex Einsidlensis I (Einsiedeln 362)	10th cent.
	Lacking *Eu.* 753-836, 1034-94.	
ε	Codex Einsidlensis II (Einsiedeln 362)	10th cent.
	Lacking *Eu.* 1-27, 38-101.	
v	Codex Valentiennensis (Valenciennes 448 [420])	11th cent.
	(F and E are classed by some as 'mixed'.)	

The manuscripts contain corrections by later hands (D^2 E^2 etc. in the apparatus). In the case of A particularly important is a certain Jovialis or Joviales, who corrected the Bembinus and introduced changes from the Calliopian tradition. The precise extent of his responsibility for the alterations in A is the subject of disagreement;[182] I use the abbreviation 'Iov.' in the wider way in which it is employed in the Oxford Text.

It is traditional, following the manuscripts, to mark act- and scene-divisions in the plays. It seems certain that the division of the plays into five acts was not the work of Terence, who wrote them for continuous performance, but was introduced afterwards by Roman scholars who knew that the Greek originals had been so divided; Donatus affirms that Varro knew of such divisions, but admits to the difficulty of dividing them.[183] Division into scenes is marked in the manuscripts where characters enter by a scene heading indicating the names and often the roles of the characters in that scene; it is at these points that some manuscripts have the miniature illustrations.

To the evidence of the manuscripts we can sometimes add the testimony of Donatus (cf. apparatus 219, 222, 312). There are also Eugraphius' commentary (cf. 300, 314, 926), the work of scholiasts, especially those in A, the scholia Bembina (cf. 380, 559),[184] and quotations, mainly in ancient grammarians (cf. 41, 274), but also in other writers (cf. 605). The problem with such quotations is, of course, that those who quoted them may have been employing a text which was already corrupt, quoting from memory, or even altering Terence to suit their own Latinity. One further source is glossaries (*glossae*), collections of unfamiliar words. One of these,

---

182   Marti (1961) 124-6 summarizes the various views.
183   See Don.'s remarks in his prefaces to *An.*, *Eu.*, *Ad.*, and *Hec.* (I 38, 40; I 266; II 4; II 192). For act- and scene-divisions in general, see Beare ch. XXV; Duckworth 98-101.
184   For the scholia in A see Mountford. The scholia of D, G, C and E, and of a 'mixed' manuscript at Munich (M), are in Schlee.

indicated by the abbreviation 'gl. l' in the Oxford Text (and in this edition), provides the correct reading once (493) and lends support to a minority view once (570).[185]

In spite of - perhaps because of - the existence of so many manuscripts, no really comprehensive critical edition of the text of Terence has yet appeared. The best is still that of F. Umpfenbach (Berlin, 1870), followed by the Oxford Text of R. Kauer and W.M. Lindsay (2nd edn, Oxford, 1926; additions to the apparatus by O. Skutsch, 1958) and the Budé edition of J. Marouzeau (3 vols, Paris, 1942-9). The elaborate edition of S. Prete (Heidelberg, 1954) contains many errors.[186]

NOTE ON THE TEXT AND APPARATUS CRITICUS OF THIS EDITION

The text of this edition is printed without the marks employed in the Oxford Text to facilitate scansion in accordance with the practices of early Latin verse. In addition, I have not followed that text's practice of indicating by an apostrophe the dropping of final -s after a short vowel and before an initial consonant (whether or not a particular instance might be deemed metrically 'necessary'). I have written -um est, -a est, -o est etc. rather than -umst, -ast, -ost, since it is perfectly possible for readers to scan a line with either form before them; but I have where necessary written -ust not -us est (e.g. 546), -u's not -us es (e.g. 559) etc., since not to do so could seriously mislead the reader interested in scansion. The aim of this (perhaps not entirely consistent) procedure has been to present as uncluttered and easily readable a Latin text as possible; my excuse must be that the commentary is not primarily concerned with metrical considerations.

In matters of spelling - quoi / cui; tuos / tuus etc. - sometimes connected with metrical matters - mihi / mi; nihil / nil - I have generally followed the Oxford Text. But I have considerably altered that text's punctuation to bring it more into line with modern English practice.

The apparatus criticus makes no claims to completeness or originality, but is highly selective and taken wholly from published sources. Since, for example, "neither Δ nor Γ anywhere seems to preserve the truth significantly against the agreement of the other with the Bembinus",[187] I have not generally included instances where A and the δ manuscripts agree against γ, or where A and γ agree against δ; exceptions are occasions where the Oxford Text accepts the minority view. Where the reading I adopt has manuscript support, I have not quoted the conjectures of those who find all the manuscript readings unsatisfactory - with the

---

185 See Weir, R. (1922), 'Terence glosses in the Abolita glossary' *CQ* 16, 44-50 and Lindsay, W. M. (1925), 'Two lost manuscripts of Terence', *CQ* 19, 101-2.
186 See the review by Skutsch, O. (1956), *CR* ns 6, 129-33.
187 Reeve in Reynolds (ed.) 413.

exception of conjectures appearing in the Oxford Text. Where I accept a conjecture, I cite its source, but do not give rival conjectures - with the same exceptions.

Of the manuscripts listed above, I regularly cite seven, A, D and G from δ, and P, C, F and E from γ, in that order; only occasionally do I cite the others. Σ indicates the consensus of the Calliopian manuscripts, and I use 'Don.' for Donatus and 'Eugr.' for Eugraphius. Where I use editors' names, details of their editions are to be found in the bibliography.

I have adopted a reading different from that of the Oxford Text, or differ from it significantly in matters of punctuation, at the following points:

Production notice: 3. Play: 3, 25, 30, 36, 41, 50, 57, 145, 150, 151, 168, 192, 197, 203, 232, 233, 240, 267, 268, 276, 280, 286, 288, 303, 305-6, 307, 319, 322, 324, 328, 335, 343, 356, 361, 370, 376, 385, 489, 499, 520, 546, 561, 563, 577, 651, 673, 674, 699, 708, 710, 721, 724, 725, 726, 739, 766, 781, 795, 811, 878, 886, 898, 952, 956, 959, 968, 969, 977, 986, 991, 1017, 1031, 1041, 1052, 1056, 1063, 1072, 1081.

Bibliography

A.   Texts, editions and translations

(i)   Terence

The following are cited by the surname(s) of the editor(s) or translator only.

ASHMORE, S. G. (1908), *The Comedies of Terence*[2] (New York); introduction, critical text and commentary.

BARSBY, J. A. (1999), *Terence, Eunuchus* (Cambridge); introduction, text and commentary, with appendices on metre and scansion, and on the remains of Men.'s *Eunouchos* and *Kolax*.

BENTLEY, R. (1726), *Publii Terenti Afri Comoediae* (Cambridge); critical text and Latin commentary.

DZIATZKO, K. (1884), *P. Terenti Afri Comoediae* (Leipzig); critical text.

FABIA, P. (1895), *P. Terenti Afri Eunuchus* (Paris).

FLECKEISEN, A. (1898), *P. Terenti Afri Comoediae*[2] (Leipzig); critical text.

KAUER, R. and LINDSAY, W. M. (1958), *P. Terenti Afri Comoediae*[2], with additions to the apparatus by SKUTSCH, O. (Oxford); critical text.

MAROUZEAU, J. (1942-9), *Térence*, 3 vols (Paris); critical text, French translation and notes, with a general introduction in vol. 1; *Eu.* is in vol. 1.

PRETE, S. (1954), *P. Terenti Afri Comoediae* (Heidelberg); critical text.

RADICE, B. (1976), *Terence, The Comedies* (London); introduction and English translation, and including a translation of Suetonius, *Life of Terence*.

SARGEAUNT, J. (1912), *Terence*, 2 vols (Cambridge, Mass. and London); short introduction, text and English translation; *Eu.* is in vol. 1.

UMPFENBACH, F. (1870), *P. Terenti Comoediae* (Berlin); critical text.

(ii)   Others

The following are cited by the surname(s) of the editor(s) or translator only, with the exception of Wessner's text of Donatus and Eugraphius, which is cited as Donatus (Don.) or Eugraphius (Eugr.).

ARNOTT, W. G. (1979, 1996, 2000), *Menander* (Cambridge, Mass. and London), 3 vols; introduction, text and English translation; the fragments of Men.'s *Kolax* are in II 151-203.

BARSBY, J. A. (1986), *Plautus, Bacchides* (Warminster); introduction, text, English translation and commentary.

BROTHERS, A. J. (1988), *Terence, The Self-Tormentor* (Warminster); introduction, text, English translation and commentary.

GOMME, A. W. and SANDBACH, F. H. (1973), *Menander, a Commentary* (Oxford).

GRATWICK, A. S. (1987), *Terence, The Brothers* (Warminster); introduction, text, English translation and commentary.

GRATWICK, A. S. (1999), *Terence, The Brothers*[2] (Warminster); introduction, text, English translation and commentary.

IRELAND, S. (1995), *Menander, The Bad-Tempered Man* (Warminster); introduction, text, English translation and commentary.

KÖRTE, A. (rev. THIERFELDER, A.) (1957, 1959), *Menander, Reliquiae*, 2 vols (Leipzig); the fragments of Men.'s *Eu.* are in II 66-9, and of his *Kolax* in I 110-19.

MILLER, N. P. (1987), *Menander, Plays and Fragments* (London); introduction and English translation.

MOUNTFORD, J. F. (1934), *The Scholia Bembina* (Liverpool and London).

SCHLEE, F. (1893), *Scholia Terentiana* (Leipzig).

WESSNER, P. (1902-8), *Aeli Donati quod fertur Commentum Terenti. Accedunt Eugraphii Commentum et Scholia Bembina*, 3 vols (Leipzig); vols I and II contain Donatus' commentary, prefaced in vol. I by Suetonius, *Vita Terenti*, Evanthius, *De Fabula* and *Excerpta de Comoedia* - the commentary on *Eu.* occupies I 263-497; vol. III, part 1, contains Eugraphius' commentary, with the commentary on *Eu.* occupying 87-150; vol. III, part 2, to contain the *Scholia Bembina*, was never published.

B.   Other works

Those of the works in the following list which are mentioned in the Introduction and Commentary are cited there by the surname of the author only. Other works (including additional works by authors in this list) are always cited in full.

ALLARDICE, J. T. (1929), *The Syntax of Terence* (London).

ANDRIEU, J. (1954), *Le Dialogue Antique* (Paris).

ARNOTT, W. G. (1975), *Menander, Plautus, Terence* (Oxford).

BAIN, D. (1977), *Actors and Audience: a Study of Asides and Related Conventions in Greek Drama* (Oxford).

BARSBY, J. A. (1990), 'The Characterisation of Parmeno in the Opening Scene of Terence's *Eunuch*', *Prudentia* 22, 4-12.

BARSBY, J. A. (1993), 'Problems of Adaptation in the *Eunuchus* of Terence' in SLATER, N. W. and ZIMMERMANN, B. (eds), *Intertextualität in der griechisch-römischen Komödie* (Stuttgart), 160-79.

BARSBY, J. A. (1999a), 'Love in Terence' in *Amor : Roma, Love and Latin Literature : Essays presented to E. J. Kenney* (Cambridge), 5-29.

BARTON, A. (1990), *The Names of Comedy* (Oxford).

BEACHAM, R. C. (1991), *The Roman Theatre and its Audience* (London).

BEARE, W. (1964), *The Roman Stage*[3] (London).

BIANCO, O. (1962), *Terenzio: Problemi e Aspetti dell' Originalità* (Rome), esp. 133-68.

BIEBER, M. (1961), *The History of the Greek and Roman Theater*[2] (Princeton, NJ, and London).

BROTHERS, A. J. (1969), 'Terence, *Eunuchus* 189-206', *CQ* ns 19, 314-9.

BROWN, P. G. McC. (1990), 'The Bodmer Codex of Menander and the Endings of Terence's *Eunuchus* and Other Roman Comedies' in HANDLEY, E. and HURST, A. (eds), *Relire Ménandre* (Geneva).

BROWN, P. G. McC. (1991), 'Athenian Attitudes to Rape and Seduction: the Evidence of Menander, *Dyskolos* 289-93', *CQ* ns 41, 533-4.

BROWN, P. G. McC. (1992), 'Menander, fragments 745 and 746KT, Menander's *Kolax* and Parasites and Flatterers in Greek Comedy', *ZPE* 92, 91-107.

BROWN, P. G. McC. (1993), 'The Skinny Virgins of Terence, *Eunuchus* 313-17' in *Tria Lustra: Essays and Notes presented to John Pinsent* (Liverpool), 229-34.

BÜCHNER, K. (1972), *Das Theater des Terenz* (Heidelberg).

CUPAIUOLO, G. (1984), *Bibliografia Terenziana (1470-1983)* (Naples).

CUPAIUOLO, G. (1992), 'Supplementum Terentianum', *BStudLat* 22, 32-57.

DENZLER, B. (1968), *Der Monolog bei Terenz* (Zurich).

DREXLER, H. (1938), 'Terentiana', *Hermes* 73, 39-98.

DREXLER, H. (1941), 'Zum Eunuch des Terenz', *Hermes* 76, 75-83.

DUCKWORTH, G. E. (1952), *The Nature of Roman Comedy* (Princeton, NJ).

FRANGOULIDIS, S. A. (1994), 'The Soldier as Storyteller in Terence's *Eunuchus*', *Mnemosyne* 47, 586-95.

GAISER, K. (1972), 'Zur Eigenart der römischen Komödie: Plautus und Terenz gegenüber ihren griechischen Vorbildern', *Aufstieg und Niedergang der römischen Welt* I, 2, 1027-1113 (Berlin and New York).

GILMARTIN, K. (1975-6), 'The Thraso-Gnatho Sub-Plot in Terence's *Eunuchus*', *CW* 69, 263-7.

GILULA, D. (1980), 'The Concept of the *bona meretrix*: a Study of Terence's Courtesans', *RFIC* 108, 142-65.

GOLDBERG, S. M. (1986), *Understanding Terence* (Princeton, NJ).

GRANT, J. N. (1973), 'G and the Miniatures of Terence', *CQ* ns 23, 88-103.

GRANT, J. N. (1975), 'Contamination in the Mixed MSS of Terence', *TAPLA* 105, 123-53.

GRANT, J. N. (1986), *Studies in the Textual Tradition of Terence* (Toronto, Buffalo, London).

GRATWICK, A. S. (1972), review of LEFÈVRE (1969), *CR* ns 22, 29-32.

GRATWICK, A. S. (1982), 'Drama' in KENNEY, E. J. and CLAUSEN, W. V. (eds), *The Cambridge History of Classical Literature II: Latin Literature* (Cambridge), 77-137.

HORNBLOWER, S. and SPAWFORTH, S. (eds) (1996), *The Oxford Classical Dictionary*[3] (Oxford) [*OCD*[3]].

HOUGH, J. N. (1945), ' The *numquid vis* Formula in Roman Comedy', *AJPh* 66, 282-302.

HUNTER, R. L. (1985), *The New Comedy of Greece and Rome* (Cambridge).

JACHMANN, G. (1924), *Die Geschichte des Terenztextes in Altertum* (Basle).

JAMES, S. L. (1998), 'From Boys to Men: Rape and Developing Masculinity in Terence's *Hecyra* and *Eunuchus*', *Helios* 25, 31-47.

JENKINS, E. B. (1932), *Index Verborum Terentianus* (Chapel Hill, NC).

KNOCHE, U. (1941), 'Terenz oder Menander?', *Hermes* 76, 251-69.

KONSTAN, D. (1986), 'Love in Terence's *Eunuch*: the Origins of Erotic Subjectivity', *AJPh* 107, 369-93.

LAIDLAW, W. A. (1938), *The Prosody of Terence* (London).

LEFÈVRE, E. (1969), *Die Expositionstechnik in den Komödien des Terenz*, (Darmstadt).

LEFÈVRE, E. (ed.) (1973), *Die römische Komödie: Plautus und Terenz* (Darmstadt).

LEVIN, R. (1996-7), 'The Double Plots of Terence', *CJ* 62, 301-5.

LLOYD-JONES, H. (1973), 'Terentian Technique in the *Adelphi* and *Eunuchus*', *CQ* ns 23, 279-84.

LOWE, J. C. B. (1983), 'The *Eunuchus*: Terence and Menander', *CQ* ns 33, 428-44.

LOWE, J. C. B. (1997), 'Terence's Four-Speaker Scenes', *Phoenix* 51, 152-69.

LUCK, G. (1964), *Über einige Interjektionen der Lateinischen Umgangssprache* (Heidelberg).

LUDWIG, W. (1959), 'Von Terenz zu Menander', *Philologus* 103, 1-38.

LUDWIG, W. (1968), 'The Originality of Terence and his Greek Models', *GRBS* 9, 169-82.

MALTBY, R. (1985), 'The Distribution of Greek Loan-Words in Terence', *CQ* ns 35, 110-23.

MARTI, H. (1961, 1963), 'Terenz 1909-59', *Lustrum* 6, 114-238, and 8, 5-101 and 244-247.

MARTIN, R. H. (1995), 'A Not-So-Minor Character in Terence's *Eunuchus*', *CPh* 90, 139-51.

McGLYNN, P. (1963, 1967), *Lexicon Terentianum*, 2 vols (London and Glasgow).

McLEISH, K. (1976), *Roman Comedy* (London).

NORWOOD, G. (1923), *The Art of Terence* (Oxford).

PEPE, G. M. (1971-2), 'The Last Scene of Terence's *Eunuchus*', *CW* 69, 141-5.

PHILIPPIDES, K. (1995), 'Terence's *Eunuchus*: Elements of the Marriage Ritual in the Rape Scene', *Mnemosyne* 48, 272-84.

PIERCE, K. F. (1997), 'The Portrayal of Rape in Roman Comedy' in DEACY, S. and PIERCE, K. F. (eds), *Rape in Antiquity: Sexual Violence in the Greek and Roman Worlds* (London), 163-84.

QUESTA, C. (1967), *Introduzione alla Metrica di Plauto* (Bologna).

RAND, E. K. (1932), 'The Art of Terence's *Eunuchus*', *TAPhA* 63, 54-72.

REEVE, M. D. (1983), 'Terence' in REYNOLDS, L. D. (ed.) (1983), *Texts and Transmission* (Oxford), 412-20.

SANDBACH, F. H. (1975), 'Menander and the Three-Actor Rule' in *Le Mond Grec. Hommages à Claire Préaux* (Brussels), 197-204.

SANDBACH, F. H. (1977), *The Comic Theatre of Greece and Rome* (London).

SANDBACH, F. H. (1982) in *Ancient Writers: Greece and Rome I* (New York), 547-8.

SMITH, L. P. (1994), 'Audience Response to Rape: Chaerea in Terence's *Eunuchus*', *Helios* 21, 21-38.

WEBSTER, T. B. L. (1960), *Studies in Menander*^{2} (Manchester).

WEBSTER, T. B. L. (1974), *An Introduction to Menander* (Manchester).

WHITEHORN, J. (1993), 'The Rapist's Disguise in Menander's *Eunuchus*' in SLATER, N. W. and ZIMMERMANN, B. (eds), *Intertextualität in der griechisch-römischen Komödie* (Stuttgart), 122-32.

WRIGHT, J. (1974), *Dancing in Chains: the Stylistic Unity of the Comoedia Palliata* (Rome).

ZAGAGI, N. (1994), *The Comedy of Menander* (London).

A note on abbreviations

For ancient sources I have followed the conventions set out in GLARE, P. G. W. (ed.) (1968-82), *Oxford Latin Dictionary* (Oxford) - a work here abbreviated to *OLD*. In addition, I use 'Eugr.' for Eugraphius and 'Men.' for Menander. For modern periodicals I follow the conventions used in *L'Année Philologique*.

List of Metres

As has already been stated in the Introduction (p. 40), this edition is not primarily concerned with metrical matters; the text is printed very largely without the 'aids' to scansion which appear in some modern versions, and metre is only occasionally mentioned in the commentary. However, the reader who is interested in this topic may find it helpful to refer to the following list of metres, as they relate to the text adopted in this edition.

Periocha	Iambic senarii	616	Trochaic septenarius
1-206	Iambic senarii	617	Iambic octonarius
207	Trochaic octonarius	618-20	Trochaic octonarii
208	Trochaic septenarius	621	Trochaic septenarius
209	Iambic dimeter	622	Iambic octonarius
210-11	Trochaic septenarii	623-8	Trochaic septenarii
212	Iambic octonarius	629-42	Iambic senarii
213	Iambic dimeter	643-4	Trochaic octonarii
214	Trochaic septenarius	645	Trochaic septenarius
215	Iambic dimeter	646	Iambic octonarius
216-17	Trochaic octonarii	647	Iambic dimeter
218	Trochaic septenarius	648	Iambic octonarius
219-23	Iambic octonarii	649	Trochaic septenarius
224-54	Trochaic septenarii	650-1	Iambic octonarii
255-91	Iambic septenarii	652	Iambic dimeter
292	Extrametrical	653	Iambic octonarius
293-7	Iambic octonarii	654	Trochaic octonarius
298	Trochaic septenarius	655	Trochaic septenarius
299	Iambic dimeter	656-7	Iambic octonarii
300	Iambic senarius	658	Iambic senarius
301	Iambic dimeter	659-67	Iambic octonarii
302-3	Iambic octonarii	668-702	Iambic senarii
304	Trochaic octonarius	703-26	Trochaic septenarii
305	Trochaic septenarius	727-37	Iambic octonarii
306	Iambic dimeter	738	Iambic senarius
307-19	Iambic octonarii	739-46	Trochaic octonarii
320	Iambic senarius	747	Trochaic dimeter catalectic
321-2	Iambic septenarii		
323-51	Iambic senarii	748	Trochaic octonarius
352-66	Trochaic septenarii	749	Trochaic septenarius
367-90	Iambic octonarii	750	Iambic octonarius
391-538	Iambic senarii	751-2	Trochaic septenarii
539-48	Iambic septenarii	753-4	Iambic septenarii
549-50	Trochaic septenarii	755-70	Trochaic septenarii
551-2	Iambic septenarii	771-87	Iambic octonarii
553-6	Iambic octonarii	788-816	Trochaic septenarii
557	Iambic septenarius	817-942	Iambic senarii
558-9	Trochaic octonarii	943-70	Trochaic septenarii
560	(?)	971-1001	Iambic senarii
561	Iambic septenarius	1002-24	Iambic septenarii
562-91	Iambic octonarii	1025-30	Trochaic septenarii
592-614	Iambic septenarii	1031-49	Iambic octonarii
615	Trochaic octonarius	1050-94	Trochaic septenarii

There are excellent discussions of metre and scansion in Gratwick (1987) 268–83, (1999) 209–37 and Barsby (1999) 290-304. See also Laidlaw and Questa.

TERENCE
THE EUNUCH

DIDASCALIA

Incipit Eunuchus Terenti. acta ludis Megalensibus, L. Postumio Albino L. Cornelio Merula aedilibus curulibus. egit L. Ambivius Turpio. modos fecit Flaccus Claudi tibiis duabus dextris. Graeca Menandru. facta secunda, M. Valerio C. Fannio consulibus.

C. SULPICI APOLLINARIS
PERIOCHA

Sororem falso dictitatam Thaidis
id ipsum ignorans miles advexit Thraso
ipsique donat. erat haec civis Attica.
eidem eunuchum quem emerat tradi iubet
Thaidis amator Phaedria ac rus ipse abit,   5
Thrasoni oratus biduum concederet.
ephebus frater Phaedriae puellulam
cum deperiret dono missam Thaidi,
ornatu eunuchi induitur (suadet Parmeno),
introiit, vitiat virginem. sed Atticus   10
civis repertus frater eius conlocat
vitiatam ephebo. Phaedriam exorat Thraso.

DIDASCALIA: 1 Megalensibus Σ, Don. : Romanis A. | **1-2** L. Postumio Albino L. Cornelio Merula Σ (L. Cornelio Merula **om.** (P) (C)), Don. : M. Iunio Lucio Iulio A. | **2** egit [L.] Ambivius Turpio Dziatzko : egit L. Ambivius Lucius Hatilius Praen A : egere L. Ambivius Turpio L. Atilius Praenestinus Σ, Kauer-Lindsay. | modos fecit A : modulavit Σ. | **3** Menandru A : Menandri Σ. | facta A : acta Σ. | secunda **codd.** : "haec edita tertium est" Don. | **4** C. Fannio **edd.** : Fan A : C. Mummio Fannio Σ. **PERIOCHA: 2** advexit G : abduxit A.

PRODUCTION NOTICE

Here begins Terence's *The Eunuch*; put on at the Megalensian Games, when
Lucius Postumius Albinus and Lucius Cornelius Merula were curule aediles;
produced by Lucius Ambivius Turpio; music composed by Flaccus, slave of
Claudius, on two right-hand pipes; Greek original by Menander; composed
second, when Marcus Valerius and Gaius Fannius were consuls.   5

SUMMARY
BY GAIUS SULPICIUS APOLLINARIS

A girl falsely said to be Thais' sister was brought along and given to her by a
soldier named Thraso – though he was unaware of her supposed identity.
The girl was, in fact, free-born and came from Attica. Thais' lover Phaedria   5
gives orders for a eunuch he had bought to be given to Thais, while he
himself goes off to the country – he has been asked to give place to Thraso
for two days. Phaedria's young brother, being madly in love with the girl
presented to Thais, dresses up as the eunuch (at Parmeno's prompting), gets
into the house and rapes the girl. But a citizen of Attica who is discovered to   10
be the girl's brother gives her to her seducer as his bride. Thraso prevails on
Phaedria to come to a compromise.

PERSONAE

PHAEDRIA	adulescens
PARMENO	servos
THAIS	meretrix
GNATHO	parasitus
CHAEREA	adulescens
THRASO	miles
PYTHIAS	ancilla
CHREMES	adulescens
ANTIPHO	adulescens
DORIAS	ancilla
DORVS	eunuchus
SANGA	servos
SOPHRONA	nutrix
SENEX	

CHARACTERS

PHAEDRIA	a young gentleman of Athens
PARMENO	a slave of Phaedria's father, attached to Phaedria
THAIS	a courtesan
GNATHO	a professional sponger, who has attached himself to Thraso
CHAEREA	Phaedria's younger brother
THRASO	an army officer
PYTHIAS	Thais' maid
CHREMES	a young gentleman of Attica
ANTIPHO	a young Athenian, friend of Chaerea
DORIAS	Thais' maid
DORUS	a eunuch
SANGA	a cook, slave of Thraso
SOPHRONA	an old nurse
AN OLD GENTLEMAN	an Athenian, father of Phaedria and Chaerea

Non-speaking characters: PAMPHILA, a young girl; her maid; an Ethiopian slave-girl; further maids of Thais; further slaves of Thraso, including SIMALIO, DONAX and SYRISCUS.

PROLOGVS

Si quisquam est qui placere se studeat bonis
quam plurimis et minime multos laedere,
in his poeta hic nomen profitetur suom.
tum si quis est qui dictum in se inclementius
existumavit esse, sic existumet 5
responsum, non dictum, esse, quia laesit prior.
qui bene vortendo et easdem scribendo male
ex Graecis bonis Latinas fecit non bonas,
idem Menandri Phasma nunc nuper dedit,
atque in Thesauro scripsit causam dicere 10
prius unde petitur aurum qua re sit suom,
quam illic qui petit unde is sit thesaurus sibi
aut unde in patrium monumentum pervenerit.
dehinc ne frustretur ipse se aut sic cogitet:
"defunctus iam sum; nil est quod dicat mihi." 15
is ne erret moneo et desinat lacessere;
habeo alia multa quae nunc condonabitur,
quae proferentur post, si perget laedere
ita ut facere instituit. quam nunc acturi sumus
Menandri Eunuchum, postquam aediles emerunt, 20
perfecit sibi ut inspiciundi esset copia.
magistratus quom ibi adesset, occepta est agi;
exclamat furem, non poetam, fabulam
dedisse et nil dedisse verborum tamen;
Colacem esse Naevi et Plauti veterem fabulam; 25
parasiti personam inde ablatam et militis.
si id est peccatum, peccatum inprudentia est
poetae, non quo furtum facere studuerit.
id ita esse vos iam iudicare poteritis.
Colax Menandri est; in ea est parasitus colax 30
et miles gloriosus; eas se non negat
personas transtulisse in Eunuchum suam
ex Graeca; sed eas fabulas factas prius

---

3 his AD(P)(C)E : is G, Kauer-Lindsay. (Cf. 168.) | **6** prior A(C)[1], Eugr. : prius D[2]G(P) (C)[2]E. | **12** illic Bentley : illi DG(C)[2] : ille A(C)[1](P)[2]. | **22** adesset AG : adessent D(P)(C). | **30** colax Umpfenbach, Dziatzko, Marouzeau : Colax Bentley, Kauer-Lindsay.

PROLOGUE

If there's anyone who is eager to please as many good men as possible and
to offend as few of them, our author enrols himself among their number.
Further, if there's anyone who has felt that he's been attacked too rudely, he   5
should reflect that it wasn't an attack but an answer, because he was the one
who caused offence first. The fellow who by accurate translation and poor
composition has produced bad Latin plays out of good Greek ones – he it is
who just recently put on *The Phantom* by Menander and who in *The*   10
Treasure showed the defendant putting his case about why the money was
his before the plaintiff put forward *his* plea about how the treasure belonged
to him and how it got into his father's tomb. In future he's not to delude
himself or think like this: "I'm finished with him now; there's nothing more   15
he can say to me." I warn him not to be deceived, and to stop provoking me;
I've got many another point which for the moment will be overlooked, but
which will be brought up later on if he carries on offending me in the way
that he's set out to do.

      The play we're going to put on today is Menander's *The Eunuch*.   20
After the aediles purchased it, he managed to get a chance to have a look at
it. When the magistrate was there, the performance began. He shouted out
that it was a thief, not a poet, who'd put on the play, but that he hadn't
fooled anyone; *The Toady* was an old play by Naevius and by Plautus, and it   25
was from there that the character of the sponger and of the soldier had been
lifted. Now if that's a fault, it's one of oversight on our author's part, not
one committed with any intention of stealing. That this is so you'll soon be
able to judge for yourselves. *The Toady* is a play by Menander, and in it   30
there's a toadying sponger and a boastful soldier. Our author doesn't deny
that he's transferred these characters from the Greek play into his *Eunuch*;

Latinas scisse sese, id vero pernegat.
quod si personis isdem huic uti non licet, 35
qui magis licet currentem servom scribere,
bonas matronas facere, meretrices malas,
parasitum edacem, gloriosum militem,
puerum supponi, falli per servom senem,
amare, odisse, suspicari? denique 40
nullum est iam dictum quod non sit dictum prius.
qua re aequom est vos cognoscere atque ignoscere
quae veteres factitarunt si faciunt novi.
date operam, cum silentio animum attendite,
ut pernoscatis quid sibi Eunuchus velit. 45

---

36 magis **codd.** : mage Kauer-Lindsay. | **41** sit dictum DGP(C), Diom. in **G. L.** 1. 400, Jerome **in Eccl.** 1. 9-10 : dictum sit AE(?), Don., Eugr., Kauer-Lindsay. | **44** animum attendite A(C)[1] : animadvertite DG(C)[2], Don. : animadvortite E.

but he certainly does emphatically deny that he knew that those Latin plays
had been written earlier. If he's not allowed to employ the same characters   35
as other writers, how can he still create the running slave, produce honest
wives, nasty courtesans, the greedy sponger, the boastful soldier, substitution
of a child, deception of an old man by his slave, love, hatred, suspicion? In
short, there's nothing said nowadays that hasn't been said before. So it is   40
right for you to acknowledge facts, and to make allowances if new writers do
what older ones have often done. Pay attention, and listen carefully in
silence, so you will realize what *The Eunuch* is all about.   45

ACTVS I

I i   PHAEDRIA PARMENO

PH.   quid igitur faciam? non eam ne nunc quidem
quom accersor ultro? an potius ita me comparem
non perpeti meretricum contumelias?
exclusit, revocat. redeam? non si me obsecret! ...
siquidem hercle possis, nil prius aut fortius.   50
verum si incipies neque pertendes gnaviter
atque, ubi pati non poteris, quom nemo expetet,
infecta pace ultro ad eam venies, indicans
te amare et ferre non posse, actum est, ilicet,
peristi; eludet ubi te victum senserit.   55
proin tu, dum est tempus, etiam atque etiam cogita ...
PA.   ere, quae res in se neque consilium neque modum
habet ullum, eam consilio regere non potes.
in amore haec omnia insunt vitia: iniuriae,
suspiciones, inimicitiae, indutiae,   60
bellum, pax rursum. incerta haec si tu postules
ratione certa facere, nihilo plus agas
quam si des operam ut cum ratione insanias.
et quod nunc tute tecum iratus cogitas:
"egone illam ... quae illum ... quae me ... quae non ...? sine modo!   65
mori me malim. sentiet qui vir siem." –
haec verba una mehercle falsa lacrimula,
quam oculos terendo misere vix vi expresserit,
restinguet, et te ultro accusabit et dabis
ultro supplicium.
PH.   o indignum facinus! nunc ego   70
et illam scelestam esse et me miserum sentio;
et taedet et amore ardeo, et prudens sciens
vivos vidensque pereo, nec quid agam scio.

50-6 Phaedriae cont. AD^{1}P^{1}C^1, Don. : 50 - 5 **Parmenoni, 56 Phaedriae trib.** D^{2}GP^{2}C^{2}E : 50 - 6 **Parmenoni trib. edd. plerique, necnon** Kauer-Lindsay. | **58** potes Iov., Σ : potest A^1. | **70** ultro A : ei ultro Σ.

ACT ONE

(The scene is a street in Athens, on to which face two houses, one belonging to Thais, and the other to the father of Phaedria and Chaerea. **PHAEDRIA** *comes out of his father's house, talking to his father's slave* **PARMENO**.)

I 1

PH. So what am I to do? Not go even now, when she's sending for me of her own accord? Should I rather steel myself to refuse to put up with the insulting behaviour of such 'ladies'? She's shut me out and now she's calling me back. Am I to go? No, not if she begged me to! *(More quietly, to himself.)* If you could really do that, there'd be   50
nothing better, nothing braver. But if you start off that way and don't persevere for all your worth, if, when you can't bear it any more, when nobody's asking for you, when no terms have been agreed between you, you simply go to her, making it quite clear that you're in love and can't stand it – then it's all over and done with and you're finished. She'll make a proper fool of you once she realizes you're   55
beaten. So, while there's still time, do reflect over and over again that
...

PA. *(interrupting his thoughts)* Sir, you can't use reason to control a situation which has no reason in it, and knows no limits. All these troubles – hurtful words, jealous thoughts, being at daggers drawn,   60
patching things up, fighting like cat and dog, then living in peace again – they're part and parcel of a love-affair. If you expected to turn such unpredictable matters into certainties through the exercise of reason, you'd get no further than if you devoted your energies to going mad with reason too. As for your angry words just now: "Am I ... to   65
her ... when she ... to him ... and to me ... but she's not ... Just let her! I'd rather die! She'll soon realize what a man I am!" – my goodness, with just one tiny crocodile tear (and she'll only just have managed to force that out by frantically rubbing her eyes) she'll soon put out the fire in those fine words, and she'll go on to put the blame on you, and you'll pay the penalty.   70

PH. What a shocking way to behave! Now at last I realize that she's a thoroughly bad lot and that I'm really miserable. I'm sick of it all, I'm on fire with love, and though I've got my wits and brains, though I'm very much alive and have got both eyes wide open, I'm as good as dead, and I haven't a clue what to do.

PA. quid agas? nisi ut te redimas captum quam queas
         minimo; si nequeas paullulo, at quanti queas,   75
         et ne te adflictes.
PH.   itane suades?
PA.   si sapis.
         neque praeter quam quas ipse amor molestias
         habet addas, et illas quas habet recte feras.
         sed eccam ipsa egreditur, nostri fundi calamitas –
         nam quod nos capere oportet haec intercipit.   80

I ii   THAIS   PHAEDRIA   PARMENO

TH. miseram me, vereor ne illud gravius Phaedria
         tulerit neve aliorsum atque ego feci acceperit,
         quod heri intro missus non est.
PH.   totus, Parmeno,
         tremo horreoque, postquam aspexi hanc.
PA.   bono animo es;
         accede ad ignem hunc, iam calesces plus satis,   85
TH. quis hic loquitur? ehem, tun hic eras, mi Phaedria?
         quid hic stabas? quor non recta intro ibas?
PA.   ceterum
         de exclusione verbum nullum!
TH.   missa istaec face.   90
PH. sane quia vero haec mihi patent semper fores
         aut quia sum apud te primus.
TH.   missa istaec face.   90
PH. quid 'missa'? o Thais, Thais, utinam esset mihi
         pars aequa amoris tecum ac pariter fieret,
         ut aut hoc tibi doleret itidem ut mihi dolet
         aut ego istuc abs te factum nihili penderem!
TH. ne crucia te, obsecro, anime mi, mi Phaedria.   95
         non pol quo quemquam plus amem aut plus diligam
         eo feci; sed ita erat res, faciundum fuit.

---

79 eccam **edd. plerique** : ecca **codd.** | **87** recta DGC²E, Don. : recte PC¹ : **om.** A. | **89** haec A : hae Σ, Don., Eugr. (Cf. 582.) | **95** mi **semel codd.** : **geminavit Fabricius**, cf. Don. ("vide quam familiariter hoc idem repetat blandimentum").

PA. What to do? Just buy yourself out of your captivity as cheaply as you can; if you can't do it cheaply, then for what you can get – and stop 75 torturing yourself so.

PH. Is that your advice?

PA. Yes, if you've got the sense to take it. Don't add to the troubles love brings – and put up with those it does in a proper spirit. But here's the woman herself, coming outside – that blight on our estate. She makes 80 off with everything that ought to come to us.

(**THAIS** *comes out of her house; she is thinking aloud, and at first does not see the others.*)

I 2

TH. Oh, dear me! I'm afraid Phaedria's taken it rather badly that I didn't let him in yesterday, and in quite a different spirit from my motives when I did it.

PH. Parmeno, I'm shivering and shaking all over, now I've caught sight of her.

PA. Cheer up! Go near this fire and you'll soon be more than warm 85 enough.

TH. Who's that talking? (*On seeing Phaedria and Parmeno.*) Oh, is that you here, Phaedria my dear? Why are you standing out here? Why don't you come in straight away?

PA. Not a word about shutting him out!

TH. Why don't you say something?

PH. (*sarcastically*) Because, of course, your door's always open to me and 90 I always have first place in your affections.

TH. No more of that.

PH. What do you mean 'no more'? Oh Thais, Thais, if only I had a fair share in your love and things were equal between us, so that either you'd be as upset by this as I am or else I'd think nothing of what you've done!

TH. Don't torture yourself, please, my dearest, my darling Phaedria. 95 Really, I didn't do it because I love or care for anyone more than you; but as things are, I had to.

PA.　credo, ut fit, misera prae amore exclusti hunc foras.

TH.　sicin agis, Parmeno? age; sed huc qua gratia
　　　te accersi iussi, ausculta.

PH.　　　　　　　　　　　　　fiat.

TH.　　　　　　　　　　　　　　　dic mihi　　　　　　　　　　100
　　　hoc primum; potin est hic tacere?

PA.　　　　　　　　　　　　　　　　egon? optume.
　　　verum heus tu, hac lege tibi meam adstringo fidem:
　　　quae vera audivi, taceo et contineo optume;
　　　sin falsum aut vanum aut finctum est, continuo palam est,
　　　plenus rimarum sum, hac atque illac perfluo.　　　　　　105
　　　proin tu, taceri si vis, vera dicito.

TH.　Samia mihi mater fuit; ea habitabat Rhodi.

PA.　potest taceri hoc.

TH.　　　　　　　　　ibi tum matri parvolam
　　　puellam dono quidam mercator dedit
　　　ex Attica hinc abreptam.

PH.　　　　　　　　　　　civemne?

TH.　　　　　　　　　　　　　　　arbitror;　　　　　　　　110
　　　certum non scimus. matris nomen et patris
　　　dicebat ipsa; patriam et signa cetera
　　　neque scibat neque per aetatem etiam potis erat.
　　　mercator hoc addebat: e praedonibus
　　　unde emerat se audisse abreptam e Sunio.　　　　　　　115
　　　mater ubi accepit, coepit studiose omnia
　　　docere, educere ita uti si esset filia.
　　　sororem plerique esse credebant meam.
　　　ego cum illo, quocum tum uno rem habebam hospite,
　　　abii huc, qui mihi reliquit haec quae habeo omnia.　　　120

PA.　utrumque hoc falsum est; effluet.

TH.　　　　　　　　　　　　　qui istuc?

PA.　　　　　　　　　　　　　　　　quia
　　　neque tu uno eras contenta neque solus dedit.
　　　nam hic quoque bonam magnamque partem ad te attulit.

TH.　ita est. sed sine me pervenire quo volo.

---

98 exclusti p, **edd.** : exclusit **cett. codd,** Prisc. in **G. L.** 3.50. | **104** finctum A : fictum Σ,
Don., Prisc. in **G. L.** 3.52, 3.244. | **106** taceri DPCE : tacere AG. | **110** civemne?
Phaedriae trib. GPC : **Parmenoni** ADE. | **113** potis erat Bentley : potuerat **codd.** | **117**
educere **edd.** : educare **codd.** | uti **edd. plerique** : ut **codd.,** Don.

PA.   And, I suppose, you shut him out because you were so desperately in love with him – as often happens!

TH.   Is that the way to behave, Parmeno? Carry on then; but please listen   100
to the reason I asked you to be sent for.

PA.   Very well.

TH.   (*to Phaedria*) But first, tell me this; can this fellow here keep his mouth shut?

PA.   Me? Certainly. But listen, I give you my word on one condition – when I hear what's true, I stay quiet about it and I'm very good at keeping it to myself; but if it's untrue or false or made up, then it's out straight away, I'm full of holes and I leak all over the place. So, if   105
you want your secrets kept, make sure you tell the truth.

TH.   My mother was a woman from Samos, and she lived on Rhodes.

PA.   That I *can* keep quiet about.

TH.   There, some merchant gave my mother a present of a little girl who'd been kidnapped from here in Attica.   110

PH.   Was she free-born?

TH.   I think so, but we don't know for sure. She told us the name of her mother and father herself, but she didn't know what country she came from or any of the other means of finding out who she was – because she was so young, she couldn't say. The merchant added that he'd heard from the pirates he'd bought her from that she'd been kidnapped   115
from Sunium. When my mother took her in, she started to give her a full and thorough education, and to bring her up as her own daughter – most people thought she was my sister. I came over here with a man   120
who'd become my friend, my one and only lover at the time; he left me everything I've got.

PA.   Both lies – they'll leak out.

TH.   How so?

PA.   Because you weren't content with just one man, and he wasn't the only one to give you things; my master, too, has brought you a large part of what you own – and a handsome part at that.

TH.   That's true. But let me come to the point I want to make. In the

	interea miles qui me amare occeperat	125
	in Cariam est profectus; te interea loci	
	cognovi. tute scis postilla quam intumum	
	habeam te et mea consilia ut tibi credam omnia.	
PH.	ne hoc quidem tacebit Parmeno.	
PA.	oh, dubiumne id est?	
TH.	hoc agite, amabo. mater mea illic mortua est	130

        nuper. eius frater aliquantum ad rem est avidior;
        is ubi esse hanc forma videt honesta virginem
        et fidibus scire, pretium sperans ilico
        producit, vendit. forte fortuna adfuit
        hic meus amicus; emit eam dono mihi,   135
        inprudens harum rerum ignarusque omnium.
        is venit; postquam sensit me tecum quoque
        rem habere, fingit causas ne det sedulo;
        ait, si fidem habeat se iri praepositum tibi
        apud me, ac non id metuat ne, ubi acceperim,   140
        sese relinquam, velle se illam mihi dare;
        verum id vereri. sed, ego quantum suspicor,
        ad virginem animum adiecit.

PH.   etiamne amplius?

TH. nil; nam quaesivi. nunc ego eam, mi Phaedria,
        multae sunt causae quam ob rem cupiam abducere: 145
        primum quod soror est dicta; praeterea ut suis
        restituam ac reddam. sola sum; habeo hic neminem
        neque amicum neque cognatum. quam ob rem, Phaedria,
        cupio aliquos parere amicos beneficio meo.
        id, amabo, adiuta me quo fiat facilius.   150
        sine illum prioris partis hosce aliquot dies
        apud me habere. nil respondes?

PH.   pessuma,
        egon quicquam cum istis factis tibi respondeam?

PA. eu, noster, laudo. tandem perdoluit; vir es.

PH. aut ego nescibam quorsum tu ires? "parvola   155
        hinc est abrepta; eduxit mater pro sua;

---

132 esse p, **edd. plerique**: om. cett. **codd.**, Don. | **145** cupiam A[1]DGPC, Prisc. in **G. L.** 3.338 : cupio A[2]E, Don., Kauer-Lindsay. | **150** quo fiat A[1] : quo id fiat A[2]Σ, Don., Kauer-Lindsay. | **151** prioris D[1]PC : priores AD[2]GE, Don., Kauer-Lindsay. | partis D[1]GPCE : partes AD[2], Don.

meantime a captain who'd begun to fall in love with me set off for 125
Caria, and while he was away I got to know you. You know how dear
I've held you as a friend since then, and how I trust you with all my
plans.

PH. Parmeno won't keep quiet about that, either.

PA. No doubt about it!

TH. Do pay attention, please. A little while ago my mother died over 130
there. Her brother is a bit too greedy over money; so when he saw
that this young girl had a good figure and was a skilled musician, he
hoped to get a good price for her, and he put her up for sale at once,
and sold her. As it happened, by a stroke of luck my friend was there, 135
and he bought her for me as a present – though he was completely
unaware and ignorant of all the facts. Now he's come back; but since
he's realized that I've got an attachment to you as well, he's busily
making up excuses not to give her to me. He says that, if he could
really believe that he'd take pride of place over you in my affections, 140
and if he wasn't afraid that I'd leave him once I'd got the girl, he'd be
willing to give her to me; but that that is precisely what he is afraid
of. In fact, as far as I can see, he's rather taken to the girl himself.

PA. Anything more than that?

TH. No, nothing more – I've asked her. Now, Phaedria my dear, there are 145
lots of reasons why I want to get her away from him; firstly, because
people call her my sister; also, so I can restore her to her family and
give her back to them. I'm all by myself, and I've got nobody here –
no friend, no relative; so, Phaedria, I'm eager to acquire some friends
by doing an act of kindness. Please help me over this, so it can 150
happen more easily. Let the captain take first place with me for the
next few days. (*After a pause.*) Have you nothing to say?

PH. You dreadful woman, can I give you any reply when this is what
you've done?

PA. Splendid, sir; well done! At last it's hit home; you're a man!

PH. Didn't I realize what you were leading up to? "A little girl was 155
kidnapped from here; my mother brought her up as hers; she was

soror dicta est; cupio abducere ut reddam suis."
nempe omnia haec nunc verba huc redeunt denique:
ego excludor, ille recipitur. qua gratia,
nisi si illum plus amas quam me et istam nunc times   160
quae advecta est ne illum talem praeripiat tibi?

TH. ego id timeo?

PH.   quid te ergo aliud sollicitat? cedo.
num solus ille dona dat? num ubi meam
benignitatem sensisti in te claudier?
nonne, ubi mi dixti cupere te ex Aethiopia   165
ancillulam, relictis rebus omnibus
quaesivi? porro eunuchum dixti velle te,
quia solae utuntur his reginae; repperi,
heri minas viginti pro ambobus dedi.
tamen contemptus abs te haec habui in memoria;   170
ob haec facta abs te spernor?

TH.   quid istic, Phaedria?
quamquam illam cupio abducere atque hac re arbitror
id fieri posse maxume, verum tamen,
potius quam te inimicum habeam, faciam ut iusseris.

PH. utinam istuc verbum ex animo ac vere diceres   175
"potius quam te inimicum habeam"! si istuc crederem
sincere dici, quidvis possem perpeti.

PA. labascit, victus uno verbo quam cito!

TH. ego non ex animo misera dico? quam ioco
rem voluisti a me tandem, quin perfeceris?   180
ego impetrare nequeo hoc abs te, biduom
saltem ut concedas solum.

PH.   siquidem biduom;
verum ne fiant isti viginti dies.

TH. profecto non plus biduom aut ...

PH.   'aut' nil moror.

TH. non fiet; hoc modo sine te exorem.

PH.   scilicet   185
faciundum est quod vis.

TH.   merito te amo; bene facis.

---

160 nisi si PC : nisi ADGE, Don. | **161** advecta Iov., Σ, : abducta A¹ : adducta A². | **164** in te claudier Ap, Don. : intercludier PCE : intercludier DG. | **168** his Σ : is A, Kauer-Lindsay. (Cf. 3.) | **186** bene facis **Thaidi cont.** AC¹ : **Phaedriae trib.** DGP¹C²E.

called my sister; I want to get her away from him to give her back to
her family." Actually what all this talk comes down to in the end is
this: I'm being shut out and he's being let in. Why – unless you love   160
him more than you do me and are afraid that this girl he's brought
along will snatch your precious captain away from you?

TH. I, afraid of that?

PH. What else is bothering you then? Tell me. He's not the only one who
gives you presents, is he? Have you ever known a time when you've
felt that my generosity was being cut off? When you said you wanted   165
a slave-girl from Ethiopia, didn't I drop everything else and look for
one? Again, you said you wanted a eunuch, because only queens have
them in their households; well, I found you one, and yesterday I paid
twenty minae for them both. Though you treated me badly, I   170
remembered these things; and in return for what I've done for you,
are you rejecting me?

TH. Oh, all right, Phaedria. Though I'm keen to get her away from him
and think it can best be done this way, rather than make an enemy out
of you, I'll do as you say.

PH. If only you said those words 'rather than make an enemy out of you'   175
truthfully and from the heart! If I thought they were sincerely said, I
could put up with anything.

PA. (*aside*) He's wavering! How quickly he's been beaten by a few
words!

TH. Oh dear! Aren't I speaking from my heart? What did you ever want   180
from me, even as a joke, without getting it? And I can't get this one
thing I ask from you, to give me just two days.

PH. If it really is two days; but don't let them turn into twenty.

TH. Really; no more than two or ...

PH. None of that 'or'!

TH. There won't be. Just let me win you over on this.   185

PH. I suppose I must do what you want.

TH. I'm so right to love you – you are kind.

PH. rus ibo; ibi hoc me macerabo biduom.
　　ita facere certum est; mos gerundust Thaidi.
　　tu, Parmeno, huc fac illi adducantur.

PA. 　　　　　　　　　　　　maxume.

PH. in hoc biduom, Thais, vale.

TH. 　　　　　　　　mi Phaedria, 　　　　　　190
　　et tu. numquid vis aliud?

PH. 　　　　　　　　　egone quid velim?
　　cum milite isto praesens absens uti sies;
　　dies noctesque me ames, me desideres,
　　me somnies, me exspectes, de me cogites,
　　me speres, me te oblectes, mecum tota sis; 　　195
　　meus fac sis postremo animus quando ego sum tuos.

TH. me miseram, forsitan hic mihi parvam habeat fidem,
　　atque ex aliarum ingeniis nunc me iudicet.
　　ego pol, quae mihi sum conscia, hoc certo scio,
　　neque me finxisse falsi quicquam neque meo 　　200
　　cordi esse quemquam cariorem hoc Phaedria.
　　et quidquid huius feci, causa virginis
　　feci; nam me eius spero fratrem propemodum
　　iam repperisse, adulescentem adeo nobilem;
　　et is hodie venturum ad me constituit domum. 　　205
　　concedam hinc intro atque exspectabo dum venit.

ACTVS II

II i 　　　　　　PHAEDRIA　　PARMENO

PH. fac, ita ut iussi, deducantur isti.

PA. 　　　　　　　　　　　faciam.

PH. 　　　　　　　　　　　　at diligenter.

PA. fiet.

PH. 　　　at mature.

PA. 　　　　　　fiet.

PH. 　　　　　　　satine hoc mandatum est tibi?

---

192 isto ADG²PCE, Don. : istoc p, Kauer-Lindsay : iste G¹. | **197** forsitan **codd.**, Don. :
fors an Bentley, **edd. plerique, necnon** Kauer-Lindsay. | **202** quidquid huius feci
ADGPCE, Don. : quidquid feci huius p, schol. Bemb. | **203** spero fratrem ADG : fratrem
spero PCE, Don., Kauer-Lindsay.

PH. I'll go to the country and spend two days of torture there. That's what I've decided to do; I must do what Thais wants. Parmeno, make sure those two are brought over.

PA. Certainly. (*He goes back into Phaedria's father's house.*)

PH. For the next two days then, Thais, goodbye. 190

TH. And goodbye to you too, Phaedria my dear. Is there anything else you want?

PH. Anything else I want? Only that when you're with that soldier fellow in body, you should be absent in spirit, that all day and all night you should love me, long for me, dream about me, wait for me, think of me, hope for me, find your delight in me, be with me, all of you. 195 Lastly, be my heart, since I am yours. (*He goes into his father's house.*)

TH. Oh, dear! Perhaps he's not got much faith in me, and is judging me from the characters of other women. But, really, as only I can know, I'm absolutely sure of this – I've not concocted any falsehoods, and 200 there's no-one dearer to my heart than this Phaedria of mine. Whatever I've done in this, I've done it for the young girl's sake, because I've got high hopes that I've as good as found her brother already, a young gentleman of very respectable family. He's arranged 205 to come to my house today; I'll go inside and wait for him to arrive.

(*She goes into her house. Almost immediately, Phaedria and Parmeno come out from the other house again.*)

ACT TWO

II 1

PH. As I told you earlier, make sure they're taken across.

PA. I will.

PH. Make certain of it.

PA. It'll be done.

PH. And quickly.

PA. It'll be done.

PH. Are your instructions clear?

PA.   ah,
rogitare, quasi difficile sit!
utinam tam aliquid invenire facile possis, Phaedria,   210
quam hoc peribit!

PH.   ego quoque una pereo, quod mi est carius;
ne istuc tam iniquo patiare animo.

PA.   minime, qui effectum dabo.
sed numquid aliud imperas?

PH. munus nostrum ornato verbis, quod poteris, et istum aemulum,
quod poteris, ab ea pellito.   215

PA. memini, tam etsi nullus moneas.

PH.   ego rus ibo atque ibi manebo.

PA. censeo.

PH.   sed heus tu!

PA.   quid vis?

PH.   censen posse me obfirmare et
perpeti ne redeam interea?

PA.   tene? non hercle arbitror.
nam aut iam revortere aut mox noctu te adiget horsum insomnia.

PH. opus faciam ut defetiger usque, ingratiis ut dormiam.   220

PA. vigilabis lassus; hoc plus facies.

PH.   abi; nil dicis, Parmeno.
eiciunda hercle haec est mollities animi; nimis me indulgeo.
tandem non ego illam caream, si sit opus, vel totum triduom?

PA.   hui,
universum triduom? vide quid agas!

PH.   stat sententia.

PA. di boni, quid hoc morbi est? adeon homines immutarier   225
ex amore ut non cognoscas eundem esse! hoc nemo fuit
minus ineptus, magis severus quisquam nec magis continens.
sed quis hic est qui huc pergit? attat! hicquidem est parasitus Gnatho
militis. ducit secum una virginem dono huic. papae!
facie honesta! mirum ni ego me turpiter hodie hic dabo   230
cum meo decrepito hoc eunucho. haec superat ipsam Thaidem.

---

219 adiget Don. ("legitur et *adiget* ut sit *insomnia* numeri singularis"), Bentley : adigent **codd.**, Don. **in lemm.** | **221** abi A² : abi sis A¹ : ah DPC²E : ha G : hah C¹. | **222** me Don. : mihi **codd,** | **223** illam AG¹ : illa DG²PCE, Don. | **230** ego me Σ, Don., Eugr. : egomet A, Don. **Ph.** 23. |

PA. Oh, what a question! As if it was that difficult! If only you could 210
make a profit somewhere else as easily as you're going to make a loss
here!

PH. *I'm* a total loss too, which matters more to me. Don't you get so upset
about it.

PA. Far from it; I'll make sure it's done. Any more instructions?

PH. Use your eloquence as much as you can to praise my present, and, as 215
much as you can, ensure that rival of mine is kept away from her.

PA. I haven't forgotten, even if you weren't to remind me.

PH. I'll go to the country and stay there.

PA. Good idea.

PH. But, hey!

PA. What do you want?

PH. Do you think I can make up my mind to it and put up with it, so I
don't come back before my time's up?

PA. You do that? I really don't think so. Either you'll come back directly,
or you'll be forced back pretty soon because you can't sleep at night.

PH. I'll work to get myself so tired that I'll sleep even if I don't want to. 220

PA. Then you'll be exhausted *and* unable to sleep; that's all the extra
you'll get out of that.

PH. Get away with you; you're talking nonsense, Parmeno. I really must
shake off this feeble attitude – I'm being too soft with myself. After
all, couldn't I do without her, if I had to, for three whole days?

PA. Phew! An entire three days? Watch what you're doing!

PH. My mind's made up. (*He goes off to the audience's left.*)

PA. Good god! What kind of a sickness is this? To think that a man can 225
be so changed by love that you wouldn't recognize him as the same
person! In the past, there was nobody less silly than my master,
nobody more serious or more self-controlled. (*He looks off to the
audience's right.*) But who's that coming this way? Oh! It's Gnatho,
the captain's sponger, and he's bringing the young girl with him to
give to Thais. Wow! What a beautiful creature! I'll make a poor 230
showing here today, I shouldn't wonder, with this decrepit old eunuch
of mine. This girl's better than Thais herself.

II ii   **GNATHO   PARMENO**

GN. di inmortales, homini homo quid praestat! stulto intellegens
     quid interest! hoc adeo ex hac re venit in mentem mihi:
     conveni hodie adveniens quendam mei loci hinc atque ordinis,
     hominem haud inpurum, itidem patria qui abligurrierat bona   235
     video sentum, squalidum, aegrum, pannis annisque obsitum. "oh,
     quid istuc," inquam, "ornati est?" "quoniam miser quod habui perdidi,
                                                                          [em
     quo redactus sum. omnes noti me atque amici deserunt."
     hic ego illum contempsi prae me: "quid, homo," inquam,
                                                        ["ignavissime?
     itan parasti te ut spes nulla relicua in te sit tibi?   240
     simul consilium cum re amisti? viden me ex eodem ortum loco?
     qui color, nitor, vestitus, quae habitudo est corporis!
     omnia habeo neque quicquam habeo; nil quom est, nil defit tamen."
     "at ego infelix neque ridiculus esse neque plagas pati
     possum." "quid? tu his rebus credis fieri? tota erras via.   245
     olim isti fuit generi quondam quaestus apud saeclum prius;
     hoc novom est aucupium; ego adeo hanc primus inveni viam.
     est genus hominum qui esse primos se omnium rerum volunt
     nec sunt; hos consector, hisce ego non paro me ut rideant,
     sed eis ultro adrideo et eorum ingenia admiror simul.   250
     quidquid dicunt, laudo; id rursum si negant, laudo id quoque;
     negat quis, nego; ait, aio; postremo imperavi egomet mihi
     omnia adsentari. is quaestus nunc est multo uberrimus."
PA. scitum hercle hominem! hic homines prorsum ex stultis insanos facit.
GN. dum haec loquimur, interealoci ad macellum ubi advenimus,   255
     concurrunt laeti mi obviam cuppedinarii omnes,
     cetarii, lanii, coqui, fartores, piscatores,

---

236 oh A¹ : **om. Iov., Σ.** | **240** sit A²p : siet Σ, Kauer-Lindsay : esset A¹. | **250** eis **edd.** :
is A : his Σ, Don., Prisc. in **G. L.** 3.322, 351, 355. | **255** advenimus DGP¹ C² : convenimus
C¹ E : adventamus Ap. (Cf. 289.)

(**GNATHO** *enters from the audience's right, bringing with him*
PAMPHILA *and a maid. He does not notice Parmeno, who stands some
distance away, listening.*)

II 2

GN. Heavens above, how much better one man is than another! What a
difference there is between a clever one and a fool! This is what's
made this thought occur to me: on my way here today, I met a man
from round these parts who's of my own station and position – not a   235
bad chap, who just like me had squandered his inheritance. He looked
unkempt, filthy and ill, covered in rags and weighed down by his
years. "What sort of a get-up's this?", I said. "I've lost all I ever had,
poor devil that I am, and look what I'm reduced to. All my friends
and acquaintances have abandoned me." Compared to myself, I had
nothing but contempt for him: "You lazy good-for-nothing," I said,
"have you so thoroughly convinced yourself, that you've no hope left   240
in you? Have you lost your wits along with your wealth? Don't you
see that I come from the same roots as you? Look at me – what colour
I've got, how smart I am, what clothes I'm wearing, what a fine figure
I cut! I have everything – and nothing; and though I've got nothing, I
don't want for anything either." "But I'm out of luck – I can't play
the buffoon, and I can't stand being knocked about." "What? Do you   245
think that's the way it's done? You're way out. Once upon a time, in
years gone by, there was a living to be made for that sort of chap. But
now we've got this new way to catch our prey – and in fact I was the
first to discover it. There's a class of people who want to be the first
in everything, but aren't. It's them I go for, but I don't set myself up
for them to laugh at me; instead I go out of my way to laugh in   250
response to them, and at the same time I voice my admiration for their
talents. Whatever they say, I praise it; if they go back on what
they've said, I praise that too. Someone says no, then I say no; he
says yes, then I say yes. In short, I've told myself to agree with
everything they say. This sort of thing's much the most lucrative trade
nowadays.

PA. (*aside*) A clever fellow indeed! This sort of chap makes fools go
barmy, and no mistake!

GN. Meanwhile, during this conversation we reached the market, and all   255
the delicatessen merchants, fishmongers, butchers, chefs, poulterers

quibus et re salva et perdita profueram et prosum saepe;
salutant, ad cenam vocant, adventum gratulantur.
ille ubi miser famelicus videt mi esse tantum honorem et   260
tam facile victum quaerere, ibi homo coepit me obsecrare
ut sibi liceret discere id de me; sectari iussi,
si potis est, tamquam philosophorum habent disciplinae ex ipsis
vocabula, parasiti ita ut Gnathonici vocentur.

PA. viden otium et cibus quid facit alienus?

GN.   sed ego cesso   265
ad Thaidem hanc deducere et rogare ad cenam ut veniat?
 †sed Parmenonem ante ostium Thaidis tristem video,
rivalis servom. salva res est. nimirum homines frigent.
nebulonem hunc certum est ludere.

PA.   hisce hoc munere arbitrantur
suam Thaidem esse.

GN.   plurima salute Parmenonem   270
summum suom inpertit Gnatho. quid agitur?

PA.   statur.

GN.   video.
numquid nam hic quod nolis vides?

PA.   te.

GN.   credo. at numquid aliud?

PA. quidum?

GN.   quia tristi's.

PA.   nil quidem.

GN.   ne sis. sed quid videtur
hic tibi mancupium?

PA.   non malum hercle.

GN.   uro hominem.

PA.   ut falsus animi est!

GN. quam hoc munus gratum Thaidi arbitrare esse?

---

260 mihi esse tantum honorem A[1] : me esse in tantum honorem Iov. : me esse tanto honore Σ, Don. | **264** ita A : itidem Σ. | **265** facit DGPCE, Don. ("legitur et *quid facit*") : faciat Ap, Don. **in lemm.** | **267** Thaidis **codd.** : Thainis Don., Kauer-Lindsay : meretricis Muret : opperiri Bentley : hoc astare Dziatzko. | **268** homines A[1]Σ, Eugr. : hic homines A[2], Serv. **in A.** 1.436, Kauer-Lindsay (**cum** res[es]t) : hi homines Serv. **in G.** 4.104. | **272** hic om. A[1] (**add.** Iov.). | **273** tristi's **edd. plerique**, **necnon** Kauer-Lindsay : tristis es **codd.** | quidem DGPCE, Don. **in prior. lemm.** : equidem Ap : et quidem Don. **in altero lemm.** | **274** animi est D[2], Don., Arusian. in G. L. 7. 475 : animo est D[1]GPCE : **om.** A.

and sea-food sellers came cheerfully running up to meet me – I'd done them well when I still had some money, and now I've lost it I often do so still. They greeted me, invited me to supper and said how glad they were I'd come. When that poor hungry wretch saw I was held in such 260 high esteem and made my living with such ease, he there and then began to plead with me to let him learn it all from me. I told him to follow me around so that, maybe, just as the philosophical schools take their names from the philosophers, so in future spongers will get the name of 'Gnathonists'.

PA. (*aside*) See what time on your hands and someone else's food can do? 265

GN. But why don't I deliver this girl to Thais and ask her to come to dinner? (*Catching sight of Parmeno.*) That's Parmeno, the captain's rival's man I can see at Thais' door – he does look glum! All's well, then; it's clear these two are frozen out. I think I'll have some fun at this idiot's expense.

PA. And all because of this present of theirs, they think they've got Thais 270 in their pocket!

GN. (*pompously, as he turns to Parmeno*) Gnatho bestows his warmest greetings on his dear friend Parmeno. What's your position?

PA. (*rudely*) An upright one.

GN. So I observe. (*With a glance at Pamphila.*) See anything round here that you'd rather not?

PA. (*refusing to rise to the bait*) Yes, you.

GN. So I suppose; but is there anything else?

PA. How could there be?

GN. Because you're looking glum.

PA. It's nothing, I assure you.

GN. Well, don't be. What do you think of this slave-girl?

PA. (*in spite of himself*) Not bad at all.

GN. (*aside*) I've caught the fellow on the raw.

PA. (*also aside, having overheard Gnatho's remark*) How wrong he is!

GN. How acceptable do you think this gift of ours will be to Thais? 275

PA.   hoc nunc dicis   275
     eiectos hinc nos? omnium rerum, heus, vicissitudo est.

GN. sex ego te totos, Parmeno, hos mensis quietum reddam,
     ne sursum deorsum cursites neve usque ad lucem vigiles.
     ecquid beo te?

PA.   men? papae!

GN.   sic soleo amicos.

PA.   laudo.

GN. detineo te; fortasse tu profectus alio fueras?   280

PA. nusquam.

GN.   tum tu igitur paullulum da mi operae; fac ut admittar
     ad illam.

PA.   age modo, i. nunc tibi patent fores hae quia istam ducis.

GN. numquem evocari hinc vis foras?

PA.   sine biduom hoc praetereat;
     qui mihi nunc uno digitulo fores aperis fortunatus,
     ne tu istas faxo calcibus saepe insultabis frustra.   285

GN. etiam nunc hic stas, Parmeno? eho num nam hic relictu's custos,
     ne quis forte internuntius clam a milite ad istam curset?

PA. facete dictum! mira vero, militi qui placeat.
     sed video erilem filium minorem huc advenire.
     miror quid ex Piraeo abierit – nam ibi custos publice est nunc.   290
     non temere est. et properans venit; nescioquid circumspectat.

II iii   CHAEREA   PARMENO

CH. occidi!
     neque virgo est usquam neque ego, qui illam e conspectu amisi meo.
     ubi quaeram, ubi investigem, quem perconter, quam insistam viam,
     incertus sum. una haec spes est: ubi ubi est, diu celari non potest.   295

---

275 dicis AE : dices DG²PC. | **279** men A²Σ : me A¹. | **282** i A : **om.** Σ, Don. | **286** hic stas A¹DGPCE : tu hic stas Iov., p, Kauer-Lindsay. | hic relictus A¹DGPC : tu hic relictus Iov. : relictus E. | relictu's **edd. plerique** : relictus **codd.** | **288** qui placeat A¹, Don. **in comm.** : quae placeat Iov. : qui placeant C¹P¹ : quae placeant **cett. codd.**, Don. **in lemm.**, Serv. **in A.** 1.669. | **289** advenire APCE : adventare DG. (Cf. 255.)

PA. Are you implying by that that we've been thrown out of here? Well, listen – everything that goes up must come down.

GN. I'll be giving you a rest, Parmeno, for the next six whole months, so you won't have to keep running back and forth and staying awake till dawn. Aren't I making you a happy man?

PA. Making me a happy man? Huh!

GN. That's what I usually do to my friends.

PA. (*sarcastically*) Excellent!

GN. But I'm keeping you; perhaps you'd just started out somewhere?   280

PA. No, nowhere.

GN. Then give me a little assistance; get me let in to Thais' house.

PA. Oh, come on now; go in yourself. Her door's wide open to you now because you're bringing the girl .

GN. (*maliciously, as he turns to take Pamphila and the maid into Thais' house*) Anyone you'd like me to fetch out for you? (*He goes in, slamming the door behind him.*)

PA. (*calling after him*) Just you let these next two days go by! Your luck's in now, so you can open her door under my very nose with the push of a little finger; but I'll make sure you'll be drumming your   285 heels against it quite a bit in future – and getting nowhere.

(*Gnatho returns from Thais' house.*)

GN. Still standing here, Parmeno? You've not been left here on guard, have you, in case any messenger from the captain comes running to the lady on the quiet? (*He walks off quickly to the audience's right, looking very pleased with himself.*)

PA. (*shouting after him*) Very funny! Really surprising things for a man who finds favour with the captain to say! (*He looks intently down the street in the direction in which Gnatho has just left.*) But I can see my master's younger boy coming this way. I wonder why he's left   290 Piraeus – he's on public guard duty there at the moment. There must be some reason. He's in a hurry too, and he's looking for something.

(**CHAEREA** *rushes in from the audience's right. In his excitement, he does not notice Parmeno.*)

II 3

CH. Damn! The girl's nowhere to be seen, and I'm lost too, for letting her out of my sight. Where to look for her, where to track her down, who to ask, what way to go – I just don't know. There's only one hope –   295

o faciem pulchram! deleo omnis dehinc ex animo mulieres;
taedet cotidianarum harum formarum.

PA. ecce autem alterum!
nescioquid de amore loquitur. o infortunatum senem!
hic vero est qui, si occeperit,
ludum iocumque dices fuisse illum alterum, 300
praeut huius rabies quae dabit.

CH. ut illum di deaeque senium perdant qui me hodie remoratus est,
meque adeo qui restiterim, tum autem qui illum flocci fecerim.
sed eccum Parmenonem. salve!

PA. quid tu es tristis? quidve es alacris?
unde is?

CH. egone? nescio hercle, neque unde eam neque quorsum eam;
ita prorsus sum oblitus mei. 306

PA. qui quaeso?

CH. amo.

PA. hem!

CH. nunc, Parmeno, te ostenderis qui vir sies.
scis te mihi saepe pollicitum esse: "Chaerea, aliquid inveni
modo quod ames; in ea re utilitatem faciam ut cognoscas meam",
quom in cellulam ad te patris penum omnem congerebam clanculum.

PA. age, inepte.

CH. hoc hercle factum est. fac sis nunc promissa adpareant, 311
si adeo digna res est ubi tu nervos intendas tuos.
haud similis virgo est virginum nostrarum, quas matres student
demissis humeris esse, vincto pectore, ut gracilae sient.
si quae est habitior paullo, pugilem esse aiunt, deducunt cibum; 315

---

300 dices Σ, Eugr., Prisc. in **G. L.** 3.50 : dicet A, Arusian. in **G. L.** 7. 503. | **302** senium Don. : senium **vel** seneum A[1] : senem Iov., Σ. | **303** restiterim Iov., Σ : ei restiterim A[1], Kauer-Lindsay. | **305-6** 305 (*unde ... eam*) **troch. sept.**, 306 (*ita ... mei*) **iamb. dim. faciunt edd. plerique** : 305 (*unde ... hercle*) **troch. dim.**, 306 (*neque ... mei*) **iamb. oct. faciunt** Kauer-Lindsay. | **306** prorsus Σ, Don. **in lemm.** : prorsum A, Don. **in comm.** | sum oblitus Σ, Don. : oblitus A[1] : oblitus sum A[2]. | **307** ostenderis (?) Don. : ostendes **codd.** | nunc Parmeno te ostenderis Bentley : nunc te Parmeno te ostendes GPC : nunc te Parmeno te ostendes A[1] (**prius** te **del.** A[2]) : nunc te Parmeno ostendes D : Parmeno nunc te ostendes E : nunc Parmeno ostendes te Kauer-Lindsay. | **310** omnem AP[1]C : omne DGP[2]E : "*omnem et omnem* legitur" Don. (cf. Prisc. in **G. L.** 2.163). | **312 Chaereae cont.** Don., **edd.** : **Parmenoni trib. codd.** | **314** pectore AGPC : corpore DE. | gracilae Don. ("a singulari *gracila* venit haec declinatio"), Eugr. ("legitur et *gracilae*") : graciles **codd.** | **315** si quae A: si qua Σ.

she can't stay hidden for long, wherever she is. What a gorgeous creature! From now on, I'm putting all other women out of my mind; I'm fed up with your run-of-the-mill beauties!

PA. Here's the other one – and he's chattering on about love too! Unlucky old master! This one's the sort of chap that, once he's got going, you'll say the other one was child's play, a mere joke, compared to what this one's madness will let loose.   300

CH. May all the powers in heaven damn that old fellow who held me up today, and damn me too for stopping for him and for taking any notice of him! (*Catching sight of Parmeno.*) But here's Parmeno; hullo!

PA. Why are you so glum? And so excited? Where have you come from?

CH. Me? I really don't know where I've come from or where I'm going; I'm in such a complete dream.   306

PA. How's that, may I ask?

CH. (*dramatically*) I'm in love.

PA. What!

CH. Now's the time, Parmeno, for you to show what kind of man you are. You know how you often used to promise me: "Chaerea, just find an object for your love, and I'll make sure you realize how useful I can be in such a situation" – that was when I used to bring all those piles of father's rations to your room on the quiet.

PA. Go on with you, you silly boy!   311

CH. That's how it was, really. Now, please, make sure those promises are kept, if you think it's something worth making the effort for. This girl's not like our other girls, whose mothers are keen for them to have sagging shoulders and flat chests, so they'll look thin. If a girl's a bit too much on the chubby side, they call her 'champ' and cut her food   315

tam etsi bona est natura, reddunt curatura iunceas.

itaque ergo amantur.

PA. quid tua istaec?

CH. nova figura oris.

PA. papae!

CH. color verus, corpus solidum et suci plenum.

PA. anni?

CH. anni? sedecim.

PA. flos ipse.

CH. nunc hanc tu mihi vel vi vel clam vel precario

fac tradas; mea nil refert dum potiar modo. 320

PA. quid? virgo quoia est?

CH. nescio hercle.

PA. unde est?

CH. tantundem.

PA. ubi habitat?

CH. ne id quidem.

PA. ubi vidisti ?

CH. in via.

PA. qua ratione amisisti?

CH. id equidem adveniens mecum stomachabar modo,

neque quemquam ego esse hominem arbitror quoi magis bonae

felicitates omnes advorsae sient. 325

quid hoc est sceleris? perii.

PA. quid factum est?

CH. rogas?

patris cognatum atque aequalem Archidemidem

novistin?

PA. quidni?

CH. is, dum hanc sequor, fit mi obviam.

PA. incommode hercle.

---

316 iunceas Σ, Don., Don. **An.** 941, Nonius p. 493M : iunceam A. | **319** ipse A²Σ, Probus
213 : ipsum A¹ : ipsus **edd. plerique.** | nunc hanc Hermann : hanc **codd.** : ipsam hanc
Fleckeisen, Kauer-Lindsay. | **322** amisisti AG² : amisti DG¹PCE¹, Don. : amisti eam E² :
eam amisti Kauer-Lindsay. | **324** neque Σ : nec A², Kauer-Lindsay. | quemquam ego
esse hominem Ap : ego quemquam hominem esse PC : quemquam esse ego hominem DG :
quemquam esse hominem E. | **326** quid hoc est sceleris **Chaereae cont.** A, Don. :
Parmenoni trib. Σ. | **328** novistin A, **edd. plerique** : nostin Σ, Nonius p. 235M, Kauer-
Lindsay.

down; even if she's got a good figure, they make them look like
bullrushes by the treatment they give them. And that's the way they
get their suitors.

PA. What about this one of yours?

CH. Oh, quite a new kind of looks.

PA. Goodness!

CH. There's a natural colour to her, and she's got a firm and juicy figure.

PA. How old?

CH. How old? Sixteen.

PA. The absolute flower of youth!

CH. Make sure you get her to me now – by force or by stealth or just by   320
begging her; it doesn't matter to me at all, as long as I just get her.

PA. Well, whose is she?

CH. I really don't know.

PA. Where's she from?

CH. Same answer.

PA. Where does she live?

CH. I don't even know that.

PA. Where did you see her?

CH. In the street.

PA. How did you lose her?

CH. That's what I was furious with myself about as I came along just now;
I don't think there's anyone whose good fortune's turned so   325
completely sour on him. What a curse! I've had it now.

PA. What happened?

CH. What happened? You know that relation of my father's,
Archidemides – the one as old as he is?

PA. Of course I do.

CH. While I was following this girl, he bumped into me.

PA. How tiresome!

CH.   immo enimvero infeliciter;
nam incommoda alia sunt dicenda, Parmeno.   330
illum liquet mihi deierare his mensibus
sex septem prorsum non vidisse proxumis
nisi nunc, quom minime vellem minimeque opus fuit.
eho nonne hoc monstri simile est? quid ais?
PA.   maxume.
CH. continuo accurrit ad me, quam longe quidem,   335
incurvos, tremulus, labiis demissis, gemens.
"heus! heus! tibi dico, Chaerea," inquit; restiti.
"scin quid ego te volebam?" "dic." "cras est mihi
iudicium." "quid tum?" "ut diligenter nunties
patri advocatus mane mihi esse ut meminerit."   340
dum haec dicit, abiit hora. rogo numquid velit.
"recte," inquit, abeo. quom huc respicio ad virginem,
illaec se interea commodum huc advorterat
in hanc nostram plateam.
PA.   mirum ni hanc dicit, modo
huic quae data est dono.
CH.   huc quom advenio, nulla erat.   345
PA. comites secuti scilicet sunt virginem?
CH. verum; parasitus cum ancilla.
PA.   ipsa est; ilicet.
desine; iam conclamatum est.
CH.   alias res agis.
PA. istuc ago equidem.
CH.   nostin quae sit, dic mihi, aut
vidistin?
PA.   vidi, novi, scio quo abducta sit.   350
CH. eho, Parmeno mi, nostin? et scis ubi siet?
PA. huc deducta est ad meretricem Thaidem; ei dono data est.
CH. quis is est tam potens cum tanto munere hoc?
PA.   miles Thraso,
Phaedriae rivalis.
CH.   duras fratris partis praedicas.

---

335 accurrit A¹Σ : occurrit A², Kauer-Lindsay. | **341** dicit AD¹, Eugr. : loquitur D²GPCE.
| **343** illaec **Grant** (cf. 947, **Ad.** 489) : illa **codd.**, **edd. plerique**, **necnon** Kauer-Lindsay. |
se Kauer-Lindsay : sese **codd.**, **edd. plerique**. | **347** ilicet Ap : scilicet DGPCE.

CH. Jolly unlucky, more like; it's other things we should call just 330 'tiresome', Parmeno. I'm sure I can swear I haven't seen him for the last six or seven months on end – except now, when I least wanted to or needed to. Isn't it like some ghastly stroke of fate? What do you say?

PA. It looks very like it.

CH. He ran up to me at once, from miles away, bent and shaking, his lips 335 all slobbering, moaning away at me. "Hey! Hey! Chaerea, it's you I'm speaking to," he said; I stopped. "Do you know what I want you for?" "No, tell me." "Tomorrow I've got a lawsuit." "What of it?" "Be sure to tell your father to remember to be one of my supporters in 340 the morning." While he was telling me this, an hour went by. I asked if that was all he wanted. He said "Yes", and I left. When I looked over in this direction for the girl, she'd just turned into our street, down this way.

PA. (*aside*) I'm almost sure he means this girl who's just been given to 345 Thais.

CH. When I got here, she was nowhere to be seen.

PA. I suppose she'd got some people walking with her?

CH. Yes, a sponger and a servant-girl.

PA. (*aside*) It's her; that's the end of that, then. (*To Chaerea.*) You can drop it; it's all over.

CH. You must be talking of something else.

PA. No, I'm talking about this business.

CH. Tell me, do you know who she is? Have you seen her? 350

PA. I've seen her, I know her, and I know where she's been taken.

CH. Oh, Parmeno, my dear chap, you know her? And you know where she is?

PA. Yes, she's been delivered to Thais here; she's a present for her.

CH. Who's so well-off he can give such an expensive gift as that?

PA. The captain Thraso, Phaedria's rival.

CH. That's a tough role you're telling me my brother's got.

PA. immo enim si scias quod donum huic dono contra conparet,   355
tum magis id dicas.

CH.   quodnam quaeso hercle?

PA.   eunuchum.

CH.   illum, obsecro,
inhonestum hominem, quem mercatus est heri, senem mulierem?

PA. istunc ipsum.

CH.   homo quatietur certe cum dono foras.
sed istam Thaidem non scivi nobis vicinam.

PA.   haud diu est.

CH. perii! numquamne etiam me illam vidisse! eho dum, dic mihi,   360
estne, ut fertur, forma?

PA.   sane.

CH.   at nil ad nostram hanc?

PA.   alia res.

CH. obsecro hercle, Parmeno, fac ut potiar.

PA.   faciam sedulo ac
dabo operam, adiuvabo. numquid me aliud?

CH.   quo nunc is?

PA.   domum,
ut mancupia haec, ita uti iussit frater, ducam ad Thaidem.

CH. o fortunatum istum eunuchum quiquidem in hanc detur domum!   365

PA. quid ita?

CH.   rogitas? summa forma semper conservam domi
videbit, conloquetur, aderit una in unis aedibus,
cibum non numquam capiet cum ea, interdum propter dormiet.

PA. quid si nunc tute fortunatus fias?

CH.   qua re, Parmeno?
responde.

PA.   capias illius vestem.

CH.   vestem? quid tum postea?   370

---

355 enim DGPC, Eugr. : **om.** AE. | **356** tum **codd.** : **om. edd. plerique, necnon** Kauer-Lindsay. | illum D¹PC¹ : illumne **cett. codd.** | **361** res A : res est Σ, Don. : rest Kauer-Lindsay. | **364** ita uti C¹ (?), **edd.** : ita ut **cett. codd.** | **370** capias illius A¹ : capias tu illius Iov., Σ, Don., Kauer-Lindsay.

PA. Yes, but if you knew what a present he's getting ready to match it,   355
     you'd say that all the more.

CH. What's that, then?

PA. A eunuch.

CH. Goodness, you mean that wretched-looking fellow he bought
     yesterday, that effeminate old man?

PA. That's the one.

CH. Then he'll be bundled out of the house, and his present too, that's for
     sure. But I didn't know that woman Thais was our neighbour.

PA. She hasn't been for very long.

CH. Damn it! To think that I've never even set eyes on her! Hey, though,   360
     tell me – is she as good to look at as she's said to be?

PA. Very much so.

CH. But she's nothing compared to this girl of mine?

PA. Quite a different matter.

CH. Please, Parmeno, make sure I get her, for heaven's sake!

PA. I'll do my best and apply myself to it; I'll help you. Will that be all?

CH. Where are you off to now?

PA. Back home, to take those slaves across to Thais, as your brother told
     me to.

CH. Oh, that lucky eunuch, to be taken into that house as a gift!   365

PA. How so?

CH. What a thing to ask! He'll always be seeing that exquisite fellow-
     slave of his in there, he'll talk to her, be under the same roof with her,
     sometimes have his meals with her, and now and then sleep next to
     her.

PA. What if *you* became the lucky fellow?

CH. How, Parmeno? Explain.   370

PA. You could put on his clothes.

CH. His clothes? Then what?

PA. pro illo te ducam.

CH.   audio.

PA.   te esse illum dicam.

CH.   intellego.

PA. tu illis fruare commodis quibus tu illum dicebas modo:
cibum una capias, adsis, tangas, ludas, propter dormias,
quandoquidem illarum neque te quisquam novit neque scit qui sies.
praeterea forma et aetas ipsa est facile ut pro eunucho probes.   375

CH. dixisti pulchre; numquam vidi melius consilium dari.
age, eamus intro nunciam; orna me, abduc, duc, quantum potest.

PA. quid agis? iocabar equidem.

CH.   garris.

PA.   perii! quid ego egi miser?
quo trudis? perculeris iam tu me. tibi equidem dico, mane.

CH. eamus.

PA.   pergin?

CH.   certum est.

PA.   vide ne nimium calidum hoc sit modo.   380

CH. non est profecto; sine.

PA.   at enim istaec in me cudetur faba.

CH.   ah!

PA. flagitium facimus.

CH.   an id flagitium est si in domum meretriciam
deducar et illis crucibus, quae nos nostramque adulescentiam
habent despicatam et quae nos semper omnibus cruciant modis,
nunc referam gratiam atque eas itidem fallam ut ab illis fallimur?   385
an potius haec patri aequom est fieri ut a me ludatur dolis?
quod qui rescierint, culpent; illud merito factum omnes putent.

PA. quid istic? si certum est facere, facias; verum ne post conferas
culpam in me.

CH.   non faciam.

PA.   iubesne?

CH.   iubeam? cogo atque impero.

---

371 ducam ADGE : deducam PCp. | **372** illis Iov., DGC : illius A¹PE. | **376** dixisti D²,
Umpfenbach : dixti **cett. codd.**, Kauer-Lindsay. | **377** potest Ap : potes DGPCE, Don. |
380 calidum Don., schol. Bemb. : callidum **codd.** | **384** despicatam D¹GPCE, Don. :
despectam AD². | **385** ab illis AD²E : ab his D¹GP : ab is C, Kauer-Lindsay. | **388** facias
Iov., Σ : faciam A¹. | **389** iubeam Ap : iubeo Nonius p. 264M : iubeo immo DGPCE.

PA. I could take you there instead of him.

CH. (*slowly*) I see.

PA. I could say you were him.

CH. I get it.

PA. You could enjoy the benefits you said just now that he'd enjoy: you could have your meals with her, be with her, touch her, play games with her, sleep next to her – none of the women there know you or have any idea who you are. (*With a laugh.*) Besides, you've got the looks and age to pass as the eunuch easily!   375

CH. (*excitedly*) Excellent idea! I've never known better advice. Come on, let's go indoors right now; fit me out, take me across, take me, quick as you can.

PA. (*appalled*) What are you on about? I was only joking.

CH. Rubbish!

PA. Oh, damn! What a fool I am! What have I done? Where are you shoving me? You'll knock me over in a minute. Stop, I tell you!

CH. Let's go.   380

PA. Are you going on with this?

CH. My mind's made up.

PA. Just watch out this isn't too hot to handle!

CH. It isn't, really it's not. Let me.

PA. But this will be a rod for my back.

CH. Huh!

PA. But we're doing wrong.

CH. Is it wrong if I'm taken into the house of one of *those* women and pay back those harridans who so despise us and our tender years and who   385 are always torturing us in every way they can think of? Is it wrong if I trick them in just the way that they trick us? Or is it fairer to bamboozle my father? People who got wise to *that* would find fault with me; but they'd all think *this* was a job well done.

PA. Oh, all right. If you're set on doing it, go on and do it; but don't put the blame on me afterwards.

CH. I shan't.

PA. So that's an order?

CH. An order? It's a strict command! I'll never shirk the responsibility.   390

          numquam defugiam auctoritatem. sequere.

PA.
                                        di vortant bene.   390

                              ACTVS III

III i   **THRASO   GNATHO   PARMENO**

THR. magnas vero agere gratias Thais mihi?
GN. ingentis.
THR.   ain tu, laeta est?
GN.
                    non tam ipso quidem
          dono quam abs te datum esse; id vero serio
          triumphat.
PA.   hoc proviso ut, ubi tempus siet,
          deducam. sed eccum militem.
THR.
                                    est istuc datum   395
          profecto ut grata mihi sint quae facio omnia.
GN. advorti hercle animum.
THR.   vel rex semper maxumas
          mihi agebat quidquid feceram; aliis non item.
GN. labore alieno magno partam gloriam
          verbis saepe in se transmovet qui habet salem;   400
          quod in te est.
THR.   habes.
GN.   rex te ergo in oculis ...
THR.
                                        scilicet.
GN. ... gestare.
THR.   vero; credere omnem exercitum,
          consilia.
GN.   mirum.
THR.   tum sicubi eum satietas
          hominum aut negoti siquando odium ceperat,
          requiescere ubi volebat, quasi... nostin?
GN.
                                        scio.   405

---

390 numquam ... sequere **Chaereae cont.**, di ... bene **Parmenoni trib. edd.** : numquam ...
sequere **Parmenoni**, di ... bene **Chaereae trib. codd.**, Don., Eugr. | **394** hoc A¹ : huc A²Σ,
Don. (Cf. 501.) | **399** magno Ap, Nonius pp. 223M, 318M : magnam DGPCE. | **401**
quod A²D²P¹C¹E : quid A¹ : qui D¹GP²C², Consentius 348. | **402** gestare AC¹ : gestire
DGP²C²E, Don. : gestiri P¹. | vero Ap : verum DGPCE.

Follow me.

PA. Heaven grant success!

(*They both go into Chaerea's father's house. After only a very short pause, Gnatho and the captain* **THRASO** *enter from the audience's right.*)

ACT THREE

III 1

THR. Is Thais really very grateful to me?

GN. Oh, enormously.

THR. And she's delighted, you say?

GN. Not so much with the actual present as with the fact it was you that gave it; she thinks that's a real triumph.

(*Parmeno comes out again.*)

PA. I'm coming out to have a look, so I can take them over when the time 395 is right. (*He catches sight of the others.*) Oh, look – it's the captain.

THR. (*smugly*) It's a real gift I've got – everything I do makes people grateful to me.

GN. (*sarcastically*) So I've noticed.

THR. (*not appreciating the sarcasm*) For instance, the king always used to be extremely grateful to me whatever I'd done; he wasn't like that with other people.

GN. By what he says, a man of wit can often transfer to himself the glory 400 other people have worked so hard to win. That's what happens with you.

THR. You've got it exactly.

GN. That's why the king regarded you ...

THR. Of course.

GN. ... as the apple of his eye.

THR. Yes, indeed; he entrusted me with his entire army, and all his plans.

GN. Amazing!

THR. Then if ever he'd got fed up with people or bored with work, when he 405 wanted to have a bit of a rest, as if ... you know?

      quasi ubi illam exspueret miseriam ex animo.

THR.   tenes.

      tum me convivam solum abducebat sibi.

GN.   hui,

      regem elegantem narras!

THR.   immo sic homo est –

      perpaucorum hominum.

GN.   immo nullorum arbitror,

      si tecum vivit.

THR.   invidere omnes mihi,   410

      mordere clanculum; ego non flocci pendere;

      illi invidere misere; verum unus tamen

      inpense, elephantis quem Indicis praefecerat.

      is ubi molestus magis est, "quaeso," inquam, "Strato,

      eon es ferox quia habes imperium in beluas?"   415

GN.   pulchre mehercle dictum et sapienter. papae!

      iugularas hominem. quid ille?

THR.   mutus ilico.

GN.   quidni esset?

PA.   di vostram fidem! hominem perditum

      miserumque et illum sacrilegum!

THR.   quid illud, Gnatho,

      quo pacto Rhodium tetigerim in convivio,   420

      numquam tibi dixi?

GN.   numquam; sed narra, obsecro.

      plus miliens audivi.

THR.   una in convivio

      erat hic, quem dico, Rhodius adulescentulus.

      forte habui scortum; coepit ad id adludere

      et me inridere. "quid ais," inquam homini, "inpudens?   425

      lepus tute es, pulpamentum quaeris?"

GN.   hahahae!

THR. quid est?

GN.   facete, lepide, laute, nil supra.

      tuomne, obsecro te, hoc dictum erat? vetus credidi.

---

422 audivi A : iam audivi Σ. | **425** inquam homini inpudens A[1] : inquam homo inpudens Iov., DGE : homo inquam inpudens PC : homo inpudens inquam (F). | **427** lepide laute ADG, Don. : laute lepide PC(F)Ep.

GN. I do; as if he'd get rid of all the troubles from his mind.

THR. That's it. On those occasions he'd take me on one side as his only companion.

GN. Goodness, what a very particular king!

THR. Oh, that's what he's like – a man of very few friends.

GN. (*aside*) A man of *no* friends, I should think, if he keeps company with you!   410

THR. Everyone was envious of me, and said nasty things behind my back, but I didn't give a damn. They were all terribly jealous – one of them, who was in command of the Indian elephants, quite uncontrollably so. When he was being more tiresome than usual, I said to him: "Tell me, Strato, are you so fierce because you're in charge of wild beasts?"   415

GN. Beautifully said, by god, and with such intelligence! Gracious! You really finished him. What did he say to that?

THR. He was struck dumb on the spot.

GN. Naturally.

PA. (*who has been listening intently to all this, aside*) Good god! What a wretched and hopeless case the man is! And the other one's outrageous!

THR. Well now, Gnatho, have I never told you that story about how I rattled the Rhodian at a banquet?   420

GN. No, never; but do tell me, please. (*Aside.*) I've heard it over a thousand times!

THR. This person I'm talking about, a young chap from Rhodes, was at a dinner-party with me. As it happened, I had a tart with me, and he began to play up to her and make fun of me. "What's that," I said to him, "you impudent puppy? You're on the menu yourself, and you're going after the tit-bits?"   425

GN. (*with exaggerated enthusiasm*) Ha, ha, ha!

THR. What's the matter?

GN. How witty and amusing! How neat! Nothing better! But tell me, was the joke yours? I thought it was an old one.

THR. audieras?

GN.   saepe, et fertur in primis.

THR.   meum est.

GN.   dolet dictum inprudenti adulescenti et libero.   430

PA.   at te di perdant!

GN.   quid ille, quaeso?

THR.   perditus.

risu omnes qui aderant emoriri; denique

metuebant omnes iam me.

GN.   haud iniuria.

THR. sed heus tu, purgor ego me de istac Thaidi,

quod eam me amare suspicata est?

GN.   nil minus.   435

immo auge magis suspicionem.

THR.   quor?

GN.   rogas?

scin, si quando illa mentionem Phaedriae

facit aut si laudat, te ut male urat?

THR.   sentio.

GN.   id ut ne fiat, haec res sola est remedio:

ubi nominabit Phaedriam, tu Pamphilam   440

continuo; si quando illa dicet "Phaedriam

intro mittamus comissatum", Pamphilam

cantatum provocemus; si laudabit haec

illius formam, tu huius contra. denique

par pro pari referto, quod eam mordeat.   445

THR. siquidem me amaret, tum istuc prodesset, Gnatho.

GN.   quando illud quod tu das exspectat atque amat,

iamdudum te amat, iamdudum illi facile fit

quod doleat; metuit semper quem ipsa nunc capit

fructum ne quando iratus tu alio conferas.   450

THR. bene dixti, ac mihi istuc non in mentem venerat.

GN.   ridiculum! non enim cogitaras. ceterum

idem hoc tute melius quanto invenisses, Thraso.

---

430 dolet ... libero **Gnathoni trib.** AL, Don. : **Thrasoni cont.** DGPC(F)E. | **433** haud A[1] : non Iov. Σ. | **449** metuit A, Don. : metuet DPCE : metuat GF. | **451** ac APCE : at DGF.

THR. You'd heard it, then?

GN. Often, and it's always regarded as one of the best.

THR. Well, it's mine.

GN. It really made that stupid, loud-mouthed youngster smart.   430

PA. (*aside*) God damn you!

GN. Tell me, what did he do?

THR. He was completely sunk. Everybody there was dying of laughter; and the upshot was that everyone was very wary of me from then on.

GN. And with good reason, too.

THR. But listen, shall I clear myself in Thais' eyes about the girl – her suspicions that I'm in love with her, I mean?   435

GN. That's the last thing you should do. On the contrary, increase them.

THR. Why ?

GN. Need you ask? You know how it cuts you to the quick if she ever mentions Phaedria or says nice things about him?

THR. Yes.

GN. This is the only way to stop that happening. When she mentions   440
Phaedria's name, you immediately mention Pamphila's; if ever she says "Let's have Phaedria in for a party", we must call on Pamphila to sing; if she praises his good looks, you praise hers in turn. In short, give her like for like, so it'll really annoy her.   445

THR. If she really loved me, then that *would* be the best thing, Gnatho.

GN. Since she waits for your presents and really likes them, she's obviously been in love with you for a long time – and for a long time, too, it's been easy for you to do something to upset her. She's always afraid that one day you'll fly into a rage and take the contributions she   450
now enjoys off somewhere else.

THR. Good advice; that hadn't occurred to me.

GN. Nonsense! You just hadn't thought it through. But how much better you'd have hit on it for yourself, Thraso!

(*Thais comes out of her house.*)

III ii   **THAIS THRASO GNATHO PARMENO PYTHIAS**

TH.   audire vocem visa sum modo militis.
      atque eccum. salve, mi Thraso.

THR.
                        o Thais mea,   455
      meum savium, quid agitur? ecquid nos amas
      de fidicina istac?

PA.
                quam venuste! quod dedit
      principium adveniens!

TH.
                plurimum merito tuo.

GN. eamus ergo ad cenam. quid stas?

PA.
                    em alterum!
      ex homine hunc natum dicas?

TH.
                ubi vis; non moror.   460

PA. adibo atque adsimulabo quasi nunc exeam.
      ituran, Thais, quopiam es?

TH.
                ehem Parmeno!
      bene fecisti; hodie itura ...

PA.
              quo?

TH.
                quid, hunc non vides?

PA. video, et me taedet. ubi vis, dona adsunt tibi
      a Phaedria.

THR.
          quid stamus? quor non imus hinc? 465

PA. quaeso hercle ut liceat, pace quod fiat tua,
      dare huic quae volumus, convenire et conloqui.

THR. perpulchra credo dona aut nostri similia.

PA. res indicabit. heus! iubete istos foras
      exire quos iussi ocius. procede tu huc;
      ex Aethiopia est usque haec.   470

THR.
                hic sunt tres minae.

GN. vix.

PA.   ubi tu es, Dore? accede huc. em eunuchum tibi!
      quam liberali facie! quam aetate integra!

TH. ita me di ament, honestust.

PA.
              quid tu ais, Gnatho?

---

454 vocem visa sum modo A, Don. : visa sum vocem modo DG : visa sum modo vocem E(F).
| **459** em APF : hem DGCE. | **460** non ADE², Don. : num PCFE¹ : **om.** G¹ : nam G². |
462 ituran A²DG²PCFE : ituram A¹. | ehem Ap : hem (**vel** em) DGPCFE. | **468** nostri
AD¹G¹ : nostris D²G²LPCFE, Don., Prisc. in **G. L.** 3. 34.

III 2

TH. I thought I could hear my captain's voice just now. And there he is – 455
hullo, my dear Thraso.

THR. Oh, Thais my dear, my sweetest, how are you? Do you love me just a
little bit because of that music-girl?

PA. (*aside*) How beautifully put! What an opening shot that was as he
arrived!

TH. Oh, an awful lot – and you deserve it.

GN. So let's go off to supper. Why are you hanging about?

PA. (*aside*) There's the other one now! You'd hardly say he was human, 460
would you?

TH. Whenever you want. I'm not holding you up.

PA. (*aside*) I'll go up to them and pretend I've just come out. (*Aloud, as
he comes forward.*) Thais, are you going somewhere?

TH. (*embarrassed*) Oh, Parmeno! You have been kind. I'm just off now
...

PA. Where to?

TH. What, can't you see the captain?

PA. Yes, I can, and the sight sickens me. I've got Phaedria's presents here
for you whenever you want them.

THR. What are we standing around for? Why don't we get going? 465

PA. I'm just asking, by your leave, to be allowed to give Thais here the
presents we want her to have, and to go up and have a few words with
her.

THR. (*sarcastically*) Very fine presents, I'm sure, and just like mine.

PA. Time will tell. (*Calling into the house.*) Hey, tell those two to come
out here quickly – the ones I gave the orders about. (*To the Ethiopian* 470
slave-girl, as she comes out.) Over here, you. (*To Thais.*) This one's
all the way from Ethiopia.

THR. Worth three minae!

GN. If that!

PA. (*calling into the house again*) Dorus, where are you? Come here.
(*Chaerea comes out, dressed in eunuch's clothes.*) Here's a eunuch
for you! What gentlemanly looks he's got! And in the bloom of
youth, too!

TH. My god, he is a good looker!

PA. What do you say, Gnatho?

numquid habes quod contemnas? quid tu autem Thraso? 475
tacent; satis laudant. fac periclum in litteris,
fac in palaestra, in musicis: quae liberum
scire aequom est adulescentem, sollertem dabo.
THR. ego illum eunuchum, si opus siet, vel sobrius ...
PA. atque haec qui misit non sibi soli postulat 480
te vivere et sua causa excludi ceteros,
neque pugnas narrat neque cicatrices suas
ostentat neque tibi obstat, quod quidam facit;
verum ubi molestum non erit, ubi tu voles,
ubi tempus tibi erit, sat habet si tum recipitur. 485
THR. adparet servom hunc esse domini pauperis
miserique.
GN. nam hercle nemo posset, sat scio,
qui haberet qui pararet alium, hunc perpeti.
PA. tace tu, quem ego esse infra infimos omnis puto
homines; nam qui huic animum adsentari induxeris 490
e flamma petere te cibum posse arbitror.
THR. iamne imus?
TH. hos prius intro ducam et quae volo
simul imperabo; poste continuo exeo.
THR. ego hinc abeo. tu istanc opperire.
PA. haud convenit
una ire cum amica imperatorem in via. 495
THR. quid tibi ego multa dicam? domini similis es.
GN. hahahae!
THR. quid rides?
GN. istuc quod dixti modo,
et illud de Rhodio dictum cum in mentem venit.
sed Thais exit.
THR. abi prae; cura ut sint domi
parata.
GN. fiat.
TH. diligenter, Pythias, 500

---

489 quem ego D²GPCFE : quem te ego A, Kauer-Lindsay : ego te p¹, Prisc. ⸱⸱ **G. L.** 3.44 : ego D¹. | **491** petere te cibum DG : te petere cibum A : te cibum petere PCFE. | **493** poste gl. I : post A : postea PCFE : postea huc schol. D : post huc DG. | **494** istanc AG : istam schol. D, PCFE : ista D¹. | **499** cura Paumier, **edd. plerique** : curre **codd.**, Don., Kauer-Lindsay.

Nothing here to pour scorn on, is there? And what about you, Thraso? 475
(*Aside, after a pause.*) They're dumbstruck – that's praise enough.
(*Aloud.*) Test him on literature, gymnastics, music; I'll prove he's
skilled in everything a young gentleman should know.

THR. Even if I was sober, I know what I could do to that eunuch, if I was
pushed!

PA. (*to Thais*) The person who's sent you these doesn't demand that you 480
live for him alone and that everyone else be shut out for his sake; he
doesn't talk of his battles and show you his scars or get in your way
like *someone* does. But when it's not too much trouble, when you
want to and when you've got the time – he's quite satisfied if you 485
receive him then.

THR. Obviously this slave's got a wretched and penniless master.

GN. Yes, I'm sure nobody could put up with this one if he'd got the money
to buy another.

PA. Oh, shut up! You're lower than all the lowest of the low to me. If 490
you're the type to bring yourself to suck up to this idiot, I think you'd
snatch the offerings from a funeral pyre!

THR. *Now* are we going?

TH. I'll take these two inside first and give my orders while I'm there; I'll
be back out straight away. (*She goes into her house with Chaerea and
the slave-girl.*)

THR. I'm going. (*To Gnatho.*) You wait for her.

PA. (*maliciously*) It isn't right for a general to be walking in the street 495
with his lady-friend! (*He walks off to the audience's left.*)

THR. (*shouting after him*) Why should I waste words on you? You're just
like your master.

GN. Ha, ha, ha!

THR. What are you laughing at?

GN. What you said just now, and that story about the chap from Rhodes,
whenever it comes to mind. But here's Thais.

(*Thais comes out again, with her maid **PYTHIAS** and some other maids.*)

THR. (*to Gnatho*) You go on ahead; make sure things are ready at home. 500

GN. Very well. (*He goes off to the audience's right.*)

TH. (*quietly, so Thraso cannot hear*) Make very sure, Pythias, if Chremes

       fac cures, si Chremes hoc forte advenerit,
       ut ores primum ut maneat; si id non commodum est,
       ut redeat; si id non poterit, ad me adducito.

PY. ita faciam.

TH.   quid? quid aliud volui dicere?
       ehem, curate istam diligenter virginem;   505
       domi adsitis facite.

THR.   eamus.

TH.   vos me sequimini.

III iii   **CHREMES   PYTHIAS**

CHR. profecto quanto magis magisque cogito,
       nimirum dabit haec Thais mihi malum magnum;
       ita me ab ea astute video labefactarier,
       iam tum quom primum iussit me ad se accersier.   510
       roget quis: "quid tibi cum illa?" ne noram quidem.
       ubi veni, causam ut ibi manerem repperit.
       ait rem divinam fecisse et rem seriam
       velle agere mecum. iam tum erat suspicio
       dolo malo haec fieri omnia. ipsa accumbere   515
       mecum, mihi sese dare, sermonem quaerere.
       ubi friget, huc evasit, quam pridem pater
       mihi et mater mortui essent. dico iam diu.
       rus Sunii ecquod habeam et quam longe a mari.
       credo placere hoc, sperat se a me avellere.   520
       postremo, ecqua inde parva periisset soror,
       ecquis cum ea una, quid habuisset cum perit,
       ecquis eam posset noscere. haec quor quaeritet,
       nisi si illa forte quae olim periit parvola
       soror hanc se intendit esse, ut est audacia?   525
       verum ea si vivit, annos nata est sedecim,
       non maior; Thais quam ego sum maiuscula est.
       misit porro orare ut venirem serio.
       aut dicat quid volt, aut molesta ne siet.

---

501 hoc A : huc DPCFE, Don., Eugr. : huic G¹. (Cf. 394.) | **509** ab ea astute video DGPCFE : video ab ea astute A. | **511** quid Σ, Don., Eugr. : quid rei A. | **520** placere A¹ : ei placere A²Σ, Kauer-Lindsay. | **529** quid Σ : quod A.

happens to arrive, that first of all you ask him to wait; if that's not
convenient, that you ask him to come back; if that's not possible,
bring him to me.

PY. I will.

TH. Now, what else did I want to tell you? Oh, look after that young girl   505
carefully, and make sure you all stay at home.

THR. Let's go.

TH. (*to the other maids*) You follow me.

(*Thraso, Thais and the other maids go off to the audience's right. Pythias is
just about to go into Thais' house when* **CHREMES** *comes on from the left.
She stands back, listening and unnoticed.*)

III 3

CHR. Really, the more I think of it, I'm sure this woman Thais is going to
cause me a lot of trouble. I can see I've been thrown quite off balance
by her clever moves, right from the time she first asked me to be   510
brought to her. (And if anyone should ask "What have you got to do
with her?", the answer is I didn't even know her.) When I arrived, she
found an excuse for me to be kept waiting there; she said she'd just
been sacrificing, and wanted to discuss an important matter with me.
Already at that stage I suspected this was all being done with malice   515
aforethought. She placed herself beside me, gave me all her attention
and tried to start up a conversation. When that fell flat, she had
recourse to asking how long my father and mother had been dead. For
quite a while, I said. Had I got an estate at Sunium, and how far was it
from the sea? I expect she rather likes it and is hoping to get it off me.   520
Finally, had any little sister of mine gone missing from there, was
anyone with her at the time, what had she got with her when she
disappeared, and was there anyone who could recognize her? Why
should she ask all this, unless her plan is to pretend to be my little   525
sister who went missing all those years ago? She's certainly got the
bare-faced cheek to do it. But if my sister is alive, she's sixteen now,
no more, and Thais is a little bit older than I am. She's sent again
now, to implore me to come. Either she'll have to tell me what she
wants, or she must stop being a nuisance. I swear I won't be coming a   530

non hercle veniam tertio. heus! heus! ecquis hic?   530
ego sum Chremes.

PY.   o capitulum lepidissimum!
CHR. dico ego mi insidias fieri?
PY.   Thais maxumo
te orabat opere ut cras redires.

CHR.   rus eo.
PY. fac amabo.
CHR.   non possum, inquam.
PY.   at tu apud nos hic mane
dum redeat ipsa.

CHR.   nil minus.
PY.   quor, mi Chremes?   535
CHR. malam rem hinc ibis?
PY.   si istuc ita certum est tibi,
amabo ut illuc transeas ubi illa est.

CHR.   eo.
PY. abi, Dorias, cito hunc deduce ad militem.

III iv   **ANTIPHO**

AN. heri aliquot adulescentuli coiimus in Piraeo
in hunc diem ut de symbolis essemus. Chaeream ei rei   540
praefecimus; dati anuli; locus, tempus constitutum est.
praeteriit tempus; quo in loco dictum est parati nil est;
homo ipse nusquam est, neque scio quid dicam aut quid coniectem.
nunc mi hoc negoti ceteri dedere ut illum quaeram.
idque adeo visam si domi est. quisnam hinc ab Thaide exit?   545
is est an non est? ipsus est. quid hoc hominis? qui hic ornatust?
quid illud mali est? nequeo satis mirari neque conicere;
nisi, quidquid est, procul hinc lubet prius quid sit sciscitari.

530 PY. ecquis hic schol. D, P, schol. C, F²E. | **531** CHR. ego sum Chremes
DG²P²C²F²E. | **536** malam rem APCE : malam in rem DGF. | **538** deduce ʄ : deduc Σ. |
539 coiimus C² : co**mus D : coimus AGPC¹FE, Don., Eugr. | **545** idque adeo A : ibo ad
eam Σ. | ab A¹ : a Iov., Σ. | **546** hominis A : hominis est Σ, Don. : hominist Kauer-
Lindsay. | qui AD¹GP : quid D²CE.

third time. (*He turns to Thais' door and knocks loudly.*) Hey! Hey! Anyone at home? It's Chremes. (*Pythias comes across from where she has been standing and greets him effusively.*)

PY. Oh, my dear young sir!

CHR.(*aside*) I said this was a trap, didn't I?

PY. Thais has asked you most particularly to come back tomorrow.

CHR.I'm going to the country.

PY. Oh, do, please.

CHR.I can't, I tell you.

PY. Then wait here at our house until she gets home.   535

CHR. That's the last thing I'll do.

PY. Why, my dear Chremes?

CHR. Oh, go to hell!

PY. If that's how your mind's made up, please come across to where she is.

CHR.(*reluctantly*) All right, I'm coming.

PY. (*calling into Thais' house*) Off you go, Dorias, and take this gentleman to the captain's, quick as you can.

(**DORIAS** *comes out of the house and goes off with Chremes to the audience's right. Pythias goes into the house. After a few moments,* **ANTIPHO** *comes on from the left.*)

III 4

AN. Yesterday some of us young lads met up at Piraeus to arrange our   540
contributions for a dinner-party today. We put Chaerea in charge, gave our pledges and settled the place and time. That time's gone past, and nothing's ready in the place we fixed; Chaerea himself is nowhere to be seen, and I don't know what to say or think. Now the others have given me the job of searching for him, so I'm coming to   545
see if he's at home. (*The door of Thais' house opens, and Chaerea comes out.*) But who's that coming out of Thais' place? Is it Chaerea or isn't it? It's him! What sort of a creature does he look like? What kind of get-up's that? What mischief's he been up to? I'm too amazed for words, and just can't think what it's all about. But whatever it is, it'll be fun to try to find out from back here. (*He steps back and stands listening as Chaerea excitedly tells his story.*)

III v   CHAEREA   ANTIPHO

CH. numquis hic est? nemo est. numquis hinc me sequitur? nemo homo
                                                                    [est.
          iamne erumpere hoc licet mi gaudium? pro Iuppiter!   550
          nunc est profecto interfici quom perpeti me possum,
          ne hoc gaudium contaminet vita aegritudine aliqua.
          sed neminemne curiosum intervenire nunc mihi
          qui me sequatur quoquo eam, rogitando obtundat, enicet,
          quid gestiam aut quid laetus sim, quo pergam, unde emergam, ubi
                                                            [siem 555
          vestitum hunc nactus, quid mi quaeram, sanus sim anne insaniam!
AN. adibo atque ab eo gratiam hanc quam video velle inibo.
          Chaerea, quid est quod sic gestis? quid sibi hic vestitus quaerit?
          quid est quod laetus es? quid tibi vis? satine sanu's? quid me
                                                          [adspectas?
          †quid taces?
CH.   o festus dies hominis! amice, salve.   560
          nemo est quem ego nunciam magis cuperem videre quam te.
AN. narra istuc quaeso quid sit.
CH.   immo ego te obsecro hercle ut audias.
          nostin hanc quam amat frater?
AN.   novi; nempe, opinor, Thaidem?
CH. istam ipsam.
AN.   sic commemineram.
CH.   quaedam hodie est ei dono data
          virgo; quid ego eius tibi nunc faciem praedicem aut laudem, Antipho,
          cum ipsum me noris quam elegans formarum spectator siem?   566
          in hac commotus sum.
AN.   ain tu?
CH.   primam dices, scio, si videris.

---

553 neminemne curiosum AC¹, Don. : neminem hic curiosum DGC²FE : neminem **
curiosum P. | 554 quoquo eam A : quoque eam P¹C¹ : quique iam D²GP²C²FE. | 558
gestis quid Iov. : gestis quidve A : gestis aut quid Σ. | 559 es schol. D, schol. G, schol. E :
sis **codd.** | satine sanu's **edd. plerique** : satin sanus A : satisne sanus es DG : satin sanus
es PCFE. | 560 o festus dies hominis **codd.**, Don. : **varie corr. edd.** | 56₁ nemost A¹,
Don. : nemost hominum A², Kauer-Lindsay : nemost omnium Σ. | nunciam A¹ : nunc
Iov., Σ, Kauer-Lindsay. | 562 sit **edd. plerique** : siet **codd.** | 564 quaedam hodie A :
hodie quaedam Σ.

III 5

CH. (*looking round in all directions*) Anyone about? Nobody. Anyone
   following me from in there? No-one at all. Now can I let my joy   550
   come out? Good god, now's the time I could honestly put up with
   death, to stop life spoiling this happiness of mine with any pain. To
   think that there's no nosey-parker here now interrupting, to follow me
   round everywhere I go, to batter my ears with questions, to plague me
   to death by asking why I'm so overjoyed, why I'm happy, where I'm   555
   going, where I've come from, where I got these clothes, what I'm
   after, whether I'm in my right mind or off my head!

AN. I'll go and do him the favour I can see he wants. (*Coming forward.*)
   Chaerea, what's the reason for this wild joy? What's the meaning of
   these clothes? What's the reason for such happiness? What do you
   mean by it? Are you quite sane? What are you staring at me for?
   Why don't you say something?   560

CH. Oh, happy day! My dear old friend, hullo. There's nobody I'd want
   to see just now more than you.

AN. Tell me what this is all about, *please*.

CH. No, no, I'm the one who's begging *you* – to listen. You know this
   woman my brother's in love with?

AN. Yes; you mean Thais, I presume?

CH. That's the one.

AN. I thought so.

CH. A young girl's been given her today as a present. Why should I sing
   the praises of her looks to you, Antipho, when you know what a   566
   fastidious observer of the female form I am? I'm in a real state over
   this one.

AN. Honestly?

CH. I know you'll say she's the tops if you see her. To cut a long story

quid multa verba? amare coepi. forte fortuna domi
erat quidam eunuchus quem mercatus fuerat frater Thaidi,
neque is deductus etiamdum ad eam. submonuit me Parmeno 570
ibi servos quod ego arripui.

AN. quid id est?

CH. tacitus citius audies:
ut vestem cum illo mutem et pro illo iubeam me illoc ducier.

AN. pro eunuchon?

CH. sic est.

AN. quid ex ea re tandem ut caperes commodi?

CH. rogas? viderem, audirem, essem una quacum cupiebam, Antipho.
num parva causa aut prava ratio est? traditus sum mulieri. 575
illa ilico, ubi me accepit, laeta vero ad se abducit domum,
commendat virginem.

AN. quoi? tibine?

CH. mihi.

AN. satis tuto tamen!

CH. edicit ne vir quisquam ad eam adeat, et mihi ne abscedam imperat,
in interiore parte ut maneam solus cum sola. adnuo,
terram intuens modeste.

AN. miser!

CH. "ego", inquit, "ad cenam hinc eo." 580
abducit secum ancillas; paucae quae circum illam essent manent
noviciae puellae. continuo haec adornant ut lavet.
adhortor properent. dum adparatur, virgo in conclavi sedet
suspectans tabulam quandam pictam; ibi inerat pictura haec, Iovem
quo pacto Danaae misisse aiunt quondam in gremium imbrem aureum.
egomet quoque id spectare coepi, et quia consimilem luserat 586
iam olim ille ludum, inpendio magis animus gaudebat mihi,
deum sese in hominem convortisse atque in alienas tegulas
venisse clanculum, per inpluvium fucum factum mulieri.
at quem deum! 'qui caeli templa summa sonitu concutit.' 590
ego homuncio hoc non facerem? ego illud vero ita feci, ac lubens.

---

569 fuerat frater A : frater fuerat Σ. | **570** etiam dum A¹, gl. I : etiam nunc Iov. : etiam tum
DPCFE : etiam non tunc G. | **572** cum illo Σ : cum eo A. | illoc DC²FE, Don. : illuc G :
illic PC¹ : **om.** A. | **575** prava ratio Paumier : parva ratio **codd.**, Don. | **581** circum
ADPCF² : circa GE : cum F¹. | **582** haec A¹F²E, Don. : hae Iov., DGPCF¹. (Cf. 89.)

short, I fell in love. As luck would have it, there was a eunuch at
home that my brother had bought for Thais, and he'd still not been   570
taken across to her. There and then our servant Parmeno came up
with a suggestion that I jumped at.

AN. What was that?

CH. Keep quiet, and you'll hear all the sooner. The idea was to change
clothes with him and get myself taken over there instead.

AN. Instead of the eunuch?

CH. Yes.

AN. And what good could you get out of that?

CH. What a stupid question! I could see, hear and be with my heart's
desire, Antipho. That's not a trifling reason is it? Or a bad idea? I   575
was handed over to Thais, and as soon as she'd got me, she happily
took me into her house and gave me the girl to look after.

AN. Who? You?

CH. Yes, me.

AN. Real safe keeping, that!

CH. She gave orders that no man was to go near her, and told me not to
leave her, but to stay in the inner rooms of the house – just me and
her. I nodded my agreement, staring modestly at the floor.   580

AN. You wretch!

CH. She said "I'm off out to supper", and took her maids with her; a few
new ones stayed behind to be with the new arrival. They immediately
got her ready to have a bath, and I encouraged them to hurry up.
While everything was being got ready, the girl sat in her room looking
up at a picture; the painting in it was of how long ago – so they say –
Jupiter sent a shower of golden rain into Danae's lap. I started to   586
look at it too, and because he'd once played a similar game I began to
feel really glad, to think that a god had turned himself into a man and
secretly come down on to another man's roof and down through the
skylight to play a trick on a woman. And what a god! 'He who with   590
his thunder shakes the highest realms of heaven.' Couldn't I – mere
mortal that I was – do that? So that was just what I did do, and gladly.

dum haec mecum reputo, accersitur lavatum interea virgo.
iit, lavit, rediit; deinde eam in lecto illae conlocarunt.
sto exspectans siquid mi imperent. venit una, "heus tu," inquit, "Dore,
cape hoc flabellum, ventulum huic sic facito, dum lavamur; 595
ubi nos laverimus, si voles, lavato." accipio tristis.

AN. tam equidem istuc os tuom inpudens videre nimium vellem,
qui esset status, flabellulum tenere te asinum tantum.

CH. vix elocuta est hoc, foras simul omnes proruont se,
abeunt lavatum, perstrepunt, ita ut fit domini ubi absunt. 600
interea somnus virginem opprimit. ego limis specto
sic per flabellum clanculum; simul alia circumspecto
satine explorata sint. video esse; pessulum ostio obdo.

AN. quid tum?

CH.   quid 'quid tum?', fatue?

AN.   fateor.

CH.   an ego occasionem
mi ostentam, tantam, tam brevem, tam optatam, tam insperatam 605
amitterem? tum pol ego is essem vero qui simulabar.

AN. sane hercle ut dicis. sed interim de symbolis quid actum est?

CH. paratum est.

AN.   frugi es. ubi? domin?

CH.   immo apud libertum Discum.

AN. perlonge est, sed tanto ocius properemus. muta vestem.

CH. ubi mutem? perii, nam domo exsulo nunc. metuo fratrem 610
ne intus sit; porro autem pater ne rure redierit iam.

AN. eamus ad me; ibi proxumum est ubi mutes.

CH.   recte dicis.
eamus, et de istac simul, quo pacto porro possim
potiri, consilium volo capere una tecum.

AN.   fiat.

---

593 lecto DL : lectum GPCFE, Don. : lectulo (**om.** illae) A. | **595** lavamur AD, Don. : lavamus GPCFE. | **598** flabellulum Guyet : flabellum **codd.** (fabellum A[1]). | **605** ostentam Serv. **in** G. 1.248 : ostentatam **codd.** | **606** vero A : vere Σ.

While I was thinking about all this, the girl was summoned to go for the bath. She went off, had it and came back; then the girls laid her on a couch. I stood there waiting to see if they'd got any orders for me. One of them came up and said: "Hey, Dorus, take this fan and 595 fan her like this while we have our baths; once we've had ours, you can have one too if you like." So, grumpily, I took it.

AN. I'd really love to have seen your brazen face, and how you stood there, holding that fan, you great ass!

CH. She'd hardly said that when they all rushed out at once, off for their 600 bath, making a fearful racket, as servants do when their masters are away. Meantime the girl went to sleep. I looked at her surreptitiously out of the corner of my eye through the fan, like this; at the same time I looked around to see if everything was all right. I saw it was, and bolted the door.

AN. What next?

CH. What do you mean 'What next?', you idiot?

AN. Yes, I suppose so.

CH. Was I going to let the opportunity slip when it was given me on a plate 605 – when it was such a splendid one, so short lived, so longed for and so unexpected? Then I really would have been what I was pretending to be!

AN. Absolutely, just as you say. But, meanwhile, what's been done about the dinner-party?

CH. It's all ready.

AN. You're a splendid fellow! Where is it? At your place?

CH. No, at the freedman Discus's.

AN. That's an awful long way. We'll have to get a move on even more. Get changed.

CH. Get changed where? It's a damn nuisance. I've got to keep away 610 from the house at the moment – I'm afraid my brother might be inside, and even that my father might be back from the country by now.

AN. Let's go to my house; it's the nearest place you can change.

CH. Good idea; let's go. On the way I want your advice about how I can have the girl to myself in future.

AN. All right.

(*They go off to the audience's right. After a short pause, Dorias comes on from the same direction, carrying a jewel-box.*)

ACTVS IV

IV i   **DORIAS**

DORI. ita me di ament, quantum ego illum vidi, non nil timeo misera   615
      nequam ille hodie insanus turbam faciat aut vim Thaidi.
      nam postquam iste advenit Chremes adulescens, frater virginis,
      militem rogat ut illum admitti iubeat; ill' continuo irasci
      neque negare audere; Thais porro instare ut hominem invitet.
      id faciebat retinendi illius causa, quia illa quae cupiebat   620
      de sorore eius indicare ad eam rem tempus non erat.
      invitat tristis; mansit. ibi illa cum illo sermonem ilico.
      miles vero sibi putare adductum ante oculos aemulum;
      voluit facere contra huic aegre: "heus," inquit, "puere, Pamphilam
      accerse ut delectet hic nos." illa: "minime gentium!   625
      in convivium illam?" miles tendere; inde ad iurgium.
      interea aurum sibi clam mulier demit, dat mi ut auferam.
      hoc est signi: ubi primum poterit, se illinc subducet, scio.

IV ii   **PHAEDRIA**   **<DORIAS>**

PH. dum rus eo, coepi egomet mecum inter vias,
      ita ut fit ubi quid in animo est molestiae,   630
      aliam rem ex alia cogitare et ea omnia in
      peiorem partem. quid opust verbis? dum haec puto,
      praeterii inprudens villam. longe iam abieram
      quom sensi; redeo rursum, male me vero habens.
      ubi ad ipsum veni devorticulum, constiti;   635
      occepi mecum cogitare: "hem! biduom hic
      manendum est soli sine illa? quid tum postea?
      nil est. quid 'nil'? si non tangendi copia est,
      eho ne videndi quidem erit? si illud non licet,
      saltem hoc licebit. certe extrema linea   640
      amare haud nil est." villam praetereo sciens.
      sed quid hoc quod timida subito egreditur Pythias?

---

615 di ament A[1]G : di bene ament A[2]DPCFE. | **618** illum A : eum Σ. | **622** ilico A :
incipit Σ : occipit(?) Don. | **624** puere **edd. plerique** : puer **codd.**, Don., Eugr. | **625** illa
Guyet, **edd. plerique** : illa exclamat **codd.**, Don. | **626** tendere A[2]Σ : intendere A[1].

ACT FOUR

IV 1

DORI. So help me, from what I've seen of him, I'm terribly afraid the   615
man's mad, and he'll cause a riot today or attack Thais. After that
young gentleman Chremes, the girl's brother, arrived, she asked the
captain to say he should be let in; he immediately flew into a rage but
didn't dare say no, and she kept pressing him to invite him. She was   620
doing this to keep him there, because it wasn't the time to tell him
what she wanted to about his sister. Thraso sulkily asked him in, he
stayed, and Thais started up a conversation with him there and then.
The captain obviously thought a rival had been brought in before his
very eyes, and wanted to hit back where it hurt. He said: "Hey, boy,
fetch Pamphila to entertain us here!" "Not for all the world," said   625
Thais, "Bring her to a dinner-party?" The captain was insistent, and
then a quarrel broke out. While all this was going on, my mistress
took off her jewelry without him noticing, and gave it to me to take
away. That's a sure sign – as soon as she can, she'll get herself away
from there, I know.

(*She turns to go into Thais' house, but before she can do so, Phaedria comes
on from the audience's left.*)

IV 2

PH. While I was on my way to the country, I began – as you do when   630
you've got something troubling your mind – to think of one thing after
another as I walked along, seeing all of them in a bad light. Need I
say more? While my thoughts were taken up like this, I walked right
past our farm without noticing, and I'd gone a long way before I
realized. So I came back again, feeling very cross with myself. When   635
I reached our turning, I stopped and began to think: "What! Must I
stay here all by myself for two days without her? And what will
happen then? Oh, it doesn't matter ... What do I mean, 'Doesn't
matter'? If there's no chance of my touching her, won't there even be
the chance to see her? If I can't do the one, at least I'll be able to do   640
the other. To love from the side lines is certainly better than nothing."
So I went past the farm on purpose. (*Pythias rushes out of Thais'
house.*) But why on earth's Pythias suddenly rushing out in such a
panic?

IV iii   PYTHIAS   DORIAS   PHAEDRIA

PY. ubi ego illum scelerosum misera atque inpium inveniam? aut ubi
                                                  [quaeram?
      hoccin tam audax facinus facere esse ausum!

PH.   perii! hoc quid sit vereor.

PY. quin etiam insuper scelus, postquam ludificatust virginem,   645
      vestem omnem miserae discidit, tum ipsam capillo conscidit.

PH. hem!

PY.   qui nunc si detur mihi,
      ut ego unguibus facile illi in oculos involem venefico!

PH. nescioquid profecto absente nobis turbatum est domi.
      adibo. quid istuc? quid festinas? aut quem quaeris, Pythias?   650

PY. ehem, Phaedria, ego quem quaeram? in' hinc quo dignu's cum donis
                                                 [tuis
      tam lepidis ?

PH.   quid istuc est rei?

PY. rogas me? eunuchum quem dedisti nobis quas turbas dedit!
      virginem quam erae dono dederat miles vitiavit.

PH.   quid ais?

PY. perii!

PH.   temulenta es.

PY.   utinam sic sint qui mihi male volunt!   655

DORI. au obsecro, mea Pythias, quod istuc nam monstrum fuit?

PH. insanis; qui istuc facere eunuchus potuit?

PY.   ego illum nescio
      qui fuerit; hoc quod fecit res ipsa indicat.
      virgo ipsa lacrumat neque, quom rogites, quid sit audet dicere;
      ille autem bonus vir nusquam apparet. etiam hoc misera suspicor,   660
      aliquid domo abeuntem abstulisse.

PH.   ·   nequeo mirari satis
      quo ille abire ignavos possit longius, nisi si domum
      forte ad nos rediit.

---

644 perii **Phaedriae** trib. A : **Pythiae** cont. Σ. | **651** ego A¹ : egon A², Kauer-Lindsay. |
in hinc A¹ : abi hinc A²P : i*hinc C : i hinc G²FE : i nunc G¹ : ii nunc D. | **652** tam lepidis
G¹ : tam laepidis A : tam inlepidis G²PCFE. | **656** quod Iov., P(?) : quid A¹DGC¹FE. |
monstrum Aε¹ : monstri DGPCFE. | **662** possit AC, Don. : posset DGPFE.

IV 3

PY.   Oh, I'm in a terrible state! Where can I find that wicked monster? Where can I look for him? To think that he had the effrontery to do such a shameless thing as this!

PH.   Heavens! What's all this? I'm worried.

PY.   What's more, on top of that, after he'd had his way with the girl, the   645
villain tore the poor thing's clothes and pulled out her hair.

PH.   What!

PY.   If I could get my hands on him now, it would be so easy to scratch the poisonous creature's eyes out!

PH.   There's obviously been some great rumpus in the house while I've been away. I'll go and talk to her. (*He crosses to her.*) What's all   650
this? Why are you in such a rush? Who are you after, Pythias?

PY.   Good lord, Phaedria! Who am I after? You can go to hell, and your lovely presents, too!

PH.   What on earth's the matter?

PY.   Need you ask? The havoc that eunuch you gave us has caused! He's raped the young girl the captain gave my mistress.

PH.   What?

PY.   I'm done for.   655

PH.   You must be drunk.

PY.   How I wish my enemies were in the state that I am!

DORI.   But please, Pythias my dear, what sort of a monstrous thing is that to have happened?

PH.   You're off your head. How could a eunuch do that?

PY.   I don't know who it was that did it, but the facts prove what it was he did. The girl's in tears; when you ask her, she doesn't dare say what's the matter; and that fine fellow of yours is nowhere to be seen.   660
Oh dear, I've got a suspicion, too, that he stole something from the house as he made off.

PH.   I'd be very surprised if that wretched specimen could go anywhere very far, unless he's gone back to our house.

PY.   vise, amabo, num sit.
PH.   iam faxo scies.
DORI. perii, obsecro! tam infandum facinus, mea tu, ne audivi quidem!
PY.   at pol ego amatores audieram mulierum esse eos maxumos,   665
    sed nil potesse; verum miserae non in mentem venerat,
    nam illum aliquo conclusissem neque illi commisissem virginem.

IV iv   PHAEDRIA   DORVS   PYTHIAS   DORIAS

PH. exi foras, sceleste. at etiam restitas,
    fugitive? prodi, male conciliate.
DORVS   obsecro.
PH.   oh,
    illud vide, os ut sibi distorsit carnufex!   670
    quid huc tibi reditio est? quid vestis mutatio?
    quid narras? paullum si cessassem, Pythias,
    domi non offendissem, ita iam adornarat fugam.
PY. haben hominem, amabo?
PH.   quidni habeam?
PY.   factum bene!
DORI. istuc pol vero bene.
PY.   ubi est?
PH.   rogitas? non vides?   675
PY. videam? obsecro, quem?
PH.   hunc scilicet.
PY.   quis hic est homo?
PH. qui ad vos deductus hodie est.
PY.   hunc oculis suis
    nostrarum numquam quisquam vidit, Phaedria.
PH. non vidit?
PY.   an tu hunc credidisti esse, obsecro,
    ad nos deductum?
PH.   namque alium habui neminem.
PY.   au   680

---

663 sit APCF, Don. : siet DGE. | scies AD : scias GPCFE². | **671** quid huc tibi A : quid
huc Σ. | mutatio Σ : mutatio est A. | **673** adornarat PCFE² : adornabat DGp¹ : adornat E¹:
ornarat A, Kauer-Lindsay. | **674** haben **edd. plerique** : habesne **codd.** | factum bene A¹:
o factum bene A²Σ, Kauer-Lindsay. | **680** namque alium A : nam quem alium DGP²C²F²E:
nam qualium C¹.

PY.   Oh, please, go and see if he's there.

PH.   I'll make sure you know this minute. (*He goes into his father's house.*)

DORI. Heavens, I ask you!   My dear, I've never heard of such an unspeakable thing to do.

PY.   Yes, I'd heard those types were really great lovers of women, but that   665
they couldn't manage it. Oh dear, it hadn't even occurred to me, or I'd have locked him up somewhere and never given him the girl to look after.

(*Phaedria comes out of the house again, dragging* **DORUS** *with him.*)

IV 4

PH.   Out of it, you nasty piece of work! Still refusing to budge, you runaway? Come on out – you really were a bad buy.

DORUS Oh, please!

PH.   Look at that! What a face he's pulled, the scoundrel! What do you   670
mean by coming back here? And by changing your clothes? What have you got to say for yourself? If I'd been a bit slower, Pythias, I wouldn't have found him inside – he'd already got himself ready to make a run for it.

PY.   Oh, please, have you got the fellow?

PH.   Of course I have.

PY.   Well done!   675

DORI. Yes, well done indeed!

PY.   Where is he?

PH.   What a silly thing to ask! Can't you see him?

PY.   See him? See *who*, if you please?

PH.   This chap, of course.

PY.   Who on earth's he?

PH.   The fellow who was brought across to you today.

PY.   But no-one in our house has ever set eyes on *him*, Phaedria.

PH.   Never set eyes on him?

PY.   For goodness' sake, did you think this was the man who was brought   680
to us?

PH.   I didn't have anyone else.

ne comparandus hicquidem ad illum est; ille erat
honesta facie et liberali.

PH. visus est
dudum, quia varia veste exornatus fuit.
nunc tibi videtur foedus, quia illam non habet.

PY. tace, obsecro. quasi vero paullum intersiet. 685
ad nos deductus est hodie adulescentulus
quem tu videre vero velles, Phaedria.
hic est vietus vetus veternosus senex
colore mustelino.

PH. hem! quae haec est fabula?
eo rediges me ut quid egerim egomet nesciam? 690
eho tu, emin ego te?

DORVS emisti.

PY. iube mi denuo
respondeat.

PH. roga.

PY. venisti hodie ad nos? negat.
at ille alter venit annos natus sedecim,
quem secum adduxit Parmeno.

PH. agedum hoc mi expedi
primum: istam quam habes unde habes vestem? taces? 695
monstrum hominis, non dicturu's?

DORVS venit Chaerea ...

PH. fraterne?

DORVS ita.

PH. quando?

DORVS hodie.

PH. quam dudum?

DORVS modo.

PH. quicum?

DORVS cum Parmenone.

PH. norasne eum prius?

DORVS non, nec quis esset umquam audieram dicier.

PH. unde igitur fratrem meum esse scibas?

---

681 ne DGPCF, Nonius p. 256M, 496M : nec AE. | **684** tibi videtur A[1], Nonius p. 304M :
eo videtur PC[1], Serv. **in A**. 3.216 : eo tibi videtur DGFE : tibi videtur eo Iov. | **690** rediges
A : redigis DG(?)PCFE. | egerim **codd.** : emerim Don. | **699** nec ... dicier **om.** AP[1]C[1],
secl. edd. nonnulli, necnon Kauer-Lindsay.

PY. But there's no comparison between this one and the other one. The other one had handsome, gentlemanly looks.

PH. He seemed like that then because he was all dressed up in coloured clothes. He looks ugly to you now because he hasn't got them on.

PY. Oh, do be quiet, please! As if there wasn't a world of difference! The 685 young man who was brought to us today was the sort you'd be pleased to see yourself, Phaedria. This one's a wrinkled, ancient, spent old man with the colour of a weasel.

PH. What nonsense is this? Are you trying to get me into a state where I 690 don't even know myself what I've been doing? (*To Dorus.*) Hey, you, did I buy you?

DORUS Yes.

PY. Tell him to answer me a question now.

PH. Ask away.

PY. Did you come to our house today? (*Dorus shakes his head.*) He says he didn't. But that other one did, a sixteen-year-old, who Parmeno brought with him.

PH. (*To Dorus*) Now explain this to me first: where did you get those 695 clothes you're wearing? Won't you answer? You horror, aren't you going to say?

DORUS Chaerea arrived ...

PH. My brother?

DORUS Yes.

PH. When?

DORUS Today.

PH. How long ago?

DORUS Just now.

PH. Who with?

DORUS Parmeno.

PH. Did you know him before?

DORUS No, and I'd never heard anyone say who he was.

PH. So how did you know he was my brother? 700

DORVS   Parmeno   700
dicebat eum esse. is dedit mi hanc.

PH.   occidi!

DORVS meam ipse induit; post una ambo abierunt foras.

PY. iam satis credis sobriam esse me et nil mentitam tibi?
iam satis certum est virginem vitiatam esse?

PH.   age nunc, belua,
credis huic quod dicat?

PY.   quid isti credam? res ipsa indicat.   705

PH. concede istuc paullulum ... audin? etiam paullulum ... sat est.
dic dum hoc rursum: Chaerea tuam vestem detraxit tibi?

DORVS factum.

PH.   et eam est indutus?

DORVS   factum.

PH.   et pro te huc deductust?

DORVS   ita.

PH. Iuppiter magne, o scelestum atque audacem hominem!

PY.   vae mihi!
etiam nunc non credis indignis nos inrisas modis?   710

PH. mirum ni tu credas quod iste dicat. quid agam nescio.
heus, negato rursum. possumne ego hodie ex te exsculpere
verum? vidistine fratrem Chaeream?

DORVS   non.

PH.   non potest
sine malo fateri, video; sequere hac. modo ait, modo negat.
ora me.

DORVS   obsecro te vero, Phaedria.

PH.   i intro nunciam.   715

DORVS oiei!

PH.   alio pacto honeste quomodo hinc abeam nescio.
actum est, si quidem tu me hic etiam, nebulo, ludificabere.

---

703 sobriam esse me Σ : me sobriam esse A : sobriam me Don. | **705** quod A²Σ : quid A¹.
| dicat **codd.** : dicit Don. | **706** etiam Muret : etiam nunc **codd.** | **708** et eam est
DGPCFE (cf. 1015-16) : et ea est A²p¹, Prisc. in **G. L.** 3.318, Kauer-Lindsay : etast A¹. |
deductust Σ : deductus A. | **710** etiam nunc **codd.**, Don. ad 709 : etiam **edd. plerique**,
necnon Kauer-Lindsay. | credis **codd.**, Don. ad 709 : credes **edd. plerique**, **necnon** Kauer-
Lindsay. | nos inrisas Marouzeau : nos esse inrisas **codd.**, **edd. plerique**, **necnon** Kauer-
Lindsay. | **715** i intro D²CFE : intro D¹GP : in intro A.

DORUS Parmeno said he was. He was the man who gave me these clothes.

PH. This is the end!

DORUS Your brother put mine on, and then they both went off together.

PY. Now do you believe that I'm quite sober and haven't been telling you lies? Isn't it quite clear now that the girl's been raped?

PH. Come on now, you silly donkey, do you believe what he tells you?   705

PY. Why should I believe *him*? It's the facts that prove it.

PH. (*to Dorus*) Come over here a bit, do you hear? A bit more – that's enough. Now tell me this again – Chaerea took your clothes?

DORUS Yes.

PH. And put them on?

DORUS Yes.

PH. And was brought over here instead of you?

DORUS Right.

PH. (*aside*) Good god, the bare-faced scoundrel!

PY. Oh, dear! Do you still refuse to believe the scandalous way we've   710
been made fools of even now?

PH. (*sarcastically*) It would be surprising if you didn't believe what this creature says! (*Aside.*) I don't know what to do. (*To Dorus.*) Listen, say no this time. (*Aloud.*) Can't I worm the truth out of you today? Did you see my brother Chaerea?

DORUS No.

PH. I can see he's incapable of telling the truth without a flogging. Come with me. One minute he says yes, the next minute no. (*Aside, to Dorus.*) Beg for mercy.   715

DORUS Phaedria, I beg of you ...

PH. Get inside at once! (*He pushes him roughly into his father's house.*)

DORUS (*as he disappears*) Ow!

PH. (*aside*) I don't know how else I can get out of this honourably. (*Aloud, shouting into the house after Dorus.*) If you go on making a fool of me here, you worthless idiot, you've had it. (*He follows Dorus inside.*)

PY. Parmenonis tam scio esse hanc techinam quam me vivere.

DORI. sic est.

PY. inveniam pol hodie parem ubi referam gratiam.
sed quid nunc faciundum censes, Dorias?

DORI. de istac rogas   720
virgine?

PY. ita; utrum taceamne an praedicam?

DORI. tu pol, si sapis,
quod scis nescis, neque de eunucho neque de vitio virginis.
hac re et te omni turba evolves et illi gratum feceris.
id modo dic, abisse Dorum.

PY. ita faciam.

DORI. sed videon Chremem?
Thais iam aderit.

PY. quid ita?

DORI. quia, quom inde abeo, iam tum inceperat   725
turba inter eos.

PY. aufer aurum hoc. ego scibo ex hoc quid siet.

IV v   CHREMES PYTHIAS

CHR. attat data hercle verba mihi sunt; vicit vinum quod bibi.
at dum accubabam, quam videbar mi esse pulchre sobrius!
postquam surrexi, neque pes neque mens satis suom officium facit.

PY. Chreme!

CHR. quis est? ehem Pythias! vah, quanto nunc formonsior   730
videre mihi quam dudum.

PY. certe tu quidem pol multo hilarior.

CHR. verbum hercle hoc verum erit: 'sine Cerere et Libero friget Venus'.
sed Thais multo ante venit?

PY. anne abiit iam a milite?

CHR. iamdudum; aetatem. lites factae sunt inter eos maxumae.

---

718 techinam **edd. plerique** : technam **codd.** (Cf. **Hau.** 471.) | 721 utrum taceamne an praedicam C : utrum taceamne an praedicem APFE : utrumne taceam an praedicam G : utrumne taceam an praedicemne Kauer-Lindsay. | 722 scis ADG[1] : scias D[2]PCFEp[2]. | 724 Chremem DG : Chremen APCFE, Kauer-Lindsay. (Cf. 909.) | 725 inceperat ADGPCFE : occeperat p[1], Kauer-Lindsay. | 726 aufer Av ; tu aufer **cett. codd.**, Kauer-Lindsay. | 728 esse pulchre Σ : pulchre esse A. | 731 certe Iov., Σ, Don. : certo A[1].

PY. As sure as I'm alive, I know this is a trick of Parmeno's.

DORI. I'm sure it is.

PY. I swear I'll find a way to pay him back fair and square today. But 720 what do you think we should do now, Dorias?

DORI. About the girl, you mean?

PY. Yes. Should I keep quiet or tell the mistress first?

DORI. Gracious, if you've got any sense you'll know nothing of what you know, either about the eunuch or about the girl being raped. That way you'll get yourself out of all the trouble and you'll be doing her a favour. Just say Dorus has disappeared.

PY. Yes, I'll do that.

DORI. (*looking off to the audience's right*) But is that Chremes I can see? That means Thais will be here shortly. 725

PY. How so?

DORI. Because when I left the captain's, a row had already blown up between the two of them.

PY. You take these jewels indoors. I'll find out from Chremes what's going on.

(*Dorias goes into Thais' house, just as Chremes comes on from the audience's right, obviously rather drunk.*)

IV 5

CHR. Goodness, I've really been made a fool of – that wine I drank's finished me. How wonderfully sober I seemed to be while I was still at the table! But since I've got up, my feet and my brain aren't doing what they should do at all.

PY. Chremes! 730

CHR. Who's that? Oh, Pythias! My, my! How much prettier you look than you did a little while ago.

PY. And you definitely seem a lot merrier.

CHR. Well, it really is a true saying: 'No food and drink, and love's out in the cold.' Thais came back some time ago, I s'pose?

PY. Has she left the captain's already?

CHR. Oh, long ago – ages. There was a fearful row between them.

PY. nil dixit tu ut sequerere sese?

CHR.   nil, nisi abiens mi innuit.   735

PY. eho nonne id sat erat?

CHR.   at nescibam id dicere illam, nisi quia

correxit miles, quod intellexi minus. nam me extrusit foras.

sed eccam ipsam; miror ubi ego huic antevorterim.

IV vi   **THAIS   CHREMES   PYTHIAS**

TH. credo equidem illum iam adfuturum esse, ut illam a me eripiat.

[sine veniat!

atqui, si illam digito attigerit uno, oculi ilico effodientur.   740

usque adeo ego illius ferre possum ineptiam et magnifica verba,

verba dum sint; verum enim, si ad rem conferentur, vapulabit.

CHR. Thais, ego iamdudum hic adsum.

TH.   o mi Chreme, te ipsum exspectabam.

scin tu turbam hanc propter te esse factam, et adeo ad te attinere hanc

omnem rem?

CHR.   ad me? qui? quasi istuc ...

TH.   quia, dum tibi sororem studeo

reddere ac restituere, haec atque huiusmodi sum multa passa.   746

CHR. ubi ea est?

TH.   domi apud me.

CHR.   hem!

TH.   quid est?

educta ita uti teque illaque dignum est.

CHR.   quid ais?

TH.   id quod res est.

hanc tibi dono do neque repeto pro illa quicquam abs te preti.

CHR. et habetur et referetur, Thais, ita uti merita es, gratia.   750

TH. at enim cave ne, priusquam hanc a me accipias, amittas, Chreme;

nam haec ea est quam miles a me vi nunc ereptum venit.

abi tu, cistellam, Pythias, domo ecfer cum monumentis.

CHR. viden tu illum, Thais ...

PY.   ubi sita est?

---

735 tu Ap² : tum DGPCFE. | 737 quod A²Σ : quo A¹. | 739 a me Σ : **om.** A, Kauer-Lindsay. | 749 tibi dono do A²PCFEp : tibi do dono A¹ : dono tibi D¹G¹ : dono tibi do D²G². | 750 Thais ita DG¹ : Thais tibi ita A : tibi Thais ita G² : Thais a me ita PCFE.

PY. Didn't she tell you to follow her?   735

CHR. She didn't say anything; she just gave me a nod as she left.

PY. And wasn't that enough for you?

CHR. I didn't know she meant that – except the captain put me right on what I didn't understand – and threw me out! But here she comes ... I wonder where I overtook her.

(*Thais comes on from the audience's right, accompanied by her maids. The maids go into Thais' house, while Thais herself remains on stage.*)

IV 6

TH. I expect he'll be here very soon to take the girl away from me. Well, let him come! But if he so much as lays a finger on her, I'll gouge his   740 eyes out on the spot. I can put up with his stupidity and his pompous talk just as long as it *is* just talk; but if his talk turns to action, he'll get a good hiding.

CHR. Thais, I've been here for ages.

TH. Chremes my dear, the very person I've been expecting. You realize it's because of you this rumpus has broken out, and that this whole business has to do with you?

CHR. With me? How? Do you mean ... ?

TH. Because while I've been trying to give you back your sister and   746 restore her to you, I've been putting up with all this, and with a lot more of the same sort of thing besides.

CHR. Where is she?

TH. At home with me.

CHR. What!

TH. What's the matter? She's been brought up to be a credit to you and to her.

CHR. Really?

TH. Yes, that's the truth. And I'm giving her to you as a free gift, and not asking for any payment from you in return.

CHR. I'm grateful to you, Thais, and shall pay you back – as you've   750 deserved.

TH. But be careful you don't lose her before you get her back from me, Chremes – she's the one the captain's coming to take away from me by force. Pythias, go and bring out the little box with her keepsakes.

CHR. (*looking anxiously off to the audience's right*) Thais, do you see ...

PY. Where's it kept?

TH. in risco. odiosa cessas.

CHR. ... militem secum ad te quantas copias adducere? 755

attat.

TH. num formidulosus, obsecro, es, mi homo?

CHR. apage, sis!

egon formidulosus? nemo est hominum qui vivat minus.

TH. atqui ita opust.

CHR. ah, metuo qualem tu me esse hominem existumes.

TH. immo hoc cogitato: quicum res tibi est peregrinus est,

minus potens quam tu, minus notus, minus amicorum hic habens. 760

CHR. scio istuc. sed tu quod cavere possis stultum admittere est.

malo ego nos prospicere quam hunc ulcisci accepta iniuria.

tu abi, atque obsera ostium intus, dum ego hinc transcurro ad forum.

volo ego adesse hic advocatos nobis in turba hac.

TH. mane.

CHR. meliust.

TH. mane.

CHR. omitte; iam adero.

TH. nil opus est istis, Chreme. 765

hoc modo dic, sororem esse illam tuam et te parvam virginem

amisisse, nunc cognosse. signa ostende.

PY. adsunt.

TH. cape.

si vim faciat, in ius ducito hominem; intellextin?

CHR. probe.

TH. fac animo haec praesenti dicas.

CHR. faciam.

TH. attolle pallium.

perii! huic ipsi est opus patrono, quem defensorem paro. 770

---

758 atqui A, Prisc. in **G. L.** 3.101 : atque Σ. | **765** CHR. meliust. TH. mane. CHR. omitte; iam adero. Σ (mane mane G), Don. : CHR. meliust. TH. omitte. CHR. iam adero. A. | **766** esse illam tuam Σ, Don. : illam tuam esse A, Kauer-Lindsay. | **770** est opus patrono A : opus est patrono DG : opus patrono est PCFE.

TH. In the chest. You're so annoyingly slow. (*Pythias goes into Thais'
house.*)

CHR. ... what a huge army the captain's bringing with him against you? Oh,   755
Lord!

TH. Goodness, you're not frightened are you, my dear man?

CHR. Get away with you! Me, frightened? There's no man alive who's less
frightened than me.

TH. That's the way.

CHR. Oh dear, I'm afraid you don't think I'm much of a man.

TH. No, no; but just think of it this way – this fellow you're dealing with
is a foreigner, with less influence than you; he's less well known and   760
has fewer friends here than you have.

CHR. I know that, but it's stupid to let something happen when you can
guard against it. I'd rather us take measures first than get our own
back on him after we've been hurt. You go inside and bolt the door
while I run across to the market-place. I want us to have supporters
with us in this dust-up.

TH. Stay here.

CHR. No, my way's better.   765

TH. (*holding him back*) Do stay!

CHR. Let go of me; I'll be back straight away.

TH. But there's no need of any friends, Chremes. Just tell him that she's
your sister, that you lost her when she was a little girl, and that you've
now recognized her. (*To Pythias, as she brings the box out of the
house.*) Show him the tokens.

PY. Here they are.

TH. Take them. (*Pythias hands Chremes the box and returns into Thais'
house.*) If he tries force, drag the fellow off to court. Do you
understand?

CHR. Perfectly.

TH. Make sure you say all this with a firm resolve.

CHR. I shall.

TH. Get ready for action. (*Aside.*) Good Lord! The man I'm planning to   770
be my defender needs a protector himself.

(*They move back towards the door of Thais' house as Thraso marches on
from the audience's right, accompanied by Gnatho and a disreputable-
looking group of servants.*)

IV vii THRASO GNATHO SANGA CHREMES THAIS

THR. hancin ego ut contumeliam tam insignem in me accipiam, Gnatho?
mori me satiust. Simalio, Donax, Syrisce, sequimini.
primum aedis expugnabo.

GN. recte.

THR. virginem eripiam.

GN. probe.

THR. male mulcabo ipsam.

GN. pulchre.

THR. in medium huc agmen cum vecti, Donax;
tu, Simalio, in sinistrum cornum; tu, Syrisce, in dexterum.   775
cedo alios! ubi centurio est Sanga et manipulus furum?

SA. eccum adest.

THR. quid, ignave? peniculon pugnare, qui istum huc portes, cogitas?

SA. egon? imperatoris virtutem noveram et vim militum;
sine sanguine hoc non posse fieri; qui abstergerem volnera?

THR. ubi alii?

GN. qui, malum, 'alii'? solus Sannio servat domi.   780

THR. tu hosce instrue hic. ero post principia; inde omnibus signum dabo.

GN. illuc est sapere; ut hosce instruxit, ipsus sibi cavit loco.

THR. idem hoc iam Pyrrhus factitavit.

CHR. viden tu, Thais, quam hic rem agit?
nimirum consilium illud rectum est de occludendis aedibus.

TH. sane quod tibi nunc vir videatur esse hic, nebulo magnus est.   785
ne metuas.

THR. quid videtur?

GN. fundam tibi nunc nimis vellem dari,
ut tu illos procul hinc ex occulto caederes; facerent fugam.

THR. sed eccam Thaidem ipsam video.

GN. quam mox inruimus?

THR. mane;

---

775 cornum AG^{1}P^{1}C^1 : cornu DG^{2}P^{2}C^{2}F^{2}E. | dexterum A : dextrum Σ. (Cf. 835.) | **776** eccum adest **Sangae trib.** AC^{2}F^2 : **Gnathoni** GP^{1}C^{1}E (GN. Sanga eccum adest E) : **Simalioni** D. | **777** portes APCF : portas DGE. | **779** non posse fieri Σ, Prisc. in **G. L.** 2.486 : fieri non posse A, Don. | **780** domi A^{1}D^1, Don. **in comm.**, Nonius p. 61M : domum Iov., GPCFE, Don. **in lemm.** | **781** hic Grant : hic ego APCFE : ego hic DG, Kauer-Lindsay. | **782** illuc DG^{1}PCFE : illud AG^2. | ipsus G : ipse ADPCFE, Don. | **783** idem ... factitavit **Thrasoni trib.** A : **Gnathoni cont.** Σ.

IV 7

THR. Am I to put up with such a glaring insult as this, Gnatho? I'd rather die! Simalio, Donax, Syriscus, follow me. First I'll take the house by storm.

GN. Good.

THR. Then carry off the girl.

GN. Excellent!

THR. And make mincemeat of the woman.

GN. Splendid!

THR. Over here to the centre of the line with your crowbar, Donax; Simalio, you on the left wing; Syriscus, you on the right. Bring on the rest. Where's centurion Sanga and his band of thieves?   775

SA. Here!

THR. What's this, you coward? You've brought a sponge with you! Are you planning to go into battle with that?

SA. Me? I know the general's courage and his army's might. And I know this business can't be managed without shedding blood; so what would I clean up the wounds with?

THR. Where are the others?   780

SA. What the hell do you mean, 'others'? There's only Sannio keeping guard at home.

THR. You draw the men up here. I'll be behind the front rank; I'll give the signal to all of them from there.

GN. That's a wise move. (*Aside.*) Now he's drawn them up, he's stationed himself so he's looking after his own skin!

THR. It's the same thing Pyrrhus used to do.

CHR. Thais, can you see what he's up to? It's obviously the right plan, that one about barricading the house.

TH. He may seem a man of mettle to you now, but he's really a great big windbag. Don't be afraid of him.   785

THR. (*to Gnatho*) What do you think?

GN. I really wish you'd got some slingshot now, so you could hit them at long range from your concealed position here – they'd soon run for it.

THR. But look, I can see Thais herself.

GN. How soon do we make the assault?

THR. Wait a minute. It's right for the wise man to try every move before he

omnia prius experiri quam armis sapientem decet.
qui scis an quae iubeam sine vi faciat?

GN.   di vostram fidem,   790
quanti est sapere! numquam accedo quin abs te abeam doctior.

THR. Thais, primum hoc mihi responde: cum tibi do istam virginem,
dixtin hos dies mihi soli dare te?

TH.   quid tum postea?

THR. rogitas? quae mi ante oculos coram amatorem adduxti tuom ...

TH. quid cum illoc agas?

THR.   ... et cum eo te clam subduxti mihi?   795

TH. lubuit.

THR.   Pamphilam ergo huc redde, nisi vi mavis eripi.

CHR. tibi illam reddat aut tu eam tangas, omnium ...?

GN.   ah, quid agis? tace.

THR. quid tu tibi vis? egon non tangam meam?

CHR.   tuam autem, furcifer?

GN. cave sis! nescis cui maledicas nunc viro.

CHR.   non tu hinc abis?
scin tu ut tibi res se habeat? si quicquam hodie hic turbae coeperis, 800
faciam ut huius loci dieique meique semper memineris.

GN. miseret tui me, qui hunc tantum hominem facias inimicum tibi.

CHR. diminuam ego caput tuum hodie, nisi abis.

GN.   ain vero, canis?
sicin agis?

THR.   quis tu homo es? quid tibi vis? quid cum illa rei tibi est?

CHR. scibis. principio eam esse dico liberam ...

THR.   hem!

CHR.   ... civem Atticam ...

THR.   [hui!

CHR. ... meam sororem.

THR.   os durum!

CHR.   miles, nunc adeo edico tibi   806
ne vim facias ullam in illam. Thais, ego eo ad Sophronam
nutricem, ut eam adducam et signa ostendam haec.

THR.   tun me prohibeas

---

793 hos dies mihi Σ : hos mihi dies A. ǀ **795** te clam A ; clam te Σ, Kauer-Lindsay. ǀ **798** quid ... vis? **Thrasoni trib.** G¹v : **Chremeti trib.** DG²PCFE : **Gnathoni cont.** A. ǀ **800** coeperis APC : feceris G²FE : feris G¹ : comperis D. ǀ **803** ego caput tuum GPCFE², Don. : ego caput tibi D : ego tibi caput A : tibi ego caput tuum E¹ : ego caput p. ǀ **804** sicine A¹ : sic A²Σ.

resorts to arms. How do you know she won't do what I tell her   790
without my using force?

GN. Good heavens, what a great thing it is be have wisdom! I never come
near you without going away the wiser for it!

THR. Thais, first of all, answer me this: when I gave you that girl, did you
say you'd keep yourself for me alone for these next few days?

TH. What of it?

THR. You dare ask that when you brought your lover in before my very eyes
...

TH. (*to Chremes*) What would you do with a creature like him?   795

THR. ... and slipped away with him before I could notice?

TH. I wanted to.

THR. So give me back Pamphila, unless you'd rather her be taken away
from you by force.

CHR. Thais give you her back? Or you lay a finger on her, you ...

GN. What are you doing? Shut up!

THR. What do you mean? Can't I get my hands on my own property?

CHR. Your own property, you jailbird?

GN. Do watch out! You don't know what sort of a man you're swearing
at.

CHR. (*to Gnatho*) Get lost, you! (*To Thraso.*) Do you know what position   800
you're in? If you start any trouble here today, I'll make sure you
remember this place, this time and me for the rest of your life.

GN. I feel sorry for you, making an enemy of such a mighty man as this.

CHR. (*to Gnatho*) I'll smash your head in if you don't clear off!

GN. Really, you miserable hound? Is this the way to carry on?

THR. Who the hell are you? What do you want? What have you got to do
with the girl?

CHR. You'll soon know. To start with, I tell you she's free-born ...

THR. What!

CHR. ... of Attic citizen stock ...

THR. Phew!

CHR. ... and my sister.   806

THR. You bare-faced liar!

CHR. Captain, I give you notice right now not to try any force against her.
Thais, I'm going to find the nurse Sophrona, to bring her here and
show her these tokens.

THR. Would you stop me touching what's mine?

       meam ne tangam?

CHR.   prohibebo, inquam.

GN.   audin tu? hic furti se adligat.

       sat hoc tibi est?

THR.   idem hoc tu, Thais?

TH.   quaere qui respondeat.   810

THR. quid nunc agimus?

GN.   quin redeamus; haec tibi iam aderit supplicans

       ultro.

THR.   credin?

GN.   immo certe; novi ingenium mulierum.

       nolunt ubi velis, ubi nolis cupiunt ultro.

THR.   bene putas.

GN. iam dimitto exercitum?

THR.   ubi vis.

GN.   Sanga, ita ut fortis decet

       milites, domi focique fac vicissim ut memineris.   815

SA.   iamdudum animus est in patinis.

GN.   frugi es.

THR.   vos me hac sequimini.

ACTVS V

V i   **THAIS   PYTHIAS**

TH. pergin, scelesta, mecum perplexe loqui?

       "scio; nescio; abiit; audivi; ego non adfui."

       non tu istuc mihi dictura aperte es quidquid est?

       virgo conscissa veste lacrumans opticet;   820

       eunuchus abiit. quam ob rem? quid factum est? taces?

PY. quid tibi ego dicam misera? illum eunuchum negant

       fuisse.

TH.   quis fuit igitur?

---

810 sat edd. plerique : satis **codd.**, Don. ǀ idem hoc tu A^2p, Don. : idem tu hoc DGPCFE : quid nunc tu A^1. ǀ **ais ante** Thais **codd.** (agis P), Don. : **om.** Dziatzko, **edd. plerique.** ǀ **811 totum versum Gnathoni trib.** DGF^lE. ǀ haec tibi iam AL : iam haec tibi PCFEp, Don. **ad** 1025, Kauer-Lindsay : haec iam tibi D : haec tibi G. ǀ **816** iamdudum animus est Σ : iamdudumst animus A. ǀ vos ... sequimini **Thrasoni trib.** A : **Sangae** Σ. ǀ **821** quid Iov., Σ, Don. : aut quid A. ǀ **822** dicam misera APCF : misera dicam DGE.

CHR. Yes, I tell you; I will. (*He strides purposefully off to the audience's right.*)

GN. Do you hear that? He's implicating himself in the theft. Isn't that enough for you? 810

THR. Is that your view too, Thais?

TH. Find someone else to give you an answer! (*She goes inside and slams the door.*)

THR. What do we do now?

GN. Why don't we go home? She'll soon be back of her own accord, begging your forgiveness.

THR. You really think so?

GN. I'm sure of it. I know the way women's minds work; when you want something, they don't, and when you don't, they do, just to be perverse.

THR. Good thinking.

GN. Do I dismiss the troops now?

THR. Whenever you like.

GN. Sanga, like all brave soldiers should, make sure you turn your thoughts to hearth and home. 815

SA. My mind's been on my cooking-pots for ages now.

GN. Splendid fellow!

THR. Follow me this way.

(*They march off to the audience's right. When they have gone, Thais and Pythias come out of the house.*)

ACT FIVE

V 1

TH. You worthless creature, are you going to go on talking to me in riddles? "I know; I don't know; he went off; so I've heard; I wasn't there." Won't you tell it to me straight, whatever it is? The girl's in 820 tears, her clothes are all torn, she won't open her mouth – and the eunuch's disappeared. Why? What's happened? Have you nothing to say?

PY. Oh dear, what can I tell you? They say he wasn't a eunuch.

TH. So who was he?

PY.   iste Chaerea.

TH. qui Chaerea?

PY.   iste ephebus frater Phaedriae.

TH. quid ais, venefica?

PY.   atqui certe comperi.   825

TH. quid is, obsecro, ad nos? quam ob rem adductust?

PY.   nescio,

 nisi amasse credo Pamphilam.

TH.   hem! misera, occidi,

 infelix, siquidem tu istaec vera praedicas.

 num id lacrumat virgo?

PY.   id opinor.

TH.   quid ais, sacrilega?

 istucine interminata sum hinc abiens tibi?   830

PY. quid facerem? ita ut tu iusti, soli credita est.

TH. scelesta, ovem lupo commisisti. dispudet

 sic mihi data esse verba. quid illuc hominis est?

PY. era mea, tace, tace, obsecro; salvae sumus.

 habemus hominem ipsum.

TH.   ubi is est?

PY.   em ad sinisteram.   835

 viden?

TH.   video.

PY.   conprendi iube, quantum potest.

TH. quid illo faciemus, stulta?

PY.   quid facias, rogas?

 vide, amabo, si non, quom aspicias, os inpudens

 videtur! non est? tum quae eius confidentia est!

V ii   CHAEREA THAIS PYTHIAS

CH. apud Antiphonem uterque, mater et pater,   840

 quasi dedita opera domi erant, ut nullo modo

 intro ire possem quin viderent me. interim

 dum ante ostium sto, notus mihi quidam obviam

---

831 tu iusti A¹ε, Don. : tu iussisti A²DGE : iussisti PCF. | **833** illuc D¹P¹C, Don. : illud G¹: illut A : illic D²G²P²FE. | **835** sinisteram **edd.** : sinistram **codd.** (Cf. 775.) | **837** illo APC¹E, Prisc. in **G. L.** 3.189 : illi DGC²F.

PY.   That Chaerea.

TH.   What Chaerea?

PY.   That young brother of Phaedria's.

TH.   What's that, you poisonous gossip?   825

PY.   But I've found out for certain.

TH.   What's he got to do with us, for goodness' sake? Why was he brought
here ?

PY.   I don't know, except I suppose he'd fallen in love with Pamphila.

TH.   What? What dreadful bad luck for me! I'm sunk if what you say is
true. Is that what the girl's crying about?   830

PY.   I suppose so.

TH.   What? You wicked creature! Isn't that just what I threatened you
about when I went out?

PY.   What was I to do? I put her in his care – and his alone – just as you
ordered.

TH.   You useless thing, you put a lamb in the care of a wolf! I'm utterly
ashamed of having a trick played on me like this. What kind of a man
is that?

PY.   (*looking off to the audience's left*) Quiet, madam, quiet, please.
We're saved. We've got the fellow.   835

TH.   Where is he?

PY.   Look, over there to the left; can you see him?

TH.   Yes, I can.

PY.   Have him arrested, quick as you can.

TH.   What will we do with him then, you stupid woman?

PY.   What will you do with him? What a thing to ask! Just see if he
doesn't seem an impudent rascal when you get a good look at him.
Isn't he? And how cock-sure he is!

(*Chaerea comes on from the audience's right, still dressed as the eunuch.*)

V 2

CH.   Antipho's mother and father were both at home, as if on purpose, so   840
there was no way I could go in without them seeing me. Then while I
was standing in front of their door, an acquaintance of mine came

venit. ubi vidi, ego me in pedes quantum queo
in angiportum quoddam desertum, inde item   845
in aliud, inde in aliud; ita miserrimus
fui fugitando, nequis me cognosceret.
sed estne haec Thais quam video? ipsa est. haereo
quid faciam. quid mea autem? quid faciet mihi?

TH. adeamus. bone vir Dore, salve. dic mihi,   850
  aufugistin?

CH.   era, factum.

TH.   satine id tibi placet?

CH. non.

TH.   credin tu impune habiturum?

CH.   unam hanc noxiam
  amitte; si aliam admisero umquam, occidito.

TH. num meam saevitiam veritus es?

CH.   non.

TH.   quid igitur?

CH. hanc metui ne me criminaretur tibi.   855

TH. quid feceras?

CH.   paullum quidem.

PY.   eho, 'paullum', inpudens?
  an 'paullum' hoc esse tibi videtur, virginem
  vitiare civem?

CH.   conservam esse credidi.

PY. 'conservam'? vix me contineo quin involem in
  capillum, monstrum. etiam ultro derisum advenit.   860

TH. abin hinc, insana?

PY.   quid ita vero? debeam,
  credo, isti quicquam furcifero, si id fecerim,
  praesertim quom se servom fateatur tuom.

TH. missa haec faciamus. non te dignum, Chaerea,
  fecisti; nam si ego digna hac contumelia   865
  sum maxume, at tu indignus qui faceres tamen.
  neque edepol quid nunc consili capiam scio
  de virgine istac; ita conturbasti mihi

---

844 ego me G^1(?), **edd.** : egomet **cett. codd.** | **849** mea ADP^{2}C^{2}FE : me P^{1}C^{1}p^1. | **859-60** involem in | capillum AP : involem | in capillum **cett. codd.** | **860** advenit A^{2}DPCF : venit A^{1}E. | **861** abin AP : abi* CF : abi DE. | **862** fecerim A^{2}Σ : fecero A^1. | **864** haec APCF : istaec DE.

towards me. As soon as I set eyes on him, I took to my heels as fast as I could down an empty alley, from that one into another one, and then   845 into another. As I ran, I was in such a state in case anybody recognized me. (*Catching sight of the others.*) But is that Thais I can see? It is! I'm stuck over what to do. But what does it matter anyway? What can she do to me?

TH. Let's go up to him. Good day, Dorus, my fine fellow . Tell me, did   850 you run away?

CH. Yes, madam, I did.

TH. And are you pleased with what you did?

CH. No.

TH. Do you think you'll get away with it?

CH. Forgive this one offence; if I ever commit another, you can do away with me.

TH. You weren't afraid I'd be harsh, then?

CH. No.

TH. So what were you afraid of?

CH. (*pointing at Pythias*) Of her – afraid she might make accusations   855 about me to you.

TH. What had you done?

CH. Something small.

PY. What! 'Small', you shameless idiot! Does it seem 'small' to you to rape a free-born girl?

CH. I thought she was another slave, like me.

PY. 'Another slave like me'? I can hardly stop myself from tearing your hair out, you monster. (*To Thais.*) He's actually come back to make   860 fun of us into the bargain!

TH. (*to Pythias*) You go back indoors – you're over-excited.

PY. Why should I do that? I'd have to pay damages to this gallows-bird, I suppose, if I did attack him, especially since he's pretending to be your slave!

TH. Let's stop this. (*After a pause.*) Chaerea, what you did was unworthy   865 of you. Even if I fully deserve such insulting treatment, it's still unbecoming of you to have acted like this. The fact is, I don't know what advice I can take about this girl now. You've turned all my

rationes omnes, ut eam non possim suis,
ita ut aequom fuerat atque ut studui, tradere, 870
ut solidum parerem hoc mi beneficium, Chaerea.

CH. at nunc dehinc spero aeternam inter nos gratiam
fore, Thais. saepe ex huiusmodi re quapiam et
malo principio magna familiaritas
conflata est. quid si hoc quispiam voluit deus? 875

TH. equidem pol in eam partem accipioque et volo.

CH. immo ita quaeso. unum hoc scito, contumeliae
non me fecisse causa, sed amoris.

TH. scio,
et pol propterea magis nunc ignosco tibi.
non adeo inhumano ingenio sum, Chaerea, 880
neque ita inperita ut quid amor valeat nesciam.

CH. te quoque iam, Thais, ita me di bene ament, amo.

PY. tum pol tibi ab istoc, era, cavendum intellego.

CH. non ausim.

PY. nil tibi quicquam credo.

TH. desinas.

CH. nunc ego te in hac re mi oro ut adiutrix sies; 885
ego me tuae commendo et committo fidei;
te mihi patronam capio. Thais, te obsecro;
emoriar si non hanc uxorem duxero.

TH. tamen si pater ...?

CH. quid? ah, volet, certo scio,
civis modo haec sit.

TH. paullulum opperirier 890
si vis, iam frater ipse hic aderit virginis;
nutricem accersitum iit quae illam aluit parvolam.
in cognoscendo tute ipse aderis, Chaerea.

CH. ego vero maneo.

TH. vin interea, dum venit,
domi opperiamur potius quam hic ante ostium? 895

---

873 quapiam et AD¹PC¹F¹ : quapiam ex D² : quapiam et ex C²F²E. | **878** non me APCF : me non DE, Kauer-Lindsay. | **883** istoc era PCFE : isto Chaerea D¹, Arusian. in **G. L. 7.** 488 : isto era AD², Don. | **884** desinas **Thaidi trib.** PCFE : **Pythiadi cont.** AD. | **886** fidei **codd.** : fide Kauer-Lindsay. (Cf. 898.) | **889** quid ah AC²F²E : quid hic D : quid P¹F¹ : ah quid P²C¹ : ha quid Don. | **894** dum venit A¹PCF : dum is venit Iov., DE.

plans so upside down that I can't hand her back to her family, as was   870
right, and as I was keen to do in order to produce some lasting benefit
to myself that way.

CH. My hope is that there'll be a permanent friendship between us from
now on, Thais. Often, as a result of something like this, and after a
bad start, really close ties are formed. Suppose some god or other   875
wanted this to happen?

TH. Yes ... I accept it in that spirit, and I want that too.

CH. Yes, please do. And be sure of one thing – I didn't do it to insult you,
but because I love the girl.

TH. I know, and that's why I'm more inclined to forgive you. My
character's not that inhuman, Chaerea, and I'm not so lacking in   880
experience that I don't know the power of love.

CH. Heaven knows, Thais, I love you too.

PY. Then, my goodness, I think you'd better beware of him, madam.

CH. I wouldn't dare.

PY. I don't trust you with anything.

TH. Oh, do stop!

CH. I'm begging you now to help me over this; I'm entrusting myself to   885
your care and putting myself in your hands; I take you as my
protector. Thais, I implore you – I'll die if I can't have her as my
wife.

TH. But if your father ...

CH. What? Oh, he'll be willing, I'm sure, provided she's free-born.   890

TH. If you'd like to wait for a little while, the girl's brother will be here
himself shortly. He's gone to fetch the nurse who looked after her
when she was little. So you'll be there yourself at the recognition,
Chaerea.

CH. I'll stay, of course.

TH. Would you like us to wait inside until he comes, rather than here   895
outside the door?

CH. immo percupio.

PY. quam tu rem actura, obsecro, es?

TH. nam quid ita?

PY. rogitas? hunc tu in aedis cogitas
recipere posthac?

TH. quor non?

PY. crede hoc meae fidei,
dabit hic pugnam aliquam denuo.

TH. au tace, obsecro.

PY. parum perspexisse eius videre audaciam.   900

CH. non faciam, Pythias.

PY. non credo, Chaerea,
nisi si commissum non erit.

CH. quin, Pythias,
tu me servato.

PY. neque pol servandum tibi
quicquam dare ausim neque te servare. apage te!

TH. adest optume ipse frater.

CH. perii hercle! obsecro,   905
abeamus intro, Thais; nolo me in via
cum haec veste videat.

TH. quam ob rem tandem? an quia pudet?

CH. id ipsum.

PY. 'id ipsum'? virgo vero!

TH. i prae; sequor.
tu istic mane ut Chremem intro ducas, Pythias.

V iii   PYTHIAS CHREMES SOPHRONA

PY. quid, quid venire in mentem nunc possit mihi,   910
quidnam qui referam sacrilego illi gratiam
qui hunc supposivit nobis?

CHR. move vero ocius
te, nutrix.

SO. moveo.

---

898 fidei **codd.** : fide Kauer-Lindsay. (Cf. 886.) | **901** non credo A[1] : non pol credo Iov., Σ.
 | **909** Chremem Σ : Chremen A. (Cf. 724.) | **912** supposivit Bentley, **edd.** : supposuit
codd. | vero Σ, Don. : oro A. | **913** te nutrix Σ : te mea nutrix A.

CH. Yes, very much.

PY. Goodness, what's this you're proposing to do?

TH. What on earth's the matter now?

PY. Need you ask? Are you thinking of taking him into the house again after what he's done?

TH. Why not?

PY. Take my word for it , he'll create another rumpus.

TH. Oh, do be quiet, please!

PY. You don't seem to have seen through his brazen impudence very well. 900

CH. I won't do anything, Pythias.

PY. I don't trust you, Chaerea – not until you've *not* done anything.

CH. Well, you keep an eye on me, Pythias.

PY. I swear I wouldn't dare give you anything to keep an eye on – or dare keep an eye on you myself. Keep away from me!

TH. (*looking off to the audience's right*) Here's her brother – what good 905 timing!

CH. Damn it! Please, Thais, let's go inside – I don't want him to see me in the street dressed like this.

TH. (*with a smile*) Why on earth not? Not because you feel ashamed, surely?

CH. Yes, I do.

PY. You do? A real bashful maiden!

TH. (*to Chaerea*) You go in; I'm coming. Pythias, you wait here to bring Chremes indoors. (*She follows Chaerea into her house.*)

V 3

PY. What can I think of, what way to pay back that wicked monster who 910 foisted this fellow off on us?

(*Chremes comes on from the audience's right, followed by* **SOPHRONA**, *an aged nurse.*)

CHR. Do get a move on, nurse.

SO. I *am* getting a move on.

CHR.   video, sed nil promoves.
PY.   iamne ostendisti signa nutrici?
CHR.   omnia.
PY.   amabo, quid ait? cognoscitne?
CHR.   ac memoriter.   915
PY.   probe edepol narras; nam illi faveo virgini.
          ite intro; iamdudum era vos exspectat domi.
          virum bonum eccum Parmenonem incedere
          video; vide ut otiosus it! si dis placet,
          spero me habere qui hunc meo excruciem modo.   920
          ibo intro, de cognitione ut certum sciam;
          post exibo atque hunc perterrebo sacrilegum.

V iv   **PARMENO   PYTHIAS**

PA.   reviso quidnam Chaerea hic rerum gerat.
          quod si astu rem tractavit, di vostram fidem,
          quantam et quam veram laudem capiet Parmeno!   925
          nam ut mittam quod ei amorem difficillimum et
          carissimum, a meretrice avara virginem
          quam amabat, eam confeci sine molestia,
          sine sumptu et sine dispendio; tum hoc alterum –
          id vero est quod ego mi puto palmarium –   930
          me repperisse quo modo adulescentulus
          meretricum ingenia et mores posset noscere
          mature, ut, quom cognorit, perpetuo oderit.
          quae dum foris sunt, nil videtur mundius,
          nec magis compositum quicquam nec magis elegans;   935
          quae, cum amatore quom cenant, ligurriunt.
          harum videre inluviem, sordes, inopiam,
          quam inhonestae solae sint domi atque avidae cibi,
          quo pacto ex iure hesterno panem atrum vorent,
          nosse omnia haec salus est adulescentulis.   940.
PY.   ego pol te pro istis dictis et factis, scelus,

---

916 probe A[1] : bene Iov., Σ. | illi APCF : isti DE. | **919** it **edd.** : id A : sit Σ. | **926** mittam A[1]PCF : omittam Iov., DE, Don. | ei Σ, Don., Eugr. : in A[1] : per A[2] (?). | **929** sumptu et PCF : sumptu ADE. | **931** me Iov., DP[2]C[2]F : men A[1]P[1]C[1]. | **936** amatore cum cenant D[1] : amatore suo cum cenant AD[2]PCFE[2] : amatore suo cenant E[1]. | **941** dictis et factis Σ : factis et dictis A.

CHR. Yes, I can see that, but you're not making much progress.

PY. Have you shown the nurse the tokens yet?

CHR. Yes, all of them.

PY. Please, what does she say? Does she recognize them?   915

CHR. Yes, and very clearly, too.

PY. That's splendid news – I really wish the girl well. Go in; my mistress has been waiting inside for you for quite a while. (*Chaerea and Sophrona go into Thais' house. Pythias looks off to the audience's left.*) Aha! I can see that excellent fellow Parmeno coming this way. Look how carefree he is as he strolls along! Well, if the gods approve, I hope I've hit on a way of putting the screws on him exactly as I'd   920 like. I'll go in to make sure about the recognition, then I'll come back out and really put the wind up this scoundrel.

(*She goes into Thais' house, and almost immediately Parmeno comes on from the audience's left, looking very pleased with himself.*)

V 4

PA. I'm just popping back to see how Chaerea's getting on here. If he's made a clever job of this, by god what a mighty harvest of real praise   925 Parmeno will reap! Not to mention that I've brought off a very difficult and costly love-affair for him, won him the young girl he was mad about from the clutches of a grasping madam without any trouble or expense or cost – there's this second point as well (and it's what I   930 consider my master-stroke), that I've discovered how a young gentleman can get to know the character and ways of such 'ladies' at an early age, so that when he's found it out he'll always hate them. When these creatures are out and about, there's nothing seems more refined or neat or cultivated, as they show off their dainty table   935 manners when they're dining with a lover. But to see their filthy penniless squalour, how degrading and greedy they are when they're by themselves at home, how they wolf down black bread soaked in yesterday's broth – to experience all this is salvation for young lads.   940

PY. (*aside, having come out of Thais' house again while Parmeno was still talking*) My god, I'll get my own back on you for these words of

ulciscar, ut ne inpune in nos inluseris.
pro deum fidem! facinus foedum! o infelicem adulescentulum!
o scelestum Parmenonem, qui istum huc adduxit!

PA.   quid est?

PY. miseret me; itaque ut ne viderem, misera huc ecfugi foras   945
quae futura exempla dicunt in illum indigna!

PA.   o Iuppiter!
quae illaec turba est? numnam ego perii? adibo. quid istuc, Pythias?
quid ais? in quem exempla fient?

PY.   rogitas, audacissime?
perdidisti istum quem adduxti pro eunucho adulescentulum,
dum studes dare verba nobis.

PA.   quid ita? aut quid factum est? cedo.   950

PY. dicam: virginem istam, Thaidi hodie quae dono data est,
scis eam hinc civem esse, et fratrem eius esse adprime nobilem?

PA. nescio .

PY.   atqui sic inventa est. eam istic vitiavit miser.
ille ubi id rescivit factum frater violentissimus ...

PA. quidnam fecit?

PY.   ... conligavit primum eum miseris modis.   955

PA. conligavit?

PY.   atque equidem orante ut ne id faceret Thaide.

PA. quid ais?

PY.   nunc minatur porro sese id quod moechis solet;
quod ego numquam vidi fieri neque velim.

PA.   qua audacia
tantum facinus audet?

PY.   quid ita 'tantum'?

PA.   ·   an non hoc maximum est?
quis homo pro moecho umquam vidit in domo meretricia   960
prendi quemquam?

PY.   nescio.

---

943 nova scaena PCF. (Cf. 1049.) | deum fidem Iov., Σ : fidem deum A[1]. | **946** in illum
A : in eum Σ. | **951** hodie quae Σ : quae hodie A. | **952** hinc civem esse A : civem hinc
esse DPC[2]FE : civem esse hinc C[1]. | eius esse adprime Σ : eius adprime A, Kauer-Lindsay.
| **953** istic A : iste Σ. | **956** conligavit D[1]PCF : hem conligavit AD[2]E : hem **extra metrum**
(955a) servant Kauer-Lindsay. | atque equidem **codd.**, Don. : atque quidem **edd. plerique,**
necnon Kauer-Lindsay. | **957** minatur AE[1] : minitatur DPCFE[2]. (Cf. 1020.) | **959** non
hoc AE : non tibi hoc DPCF, Kauer-Lindsay.

yours, and for what you've done, you villain, so you'll not make fools of us and get away with it. (*Aloud.*) In heaven's name, what a monstrous thing to do! Oh, that poor unfortunate young man! Oh, that wicked Parmeno who brought him here!

PA.   (*aside*) What's that?

PY.   I'm so sorry for him. Oh dear, I ran out here so as not to see the   945
shocking punishment they say's in store for him!

PA.   (*aside*) My god, what's all the panic? It means I'm done for, I'm sure. I'll go and ask her. (*Aloud, as he approaches her.*) What's all this, Pythias? What are you talking about? Who's the punishment meant for?

PY.   What a thing to ask, you reckless fool! In your eagerness to put one   950
over on us, you brought that poor young lad here instead of the eunuch – and you've destroyed him.

PA.   How so? What's happened? Tell me.

PY.   Yes, I will. Do you know that that young girl who was given to Thais today is a free-born Athenian and that her brother's of the very highest birth?

PA.   (*apprehensively*) I ... really don't know.

PY.   Well, that's who she's been found to be – and that poor young man raped her! When her brother got to know what had happened, he went   –
really wild and ...

PA.   What on earth did he do?   955

PY.   ... first of all he trussed him up in a quite dreadful manner.

PA.   Trussed him up?

PY.   Yes, and while Thais was begging him not to do it, too.

PA.   What!

PY.   And now he's threatening to do to him what's usually done to adulterers. I've never seen it done, and wouldn't want to either.

PA.   How can he be so reckless? How can he dare to do such a terrible thing?

PY.   Why 'terrible'?

PA.   Isn't it the worst thing he could do? Who ever saw anyone caught as   960
an adulterer in the house of that sort of woman?

PY.   I ... really don't know.

PA.   at ne hoc nesciatis, Pythias,
dico edico vobis nostrum esse illum erilem filium.

PY.   hem!
obsecro, an is est?

PA.   nequam in illum Thais vim fieri sinat!
atque adeo autem quor non egomet intro eo?

PY.   vide, Parmeno,
quid agas, ne neque illi prosis et tu pereas; nam hoc putant   965
quidquid factum est ex te esse ortum.

PA.   quid igitur faciam miser?
quidve incipiam? ecce autem video rure redeuntem senem.
dicam huic an non dicam? dicam hercle, etsi mihi magnum malum
scio paratum. sed necesse est huic ut subveniam.

PY.   sapis.
ego abeo intro; tu isti narra omne ordine ut factum siet.   970

V v   SENEX   PARMENO

SE.   ex meo propinquo rure hoc capio commodi:
neque agri neque urbis odium me umquam percipit.
ubi satias coepit fieri, commuto locum.
sed estne ille noster Parmeno? at certe ipsus est.
quem praestolare, Parmeno, hic ante ostium?   975

PA.   quis homo est? ehem, salvom te advenire, ere, gaudeo.

SE.   quem praestolare?

PA.   perii; lingua haeret metu.

SE.   quid est? quid trepidas? satine salve? dic mihi.

PA.   ere, primum te arbitrari quod res est velim:
quidquid huius factum est, culpa non factum est mea.   980

SE.   quid?

PA.   recte sane interrogasti; oportuit
rem praenarrasse me. emit quendam Phaedria

---

968 an non dicam dicam hercle Bentley, **edd. plerique** : an non dicam hercle **codd.**, Don. : an non ei dicam hercle Kauer-Lindsay, **qui A²** ei **in Bembino addidisse putant**. | **969** subveniam A : subveniat Σ, Kauer-Lindsay. | **970** omne ordine Faernus, **edd. plerique** : omnem ordinem **codd.** | **971** commodi Iov., Σ, Charisius 142 : commodum A¹. | **976** advenire A : advenisse Σ. | **977** metu AP¹C¹F¹E : metu. SE. hem DP²C²F², Kauer-Lindsay. | **978** quid est quid D¹Lp : quid est quid tu D²PCF : quid est quod tu E : quid A. | **979** quod A : id quod Σ.

PA. But so you all really *do* know, Pythias, I solemnly tell you that he's my master's son.

PY. What! Really? Is he?

PA. Thais mustn't let anything violent happen to *him*. But what's to stop me going in there myself?

PY. Watch what you're doing, Parmeno, in case you do no good to him   965
and come to grief yourself. They think that, whatever's happened, you were behind it.

PA. Oh lord, what can I do then? What start can I make? (*Looking off to the audience's left.*) I can see the old master coming back from the country. Shall I tell him or not? Yes, by god, I will, even if I know there's big trouble in store for me. I've simply got to help Chaerea.

PY. Very wise. I'm going indoors; you tell him everything that's   970
happened, from start to finish.

(*She goes into Thais' house, just as the* **OLD GENTLEMAN** *enters from the audience's left.*)

V 5

O.G. I get a real benefit from having my estate so near at hand – I'm never bored by country or by town. When I begin to feel I've had enough of one of them, I simply change places. But is that my man Parmeno? Yes, I'm sure it is. Parmeno, who are you waiting for outside our   975
door?

PA. (*with feigned surprise*) Who's that? Oh, sir, I'm glad you've got back safely.

O.G. Who are you waiting for?

PA. (*aside*) Damn it! I'm in such a panic I've lost my tongue.

O.G. What's the matter? What are you shaking for? Is everything all right? Out with it.

PA. Sir, first of all, I'd like you to believe the truth – whatever's happened   980
hasn't happened through any fault of mine.

O.G. What's happened?

PA. You were quite right to ask – I should have told you first. Phaedria

eunuchum quem dono huic daret.

SE. quoi?

PA. Thaidi.

SE. emit? perii hercle! quanti?

PA. viginti minis.

SE. actum est!

PA. tum quandam fidicinam amat hic Chaerea. 985

SE. hem! quid? amat? an scit iam ille quid meretrix siet?
an in astu venit? aliud ex alio malum!

PA. ere, ne me spectes; me inpulsore haec non facit.

SE. omitte de te dicere. ego te, furcifer,
si vivo ...! sed istuc quidquid est primum expedi. 990

PA. is pro illo eunucho ad Thaidem deductus est.

SE. pro eunuchon?

PA. sic est. hunc pro moecho postea
conprendere intus et constrinxere.

SE. occidi!

PA. audaciam meretricum specta.

SE. numquid est
aliud mali damnive quod non dixeris 995
relicuom?

PA. tantum est.

SE. cesso huc intro rumpere?

PA. non dubium est quin mi magnum ex hac re sit malum,
nisi, quia necessus fuit hoc facere, id gaudeo
propter me hisce aliquid esse eventurum mali.
nam iam diu aliquam causam quaerebat senex 1000
quam ob rem insigne aliquid faceret is; nunc repperit.

V vi PYTHIAS PARMENO

PY. numquam edepol quicquam iam diu quod magis vellem evenire
mi evenit quam quod modo senex intro ad nos venit errans.
mihi solae ridiculo fuit, quae quid timeret scibam.

---

986 iam ille quid APCF : ille iam quid Ep, Kauer-Lindsay : ille quid iam D. | **987** in Σ, Don. **ad 923** : is A. | **991** Thaidem A : Thaidem hanc Σ, Kauer-Lindsay. | **996** rumpere AD[1], Don., Nonius p. 382M : inrumpere D[2]PCFEp. | **998** necessus A, Don. ("*necessus* nomen est") : necesse Σ. | **999** eventurum mali APCF : venturum mali Ep : mali venturum D[1]L : mali eventurum D[2]. | **1004** ridiculo APCF, Don., Prisc. in **G. L.** 3.7 : ridiculum DE.

bought a eunuch to give to this lady here.

O.G. To who?

PA. To Thais.

O.G. Bought one? Damn it! How much for?

PA. Twenty minae.

O.G. This is the end!   985

PA. Then Chaerea's in love with a music-girl in her house.

O.G. Eh? What? In love? Does he know what this type of woman's like already? Has he come into town? This is one disaster after another.

PA. Don't look at me, sir; he didn't do it at my instigation.

O.G. Stop talking about yourself. I'll deal with you, you villain, if I get out   990
of this alive. First tell me the story – whatever it is.

PA. Chaerea was taken across to Thais instead of that eunuch.

O.G. Instead of the eunuch?

PA. Yes, and afterwards they arrested him in there as an adulterer and tied him up.

O.G. Oh, calamity!

PA. See how shamelessly these women carry on.

O.G. Is there any other catastrophe, any other blow to my finances, that   995
you've left unsaid?

PA. (*abjectly*) That's all.

O.G. I must lose no time in forcing my way in there. (*He rushes into Thais' house.*)

PA. There's no doubt great trouble's coming to me from this; but since I had to do it, I'm glad there's trouble coming to this lot too because of me. The old man's been looking for an excuse for ages now to do   1000
something drastic to them – and now he's found it.

(*Pythias comes out of Thais' house, laughing uncontrollably.*)

V 6

PY. Really, there's nothing that's happened to me for a long time that I'd like to happen more than the old fellow coming into our house just now having got it all so wrong. And I was the only one who could see the joke – only I knew what he was afraid of.

PA. quid hoc autem est?

PY.   nunc id prodeo ut conveniam Parmenonem.   1005
sed ubi, obsecro, est?

PA.   me quaerit haec.

PY.   atque eccum video; adibo.

PA. quid est, inepta? quid tibi vis? quid rides? pergin?

PY.   perii!
defessa iam sum misera te ridendo.

PA.   quid ita?

PY.   rogitas?
numquam pol hominem stultiorem vidi nec videbo. ah,
non possum satis narrare quos ludos praebueris intus.   1010
at etiam primo callidum et disertum credidi hominem.
quid? ilicone credere ea quae dixi oportuit te?
an paenitebat flagiti, te auctore quod fecisset
adulescens, ni miserum insuper etiam patri indicares?
nam quid illi credis animi tum fuisse, ubi vestem vidit   1015
illam esse eum indutum pater? quid est? iam scis te perisse?

PA. hem, quid dixisti, pessuma? an mentita es? etiam rides?
ita lepidum tibi visum est, scelus, nos inridere?

PY.   nimium.

PA. siquidem istuc impune habueris ...

PY.   verum?

PA.   ... reddam hercle.

PY.   credo;
sed in diem istuc, Parmeno, est fortasse quod minare.   1020
tu iam pendebis, qui stultum adulescentulum nobilitas
flagitiis et eundem indicas; uterque in te exempla edent.

PA. nullus sum.

PY.   hic pro illo munere tibi honos est habitus. abeo.

PA. egomet meo indicio miser quasi sorex hodie perii.

1009 nec APCF : neque DE. | **1010** non possum satis narrare A : non potest satis narrari DE
: non satis potest narrari PCF. | **1017** hem **codd.** : ehem Kauer-Lindsay. | dixisti
Umpfenbach : dixti **codd.**, Kauer-Lindsay. (Cf. 376.) | **1020** minare ADE[1] : minitare
PCFE[2] : minitaris Arusian. in **G. L.** 7. 487. (Cf. 957.) | **1022** in te exempla A : exempla in
te Σ (exemplum E).

PA.   (*aside*) What's all this?   1005

PY.   Now I'm on my way outside to meet Parmeno. Where is he, for goodness' sake?

PA.   (*aside*) It's me she's after.

PY.   Ah, there he is – I can see him. I'll go and have a word.

PA.   What is it, you stupid woman? What do you want? What are you laughing at? Must you keep on?

PY.   Oh, my goodness! Oh dear, I'm quite exhausted with all this laughing at you.

PA.   Why?

PY.   What a silly question! I've never seen – never shall see – a greater fool than you. Oh, I can't tell you what fun you've given me in there!   1010 And I thought at first you were such a cunning, clever fellow. Really! Did you have to believe what I told you there and then? Weren't you satisfied with your outrageous goings-on, with what that young man did at your suggestion, unless you told on the poor chap to his father into the bargain? What do you think he felt like when his father saw   1015 him dressed up in those clothes? Well? *Now* are you convinced your days are numbered?

PA.   Eh? What did you say, you dreadful woman? Was it all lies? Are you still laughing? Does it seem so amusing to you to make fun of me, you wicked creature?

PY.   Very amusing.

PA.   If you get away with this ...

PY.   Really?

PA.   ... by god, I'll pay you back.

PY.   I'm sure you will; but perhaps these threats of yours will have to wait   1020 till another day, Parmeno. At the moment it's you who'll be strung up, for giving a foolish young lad a reputation for shocking misconduct, and for giving him away. They'll both of them make an example of you.

PA.   I'm really done for!

PY.   This is the reward you've got for that gift you brought us. I'm off.
     (*She returns into Thais' house, still laughing.*)

PA.   What a miserable wretch I am – doomed by my own loud mouth like a mouse by its squeaking!

(*Thraso and Gnatho come on from the audience's right.*)

V vii **GNATHO   THRASO   \<PARMENO\>**

GN. quid nunc? qua spe aut quo consilio huc imus? quid coeptas, Thraso?

THR. egone? ut Thaidi me dedam et faciam quod iubeat.

GN. quid est?   1026

THR. qui minus quam Hercules servivit Omphalae?

GN. exemplum placet.
utinam tibi conmitigari videam sandalio caput!
sed fores crepuerunt ab ea.

THR. perii! quid hoc autem est mali?
hunc ego numquam videram etiam; quidnam hic properans prosilit? 1030

V viii **CHAEREA   PARMENO   GNATHO   THRASO**

CH. o populares, ecquis me vivit hodie fortunatior?
nemo hercle quisquam; nam in me plane di potestatem suam
omnem ostendere, quoi tam subito tot congruerint commoda.

PA. quid hic laetus est?

CH. o Parmeno mi, o mearum voluptatum omnium
inventor, inceptor, perfector, scis me in quibus sum gaudiis?   1035
scis Pamphilam meam inventam civem?

PA. audivi.

CH. scis sponsam mihi?

PA. bene, ita me di ament, factum.

GN. audin tu, hic quid ait?

CH. tum autem Phaedriae
meo fratri gaudeo esse amorem omnem in tranquillo; una est domus;
Thais patri se commendavit, in clientelam et fidem
nobis dedit se.

PA. fratris igitur Thais tota est?

CH. scilicet.   1040

PA. iam hoc aliud est quod gaudeamus: miles pellitur foras.

CH. tu frater, ubi ubi est, fac quam primum haec audiat.

PA. visam domum.

1031 me vivit hodie DELp, Don., Eugr. : vivit me hodie G : me hodie vivit APCF, Kauer-Lindsay, **qui versum troch. sept. faciunt.** | 1033 quoi **edd. plerique** : cuiΣ : qui Iov. : qua A¹. | **1035** scis me AP²E, Don. : scin me D²P¹CF : scisne D¹ : scisne me G. | **1041** pellitur AGL : pelletur DPCFE, Kauer-Lindsay.

V 7

GN. What now? What do we hope to gain by coming back here? What's
our plan? What are you up to, Thraso?

THR. Me? I've come to surrender myself to Thais and do whatever she tells   1026
me.

GN. What?

THR. Why can't I be her servant just as much as Hercules was Omphale's?

GN. The precedent's a good one. (*Aside.*) I'd love to see your head beaten
to a pulp by a slipper! (*Aloud.*) But there's a noise at her door.
(*Chaerea rushes out of Thais' house in a state of wild elation.*)

THR. Damn it! What new trouble's this? I've never seen this fellow before.   1030
Why's he bursting out in such a hurry?

V 8

CH. My fellow-countrymen, is there a luckier man alive today than me?
No, by god, there's not. In me the gods have shown a clear sign of all
their power – so many blessings have fallen so suddenly upon my
head!

PA. (*aside*) Why's he so happy?

CH. Oh, my dear Parmeno, deviser, initiator and perfecter of all my joys,   1035
do you know the happiness that surrounds me? Do you know it's been
discovered that my Pamphila's a free-born girl?

PA. So I've heard.

CH. Do you know she's engaged to me?

PA. Heavens, well done!

GN. (*to Thraso*) Do you hear what he's saying?

CH. Next, I'm so happy that my brother Phaedria's love-affair has reached
calm waters; we're all one household now; Thais has entrusted
herself to my father's care and put herself under our guardianship and   1040
protection.

PA. She's all your brother's then?

CH. Of course she is.

PA. Then this is something else we should be glad of – the captain's being
kicked out.

CH. Make sure my brother hears the news as soon as possible, wherever he
is.

PA. I'll go and see if he's at home. (*He goes into the old man's house.*)

THR. numquid, Gnatho, tu dubitas quin ego nunc perpetuo perierim?
GN. sine dubio opinor.
CH.   quid commemorem primum aut laudem maxume?
illumne qui mihi dedit consilium ut facerem, an me qui id ausus sim
incipere, an Fortunam conlaudem quae gubernatrix fuit,   1046
quae tot res tantas tam opportune in unum conclusit diem,
an mei patris festivitatem et facilitatem? o Iuppiter,
serva, obsecro, haec bona nobis!

V ix   PHAEDRIA   CHAEREA   THRASO   GNATHO

PH.   di vostram fidem, incredibilia
Parmeno modo quae narravit. sed ubi est frater?
CH.   praesto adest.   1050
PH. gaudeo.
CH.   satis credo. nil est Thaide hac, frater, tua
dignius quod ametur; ita nostrae omni est fautrix familiae.
PH. mihi illam laudas?
THR.   perii! quanto minus spei est, tanto magis amo.
obsecro, Gnatho, in te spes est.
GN.   quid vis faciam?
THR.   perfice hoc
precibus pretio ut haeream in parte aliqua tandem apud Thaidem.   1055
GN. difficile est.
THR.   siquid conlubuit ... novi te. hoc si feceris,
quodvis donum praemium a me optato; id optatum auferes.
GN. itane?
THR.   sic erit.
GN.   si efficio hoc, postulo ut mihi tua domus
te praesente absente pateat, invocato ut sit locus
semper.

1045 illumne A : illum Iov., Σ. | qui id A[1]D[1]G : qui Iov., D[2]LPCFE. | **1049 nova scaena** PCF. (Cf. 943.) | **1052** familiae AD[1] : familiae. PH. hui **cett. codd.** (PH. om. P[1]C[1]F), Kauer-Lindsay. | **1053** PH. mihi ... P[1]C[1]F. | **1056** conlibuit A : collibuit D[2]G[2]PCF[1]E : conlibitum Iov., Kauer-Lindsay : collibitum est F[2] : collibitum est facile est D[1] : tibi collibitum est ut aliquem locum familiaritatis apud Thaidem habeam est G[1]. | feceris A, Nonius p. 358M : effeceris Σ (efferis G). | **1057** donum praemium a me A, Don. : praemium donum a me Nonius p. 358M : donum a me praemium DE : donum a me et praemium G. | auferes A[1] : feres Iov., Σ.

THR. There's no doubt in your mind, I suppose, Gnatho, that I'm done for now for evermore?

GN. No doubt at all, I think.

CH. What should I mention first, what praise the most? The man who suggested I do it, or me who dared to take it on? Or should I heap my praise on Fortune who guided me and packed so many mighty matters so conveniently into just one day? Or should it be my father's easy-going indulgence? Jupiter, I beg you, keep these blessings safe for us.   1046

(*Phaedria comes out of his father's house.*)

V 9

PH. Heavens, what an incredible tale Parmeno's just told me. Where's my brother?   1050

CH. Here.

PH. I'm so delighted.

CH. Yes, I'm sure you are. No-one, dear brother, is more worthy of being loved than this Thais of yours; she's such a kindly helper of all our family.

PH. What need have you to sing her praises to me?

THR. Damn it! The less hope I have, the more I love her. Please, Gnatho, my hopes are pinned on you.

GN. What do you want me to do?

THR. By begging or by bribes make sure I cling on in Thais' favour, to some degree at least.   1055

GN. It's no easy matter.

THR. If you really want to ... I know you. If you can manage this, you can choose any gift, any reward you like from me; you'll get what you want.

GN. Really?

THR. Yes.

GN. If I pull this off, I demand that you keep open house for me when you're there and when you're not, and that there'll always be a place for me even when I'm not invited.

THR.　　　do fidem futurum.

GN.　　　　　　　　　　adcingar.

PH.　　　　　　　　　　　　quem ego hic audio?　　1060

o Thraso!

THR.　　　salvete.

PH.　　　　　　　tu fortasse quae facta hic sient

nescis.

THR.　　scio.

PH.　　　　　quor te ergo in his ego conspicor regionibus?

THR. vobis fretus ...

PH.　　　　　　scis quam fretus? miles, edico tibi,

si te in platea offendero hac post umquam, quod dicas mihi

"alium quaerebam; iter hac habui", periisti.

GN.　　　　　　　　　　heia, haud sic decet.　　1065

PH. dictum est.

THR.　　　　non cognosco vostrum tam superbum.

PH.　　　　　　　　　　sic ago.

GN. prius audite paucis; quod quom dixero, si placuerit,

facitote.

CH.　　　audiamus.

GN.　　　　　　tu concede paullum istuc, Thraso.

principio ego vos ambos credere hoc mihi vehementer velim,

me huius quidquid facio id facere maxume causa mea.　　1070

verum si idem vobis prodest, vos non facere inscitia est.

PH. quid id est?

GN.　　　　militem ego rivalem recipiundum censeo.

PH.　　　　　　　　　　hem!

recipiundum?

GN.　　　　　cogita modo: tu hercle cum illa, Phaedria,

ut lubenter vivis (etenim bene lubenter victitas),

quod des paullum est et necesse est multum accipere Thaidem.　　1075

1062 conspicor D, Don. : conspicior A¹G : conspicio Iov., PCFE. | 1063-5 scis ... periisti **Phaedriae trib.** Σ : **Chaereae** A. | 1063 scis A : scin Σ (sin F¹), Kauer-Lindsay. | 1064 quod A, Don. : nihil quod Iov. : nihil est quod Σ. | 1066 non ... superbum **Thrasoni trib.** AD²E : **Gnathoni** D¹GPCF. | PH. sic ago **edd. plerique** : CH. sic ago A : CH. sic erit Iov. : PH. sic erit Σ. | 1068 audiamus **Chaereae trib.** A : **Phaedriae** Σ. | paullum **vel** paulum **edd.** : paululum **codd.** (Cf. 1075.) | 1069 velim A : volim D : volo GPCFE². | 1070 facio AG, Don. : facio me D : faciam PCFE. | 1072 ego rivalem Σ, Don. : rivalem ego A, Kauer-Lindsay. | 1074 ut D¹L : et AD²PCFEp¹ : **om.** Gp². | 1075 paullum **vel** paulum **edd.** : paululum **codd.** (Cf. 1068.) | et **om.** A¹

THR. I give you my promise on that.   1060

GN. Then I'll get myself ready for action.

PH. Who's this I hear? Oh, Thraso.

THR. Good day to you both.

PH. Perhaps you're not aware of what's been happening here?

THR. Yes, I am.

PH. So why do I see you in these parts?

THR. I'm relying on you ...

PH. You know what you can rely on? Captain, I solemnly say to you, if I ever come across you in this street in future – even though you may say to me "I was looking for somebody else; I was just passing this   1065 way" – you've had it.

GN. Hey, that's no way to behave.

PH. It's my last word.

THR. This high-handed attitude isn't what I expect from you.

PH. It's how I choose to act.

GN. Listen to me briefly first. When I've had my say, if you approve of my idea, then put it into practice.

CH. (*to Phaedria*) Let's hear him.

GN. Go over there a bit, Thraso. (*To the others, when Thraso has retreated.*) First of all, I should very much like you both to understand that I'm doing what I'm doing above all with my own interests in   1070 mind. But if the same course of action is to your advantage too, it's stupid of you not to follow it.

PH. What is it?

GN. I think you should admit Thraso as a rival.

PH. What! Admit him?

GN. Just think: while you enjoy living with Thais, Phaedria – indeed, you very much enjoy it – you've not got much to give her, and she,   1075 perforce, must be given a lot. To be able to supply the needs of your

ut tuo amori suppeditare possit sine sumptu tuo ad
omnia haec, magis opportunus nec magis ex usu tuo
nemo est. principio et habet quod det, et dat nemo largius;
fatuos est, insulsus, tardus, stertit noctes et dies;
neque istum metuas ne amet mulier; facile pellas ubi velis.   1080

PH. quid agimus?

GN.   praeterea hoc etiam, quod ego vel primum puto,
accipit homo nemo melius prorsus neque prolixius.

CH. mirum ni illoc homine quoquo pacto opust.

PH.   idem ego arbitror.

GN. recte facitis. unum etiam hoc vos oro, ut me in vostrum gregem
recipiatis; satis diu hoc iam saxum vorso.

PH.   recipimus.   1085

CH. ac lubenter.

GN.   at ego pro istoc, Phaedria et tu Chaerea,
hunc comedendum vobis propino et deridendum.

CH.   placet.

PH. dignus est.

GN.   Thraso, ubi vis accede.

THR.   obsecro te, quid agimus?

GN. quid? isti te ignorabant; postquam is mores ostendi tuos
et conlaudavi secundum facta et virtutes tuas,   1090
impetravi.

THR.   bene fecisti; gratiam habeo maxumam.
numquam etiam fui usquam quin me omnes amarent plurimum.

GN. dixin ego in hoc esse vobis Atticam elegantiam?

PH. nil praeter promissum est. ite hac.

ω   vos valete et plaudite.

1076 suppeditare Iov., Σ, Don. ("aut pro *suppeditari* aut deest *se*") : suppeditari A. | **1079** noctes A¹PCF : noctesque Iov., DGE, Don. | **1081** quid agimus? **Phaedriae trib. codd.** : **Chaereae** Bentley, **edd. plerique, necnon** Kauer-Lindsay. | **1082** homo AD¹P¹C¹, Don., Nonius p. 240M : hominem D²GP²C²FE. | **1083** CH. mirum ... opust. PH. idem ... arbitror A, Don. : PH. mirum ... opust. CH. idem ... arbitror Σ. | **1084** hoc **om.** DGPCF. | **1086** ac lubenter **Chaereae trib.** Σ : **Phaedriae cont.** A. | istoc Σ, Don. : isto A. | **1087** hunc comedendum vobis propino et deridendum A : hunc comedendum et deridendum vobis propino Σ (propinebo C¹, propinabo C², prebebo PFE, praebeo D²) : hunc vobis comedendum et bibendum et deridendum propino Nonius p. 33M. | **1088** ubi vis accede APCF : accede ubi vis DGE. | **1093** elegantiam ADGE : eloquentiam LPCF, Don. **in comm.**, Eugr. | **1094** ite hac **Phaedriae cont.** A : **Gnathoni trib.** Σ, Don. ("quo vocat parasitus? ad meretricem an ad cenam militis?").

love-affair in all these respects without any cost to you, there's no-one more convenient or more useful to you than Thraso. To start with, he's got money to give, and nobody gives it more freely; he's silly, stupid and slow, and spends his nights and days snoring away. You needn't be afraid that Thais will fall in love with him, and you can 1080 easily get rid of him whenever you want.

PH. (*to Chaerea*) What do we do?

GN. Then there's this as well – what I consider the most important point of all: there's nobody who entertains better or more generously than he does.

CH. It looks as if we do really need the fellow in some ways.

PH. Yes, I agree.

GN. You're doing the right thing. I've got one thing more to ask of you – that you accept me into your circle; (*with a nod in Thraso's direction*) 1085 I've been pushing this particular stone uphill for quite long enough.

PH. We accept you.

CH. Yes, gladly.

GN. In return for that, Phaedria and you, too, Chaerea, I give you Thraso, for you to eat out of house and home and make mock of.

CH. Excellent!

PH. He deserves it.

GN. (*calling across to Thraso*) Thraso, come back over here when you like.

THR. (*as he returns*) Tell me, please, how are we doing?

GN. How are we doing? These fellows didn't know you; when I showed them your true character and praised you in accordance with your deeds and qualities, I got what we wanted. 1090

THR. Well done; I'm very grateful. I've never been anywhere without being really well liked by everyone.

GN. (*to Phaedria and Chaerea*) I told you he'd got real Attic polish, didn't I?

PH. Just what you promised. Come this way.

CANTOR Farewell, and give us your applause.

(*They all go into Thais' house.*)

Commentary

Notes with bold italic and / or Latin lemmata are intended primarily for readers using the Latin text.

PRODUCTION NOTICE

For the production notices (*didascaliae*) in general, see Introduction pp. 11-12.

1   **Megalensian Games:** So the Σ MSS and Don.; the games formed part of the festival of the Megale(n)sia, held at Rome every April in honour of the *Magna Mater* "Great Mother" goddess of Asia Minor, Cybele. The name comes from the feminine of the Greek word for "great" (μεγάλη, *megale*).

A gives "Roman Games", the games held annually in mid-September in honour of Jupiter, Rome's supreme god. The change can be accounted for either by assuming confusion with *Ph.* (which *was* produced at the Roman Games in this same year), or, more likely, by supposing that we have here evidence of a later revival of *Eu.*

2   **curule aediles:** The magistrates responsible for the games; see Introduction p. 9 and *Eu.* 20. L. Postumius Albinus and L. Cornelius Merula are again mentioned as the year's aediles in the production notice of *Ph.*

3   **produced by Lucius Ambivius Turpio:** A adds the name of Lucius Hatilius Praen[estinus] "of Praeneste", but keeps the verb in the singular (*egit* "he produced"); the Σ MSS add L. Atilius Praenestinus, but change the verb to the plural (*egere* "they produced"). Since it is unlikely that a company of actors would need more than one producer, it is probable that A, with its singular verb, is nearer the truth, and that Ambivius was sole producer of the original production (as, according to A, he was of *Hau.*); Atilius' name (which also appears in the production notices of *Hau.* (in the Σ MSS only), *Ph.* and *Ad.*, and in Don.'s version of the production notice of *An.*) could easily have crept in as that of someone known to have produced revivals of Ter.'s plays.

Ambivius himself was a famous actor (Cic. *Sen.* 48), coupled with the almost legendary Roscius by Tacitus (*Dial.* 20. 3).

music composed ... : We know little of the music for Ter.'s plays, except that it was played on pipes (*tibiae*), and probably accompanied the entire play apart from the longish sections written in the metre known as iambic senarii. Its importance is demonstrated by its mention in all the production notices, and it must have made a great contribution to the entertainment. Flaccus, slave of Claudius, was composer for all the plays.

4   **on two right-hand pipes:** The pipes were "normally played in pairs, one fingered by each hand" (*OCD*[3], 1005). The music for Ter.'s other plays was performed "on right- or left-hand equal pipes" (*An.*), "first on unequal pipes then on two right-hand ones" (*Hau.*), "on unequal pipes throughout" (*Ph.*), "on equal pipes throughout" (*Hec.*) and "on Sarranian pipes throughout" (*Ad.*). What these various terms mean is unclear, but "the 'left' and 'right' were two different sizes which played at two different pitches.

Where we find 'two right' or 'two left' they were presumably played ... in unison"
(Landels, J. G. (1999), *Music in Ancient Greece and Rome* (London), 188).

3   ***Menandru***: A retains the transliteration of the Greek genitive of Men.'s name,
        Μενάνδρου; the Σ MSS substitute the gen. of the Latin form, *Menandri*.

5   **Marcus Valerius and Gaius Fannius:** M. Valerius Messala and C. Fannius Strabo
        were consuls in 161 BC. For the second name the Σ MSS have "C. Mummius Fannius",
        probably a conflation of Fannius' name with that of L. Mummius, one of the consuls of
        146 BC. In the production notice of *Hau.* A includes the name of Cn. Cornelius
        Lentulus, the other consul of 146. These facts, taken together with A's mention of the
        Roman Games instead of the Megalensian for *Eu.* and the addition by all MSS of the
        name of a second producer for several plays, provide substantial evidence for later
        revivals.

SUMMARY

Each of Ter.'s plays is prefaced by a twelve-line summary (*periocha*), written in the second
century AD by C. Sulpicius Apollinaris, tutor of the emperor Pertinax and the writer Aulus
Gellius. Using iambic senarii, the writer imitates the diction and prosody of Ter.'s day. This
summary, like them all, does not give full details of the plot. In particular, several characters
are not given their names (the "girl falsely said to be Thais' sister" is Pamphila, the eunuch is
Dorus, "Phaedria's younger brother" is Chaerea and the "citizen of Attica" is Chremes);
more importantly, the role of the sponger Gnatho is not even mentioned.

11-12   **gives her to her seducer:** It is nowhere actually stated in the play that Chremes has
        given his consent to Pamphila's betrothal to Chaerea, though such consent would have
        been necessary and can be assumed.

12   **Thraso prevails on Phaedria ... :** It is actually Gnatho who brokers the deal at 1069-
        83.

CHARACTERS

No list of *dramatis personae* appears in any MS, but it is usual to include one in modern
editions, compiled from information given in the scene-headings (see Introduction p. 39).
Ter. habitually altered the proper names he found in his originals (cf. Introduction p. 26),
though the ones he substituted were Greek, not Latin. He seems to have had a liking for
certain names: Phaedria is also a young man (*adulescens*) in *Ph.*, Parmeno is also a slave
(*servos*) in both *Hec.* and *Ad.*, and Chremes is an old man (*senex*) in *An.*, *Hau.* and *Ph.*; there
is also a nurse (*nutrix*) called Sophrona in *Ph.* and a young girl (*virgo*) called Pamphila in *Ad.*

Don. I 472 (on 971) specifically states that the father of Phaedria and Chaerea is given
no name in Ter. In the scene-heading before 971 he is called Demea (also the name of an old
man in *Ad.*) in A, but Laches (also the name of an old man in *Hec.*) in Σ. Accordingly, I have
preferred the safer - if rather less elegant - course of referring to him simply as an "old
gentleman".

PROLOGUE

4   **if there's anyone:** The reference is to Ter.'s principal critic, Luscius Lanuvinus; see Introduction, pp. 16-17).

6   **who caused offence first:** It is clear from the prologue to Ter.'s first play *An.* (6-7 and 15-16) that Luscius had attacked it before it was even staged.

7   **by accurate translation and poor composition:** Duckworth 65 feels that this is perhaps Ter.'s "most enlightening" comment on Luscius. The barb about "accurate translation" appears to pick up Ter.'s attack at *An.* 21 on the "incomprehensible exactitude" (*obscura diligentia*) of Luscius and his supporters. It seems that by sticking too closely to the actual wording of his Greek originals Luscius had ruined the overall effect of his Latin versions.

9   **just recently put on *The Phantom* by Menander:** Proof, if proof were needed, that Luscius was a productive dramatist and not just an armchair critic and poet. Menander's *The Phantom* (Φάσμα, *Phasma*) is mentioned for identification purposes - to identify Luscius by naming one of his recent adaptations. As Don. saw (I 272), it is not necessary to assume that Ter. must be criticizing Luscius over this play.

Don. I 272 gives the play's plot. A woman living with her husband and stepson had previously had a daughter by her husband's next-door neighbour, and had arranged for the daughter to continue to live next door. In order to see the girl frequently, she had made an opening in the party wall between the two houses, disguising it as a shrine. The stepson, seeing the daughter appear through the 'shrine', assumed her to be a *phantom* of the shrine's deity; but, when he realized the truth, he fell in love with her and finally, with the agreement of all parties, married her.

Some fragments of Men.'s play exist, in particular a parchment leaf with 25 incomplete lines on each side, ascribed to the play by virtue of Don.'s account of the plot. Part of this appears to be a deferred prologue giving the background to the story, including the ruse of the 'shrine'. See Körte I 134-7; Arnott (2000) 363-411.

10-13 **who in *The Treasure*...:** Don. I 273 provides further details about this play (Θησαυρός, *Thesauros*), though he does not give the outcome. A young man who had squandered his patrimony on loose living sent his slave to his father's tomb to open it for a funeral feast which the deceased had instructed should be celebrated ten years after his death. The field in which the tomb was situated had in the meantime been bought from the young man by an old miser, whose help the slave now sought in opening the tomb. Inside, the slave found treasure and a letter. The old miser kept the treasure and the young man went to law to get it back, but in the action the former stated his case first. At this point Don. quotes two lines from the miser's speech, the only fragment of Luscius' work which has come down to us: *prior senex ... causam suam sic agit 'Atheniense bellum, cum Rhodiensibus quod fuerit, quid ego hic praedicem, quod tu scias?' etc.* "The old man ... pleaded his case first as follows: 'Why should I mention here the Athenian war which took place against the Rhodians, which you should know about?' etc."

It is not clear whether Luscius had altered the sequence of events he found in his original. Ter.'s earlier remark about his rival's "accurate translation" (7) implies that this would be unlikely; but in that case it is difficult to see what complaint Ter. would have against *Luscius* here - his criticism should rather have been directed against the

author of the Greek original. Or is Ter. implying that he himself would have changed
the sequence in the original whereas Luscius had not?

The implication of Ter.'s words is that this play was also based on an original by
Menander, who we know wrote a play of this name (fragments in Körte II 77-9, frs 198-
202).

17   **many another point:** In fact Ter. makes only one other critical reference to Luscius'
work - in the prologue to *Ph.* (6-8).

20   **Menander's *The Eunuch*:** See Introduction Section V. It is only here and in *An.* 9 that
Ter. names the author of his (principal) original; but, as the production notices make
clear, the identity of the Greek playwright would not have been a secret.

the aediles: See production notice and Introduction p. 9.

emerunt: The scansion -*ĕrunt* for the 3rd pl. of the perf. indic. act. is found only here in
Ter., but is more frequent in Plautus, and occurs occasionally later, e.g. Ov. *Fast.* 2.
502.

21   **a chance to look at it:** A reference to the preliminary performance of 22; "a look at it"
need not imply an even earlier look at the text.

Quite how Luscius managed this is not explained. Though the jibes about his age in
An. 7, *Hau.* 22 and *Ph.* 1 and 13 need not be taken too far, he was obviously older than
Ter., and he may have become doyen of Rome's comic dramatists following the death
of Caecilius (see Introduction p. 8), and thus had influence with the aediles. Friendship,
or even bribery, are other possibilities.

22   **the performance began:** Since the aediles must have been satisfied with the play when
they bought it from the actor manager, who in turn must have been satisfied when he
bought it from Ter. (see Introduction p. 9), there seems little point in this preliminary
performance - except as an occasion for Luscius to make his protest. Perhaps because
of his attacks on Ter.'s previous plays, and possibly his suspicions about this one, he
was able to demand it. (It cannot have been a mere rehearsal, since that would not have
necessitated the aediles' presence.)

There is no other record of such a performance. But since Luscius knew about
Ter.'s *An.* before it was staged (see 6n.), could there have been one on that occasion too
- with more point, since Ter. was then completely unknown?

23-4 *fabulam dedisse et nil dedisse verborum*: Play on words is a feature of Ter.'s
prologues. Here *dare* is used with *fabulam* ("to put on a play") and with *verba* ("to
trick"; cf. 950), in the form *nil dare verborum* ("to fail to trick").

25   **an old play by Naevius and by Plautus:** The translation reflects the ambiguity of the
Latin, since there are several ways of interpreting the line: (i) Naevius and Plautus both
independently wrote a play of this name; (ii) they worked together on producing the
same play; (iii) Plautus revised a play by Naevius. The first possibility is the most
likely, since a few short fragments exist both of *The Toady* of Naevius and of *The Toady*
of Plautus (though if they were reworkings of the same original, Plautus would be guilty
of precisely the same charge which Luscius is here levelling at Ter.); (ii) is the least
likely, since such collaboration, though not chronologically impossible, is
unprecedented; but (iii) may also be possible, since Gellius (3. 3. 13), talking of the
'Varronian recension' of Plautus' plays (see Introduction p. 7), agrees that earlier plays
were without doubt "revised and touched up" (*retractatae et expolitae*) by Plautus -

though whether Luscius would have approved of this procedure is another matter. See also 33n.

Plautus' *The Toady* is not among the 21 plays Varro thought were undoubtedly genuine (the 20 and incomplete 21st which have survived). This need not worry us; at *Ad.* 7 Ter. mentions Plautus' *Joined in Death (Commorientes)*, which again is not among the 21, and Varro himself had accepted that some others outside the 21 were genuinely Plautine (Gel. 3. 3. 3).

26 **of the sponger and of the soldier:** Gnatho and Thraso; see Introduction pp. 34-6.

27 **one of oversight:** An extraordinary admission by Ter. As 33-4 ("but he certainly ... been written earlier") make clear, he had simply not known about Naevius' and Plautus' *The Toady*. Even granted that there would have been many Roman comedies around (Gel. 3. 3. 11 mentions 130 in circulation under Plautus' name alone), it seems remarkable that Ter. had not checked - unless, that is, Luscius is here attempting to lay down new ground-rules, and is objecting to something which had previously been an acceptable practice.

28 **stealing:** The same Latin word, *furtum* ('theft', 'plagiarism'), is used by Ter. at *Ad.* 13 when he talks (12-14) of making use of a scene from Diphilus' *Joined in Death* which Plautus had not included in his version of that play: "See whether you think a theft (*furtum*) has been committed or whether a passage which was passed over through neglect has been reclaimed".

30 **a play by Menander:** For the surviving fragments, see Arnott (1996) 151-203, Körte I 110-19. The toadying sponger seems to have two names, Strouthias and Gnathon, in that play, and the boastful soldier is called Bias (see Introduction p. 26 and nn. 132-4). The plot cannot be reconstructed in detail, but Bias and a young man called Pheidias seem to have been rivals for the attentions of an unnamed *hetaira*. Strouthias / Gnathon is attached to Bias (or, if Strouthias and Gnathon are not one and the same, Strouthias is attached to Bias and, possibly, Gnathon to Pheidias).

31 **Our author doesn't deny:** Ter. admits to inserting characters taken from a second Greek play into his version of his main original. According to some commentators, this is the practice known as *contaminatio*, referred to at *An.* 16 and *Hau.* 17. But in that case it is strange that Luscius does not upbraid Ter. here for again doing what he upbraided him for on the two earlier occasions. This should make us wonder whether the 'usual' interpretation of *contaminatio* is not wrong. See Introduction p. 19 and nn. 98-101.

33 **those Latin plays:** Ter. must mean Naevius' and Plautus' versions of *The Toady*. See Barsby (1999) 87 and cf. 27n. above. The use of the plural "plays" adds weight to the first of the possible interpretations of 25 (where see n.).

36ff. **how can he still create:** Ter.'s defence hinges on the frequency with which stock characters appear in Greek and Roman comedy, and, even though in *Eu.* in particular he seems to revel in creating characters which are not quite the stock types they appear at first to be, the defence is still essentially valid. For the running slave see Davos at *An.* 338-45, Geta at *Ph.* 179-96 and 841-52, and Geta at *Ad.* 299-321; for the honest wife see Sostrata in *Hau.* and *Hec.*; for the nasty courtesan Bacchis in *Hau.* and Parmeno's description at *Eu.* 934-40; for the sponger and soldier Gnatho and Thraso in *Eu.*; and for the slave who deceives his master Syrus in *Hau.*

36   *qui*: The old abl. sing. form of the interrogative pronoun, meaning "How?"; cf. 121,
     273 (strengthened by *-dum*), 307 etc. Similarly, *qui*, abl. sing. of the relative pronoun,
     488, 759 (*quicum*), 911 etc.

44   **Pay attention:** Similar pleas for attention close the prologues to *An.* (24), and, coupled
     with a similar appeal for silence, to *Ph.* (30), and *Hec.* (55); another occurs at *Hau.* 35.
     That the audience could be restive is attested, e.g., by *Hec.* 29-42.

ACT ONE SCENE ONE

Only two (of the possible three) house entrances are required for the play, as also in, for
example, *Ad.*, Plautus' *The Rope* (*Rudens*) and Men.'s *The Girl from Samos* (Σαμία, *Samia*).
With a complete absence of stage directions, there is no indication to show from where
Phaedria and Parmeno enter, but it is natural to assume that they do so from Phaedria's
father's house.
      Having two characters entering part-way through a conversation is a stage device found
frequently in this type of play (cf. Phaedria and Parmeno again at 207, Thraso and Gnatho at
391, 771 and 1025, Thais and Pythias at 817); it serves to connect the stage action with the
wider off-stage world. Here the audience's interest is aroused as they are immediately
plunged into an intriguing situation. At this stage, only the bare bones of the problem are
allowed to emerge through Phaedria's complaints and Parmeno's advice, and thus to interest
is added anticipation. The details and the background are not revealed until the exposition of
the following scene.

46ff. **So what am I to do?:** Phaedria's opening speech effectively illustrates his weakness
     and irresolution, as a forerunner of the typical 'elegiac' lover (Barsby (1999) 90) totally
     enslaved to the woman he loves and unable to break free; see Introduction p. 29. But
     his words also show an endearing awareness of his own failings; he is a character
     whom the audience can warm to and sympathise with as well as smile at.
           The scene rapidly became famous, and is quoted by Cicero (*N. D.* 3. 29. 72), Horace
     (*S.* 2. 3. 259-71), Persius (5. 161-75) and Quintilian (*Inst.* 9. 2. 11, 9. 3. 16, 9. 4. 141 and
     11. 3. 182). It is from the Persius passage, and the scholiast on it, that we learn that in
     Men.'s *The Eunuch* the Phaedria character was called Chairestratos, Parmeno was Daos,
     Thais Chrysis, and Phaedria's father Simon (the last also being noted by Don. I 472).
           Don. I 278 quotes the Greek original of Phaedria's opening question as ἀλλὰ τί
     ποήσω; "But what am I to do?" (Körte II 66-7, fr. 161).

48   **such 'ladies':** The Latin word used here, *meretrix* (Gk ἑταίρα, *hetaira*), has no precise
     equivalent in English, except possibly for the antiquated 'courtesan' ('prostitute'
     certainly will not do). A *meretrix* is an independent woman, often a foreigner, who
     offers companionship and sex to a number of lovers and makes her living from the
     money and gifts they provide. It is easy to see how such women acquired an unsavoury
     reputation for greed and insincerity (cf. "one tiny crocodile tear", 67), and for exploiting
     the men they dealt with. But, as will become clear, Thais, who is the *meretrix* referred
     to here, is not quite of this traditional type (see Introduction pp. 31-2 and 199-201n.).

50ff. **If you could really ... :** Some MSS (and Don.) continue Phaedria's words down to the
     end of 56 ("over and over again that ..."); others ascribe 50-55 to Parmeno and 56 to
     Phaedria. This has led many editors, including those of the Oxford Text, to give the
     whole of 50-56 to Parmeno, thus extending his speech from 50 to 70.

The erroneous ascription of 50-55 to Parmeno was caused by failure to see that at 50 Phaedria switches from talking to his slave in the first person ("I", 46-9) to thinking aloud to himself ("you", 50-56). This self-musing stresses his awareness of his own inability to live up to the brave front he has just been assuming when talking to Parmeno directly. That Parmeno's speech begins at 56 is supported by the fact that a slave addressing his master would naturally start with "Sir", rather than insert the word after he has spoken seven lines. Those MSS which give 50-55 to Parmeno seem aware of this, since they give 56 alone - rather oddly - to Phaedria, with Parmeno beginning again at 57. For a full discussion see Barsby (1990) 10-12.

57   **Sir, you can't use reason ... :** Parmeno is a slave of Phaedria's father, who has been given the role of personal servant to Phaedria (and, it seems, to his brother Chaerea too, 308ff. n.). In all probability he was the boys' *paedagogus* (παιδαγωγός, lit. 'child-escort') when they were young, escorting them to and from school, and having general responsibility for their day-to-day upbringing; in that role he would have been continually advising (and on occasion reproving) them. His advice here (basically "Don't try to deal with your feelings by the exercise of reason; just put up with the troubles love brings like a man") is thus neither impertinent nor presumptuous. He is merely continuing in a role he has played for years.

At this early stage in the play Parmeno seems to be a typical *paedagogus* (just as Thais, though we do not yet know her name, seems to be a typical greedy, heartless *meretrix*). But later (see Introduction pp. 32-3) we will find out that he, like Thais, is not in the expected mould. Far from being a level-headed source of sound wisdom, he can rapidly be reduced to a state of panic, can be easily duped, and might better be classed as a 'bungling' rather than a 'cunning' or 'clever' slave. Even his advice here has been criticized as inconsistent or at least confused (e.g. the advice not to fight passion with reasoned thought sits uncomfortably beside the advice to 'buy himself out' at 74-5, which in turn seems at odds with the encouragement to put up with the troubles love brings at 77-8); see Barsby (1990).

59-61   **hurtful words ... :** It is a commonplace that lovers' arguments are followed by reconciliation; cf. one of Ter.'s best 'one-liners' at *An.* 555: "Lovers' quarrels are love's renewal" (*amantium irae amoris integratio est*), and a more extended explanation of the topic in Plautus' *Amphitryo* 938-43.

As often in such contexts, the language in 60-1 is military; the Latin translated as "patching things up ... in peace again" is much pithier in the original: "a truce, war, peace again."

Cicero (*Tusc.* 4. 76) quotes 59-63 as an example of the "inconsistency and fickleness of mind" (*inconstantia mutabilitasque mentis*) typical of the "disorder of the mind in love" (*perturbatio ... mentis in amore*).

70-1   **Now at last I realize ... :** To the picture of Phaedria's weakness is added evidence of his genuine misery, thus further eliciting the audience's sympathy.

74   **buy yourself out:** The language is again military, the image that of ransoming a prisoner of war.

76   ***ne ... adflictes***: Ter. frequently uses *ne* with a subjunctive for 2nd person prohibitions (cf. 212, 273 etc.), as well as *ne* with an imperative (cf. 95). The classical *noli / nolite* with an infinitive is rarer (*An.* 385, *Hec.* 46 etc.).

77-8 Don't add ... proper spirit: The fifth-century AD writer Stobaeus preserves two lines from Men.'s *The Eunuch* which are so close to Ter.'s Latin here as to be virtually certainly the original of these two lines (*Ecl.* 4. 44. 38 = Körte II 67, fr. 162):

μὴ θεομάχει μηδὲ προάγου τῶι πράγματι
χειμῶνας ἑτέρους, τοὺς δ' ἀναγκαίους φέρε.

"Don't fight against the gods, and don't add further storms
to your troubles, but put up with those you have to bear."

Ter. has removed the reference to fighting the gods, possibly because the concept of Love as a god was unfamiliar to Romans, and changed "storms" to the more prosaic "troubles". See further Barsby (1999a) 6-7.

79   But here's the woman herself: Such announcement of characters, either coming out of one of the houses as here, or approaching from the 'wings' along the street (as Parmeno on the approach of Gnatho 228, and of Chaerea 289), is another common stage device. It is probably a pointer to alert the audience to the new arrival rather than a stage direction, though it could be both. Where the character comes from a house, there is sometimes (though not here) reference to the noise made by the door as it is opened (cf. 1029, *Hau.* 173-4, 613).

79-80 that blight ... come to us: Parmeno sees Thais as a conventional *meretrix*, ruinous to Phaedria's (and thus to Phaedria's father's) finances; compare his description of Thais as a "grasping madam" (927) and of the lifestyle in such people's houses (937-40), his statement that Phaedria's father has long been wanting to "do something drastic" to Thais and her household (1001), and Chaerea's picture at 382-5. We should remember that Phaedria has bought the eunuch and the Ethiopian slave girl for Thais (165-9), and, for all their inadequacy (230-1, 471), they were not cheap (169). But, despite that, these reminders of the conventional picture (none of which, it should be noted, come from Phaedria) only serve to highlight the contrast with Thais' apparently genuine affection for Phaedria (cf. 197ff. n.) and some of her other actions in the play. See Introduction pp. 31-2.

ACT ONE SCENE TWO

Now that the audience's curiosity has been thoroughly aroused, the details of the situation can be given them. Almost half this long scene (99-149) is straight exposition by Thais, interrupted only by brief interjections from Phaedria and Parmeno, and by Phaedria's speech (162-71) which itself provides further background information, this time from his point of view. The scene also further characterizes both Phaedria and Parmeno, and Thais' closing monologue (197-206), as well as supplying yet another vital piece of information (203-4), is important for demonstrating the real nature of her feelings for Phaedria.

Opinion is divided about whether this explanatory material also appeared at this point and in this form in Men.'s *The Eunuch*, or whether Ter. has transferred it here from an 'expository' prologue in Men. which he removed in his adaptation in accordance with his normal practice. See Introduction pp. 25-6.

81-2 Oh, dear me! ... : Although Thais speaks only two lines before she notices Phaedria and Parmeno, the alert members of the audience might yet pick up a hint that she is not going to turn out quite as she has been pictured.

So far none of the characters has been named, but all three are identified, in a natural and almost casual way, early in this scene. Thus Thais provides Phaedria's name here, while Phaedria identifies Parmeno (83) and Thais (91).

83-4 **Parmeno, I'm shivering ... :** The device of a character or characters overhearing and commenting on the thinking aloud of another (or the conversation of two or more others) is the commonest of all stage conventions. It can take many forms. Sometimes, as here, it leads to the eavesdropper(s) being swiftly noticed; on other occasions the overhearing and the comments can continue for a very long time until the eavesdropper is noticed (cf. Parmeno listening to Gnatho 232-67) or comes forward and reveals himself (cf. Parmeno listening to Thraso and Gnatho and then to Thraso, Gnatho and Thais 395-461). Though in these latter instances the convention may seem to us wildly overplayed, it was facilitated by the wide stage of the early theatres - though there was in early times little in the way of elaborate doorways etc. which the listener could use to conceal himself.

85 **Go near this fire:** Usually it is the young man who is 'on fire' with love (cf. 72), but here, by a striking transference, his beloved has become the fire while he himself is shivering.

86 *ehem*: This expression of surprise ("oh", "good Lord") appears also at 462, 505, 651, 730 and 976. It is most frequently used when, as here, one character is caught unawares by the presence of, or arrival of, another. See Luck 69-70, McGlynn I 158-9.]
tun: *tune*, with the final -*e* dropped ('apocope'). This is not uncommon with -*ne*; see 99n., 651n.

95-7 **Don't torture yourself ... :** Thais' protestations, and particularly her use of terms of endearment (cf. "Phaedria my dear" in 86 above) seem genuine enough; but at this stage they could still be dismissed as 'sweet-talking' in order to get what she wants.

99 *sicin*: *sic* + -*ne*, with final -*e* dropped. Where -*n(e)* follows, *i* is inserted; cf. *hoccin* (*hoc* + -*n(e)* 644, *hancin* (*hanc* + -*n(e)* 771.

107 **from Samos ... on Rhodes:** Islands in the south-eastern Aegean, close to the west coast of Asia Minor (modern Turkey). Barsby (1999) 106 sees the move of Thais' mother to Rhodes as compatible with known events shortly before Men.'s day. In 366/5 the Athenians had established a cleruchy on Samos (Diod. 18. 8. 7), expelling the Samians who were not restored until 43 years later (Diod. 18. 18. 9). It is doubtful, however, whether the majority of Ter.'s audience would have known about, let alone been interested in, such details.

110 **Was she free-born?:** This question, coupled with Thais' guarded reply and the information that the girl (Pamphila) had been captured by pirates (a stock motif), would have been enough to alert the audience to the probability that she would indeed be found to be free-born and would be reunited with her family. Compare the same kidnapping motif employed of Palaestra in Plautus' *The Rope* 39-40.
Some (e.g. Webster (1960) 70) have found Parmeno's presence at this point awkward. They ask how the slave could later help Chaerea to get access to Pamphila by suggesting (369-75) that he change places with the eunuch, when he has been party to this discussion about the possibility that she might be free-born. But Parmeno, with his jaundiced view of Thais, would in all probability dismiss her remarks here as mere embellishment, designed to get Phaedria to comply with her request (150-2) that he give place to Thraso for a few days; cf. Brothers (1969) 314. Alternatively, if he *did* take

her remarks here seriously, that would add weight to his protestations to Chaerea (378) that the suggestion he had just made to him was only a joke.

115 **from Sunium:** It is easy to believe that this famous promontory at the extreme south-eastern tip of Attica would have been a frequent hunting-ground for pirates.

119 **my friend:** As a non-Athenian, unmarried woman living independently, Thais would need a male to look after her interests, just as Chrysis is under Demeas' protection in Men.'s *The Girl from Samos* (25). Now that her unnamed friend has died and she is alone again (147-8), Thais' chief need is to find other friends (149) and acquire a patron (770). At Athens this patron would have to be an Athenian citizen; hence her present interest in Chremes (203-5), though it is Phaedria's father who eventually fulfils the role (1039-40). (Phaedria would be too young, too poor and, with his father still alive, too lacking in influence for the part, and the wealthy Thraso is ineligible, because he too is a foreigner (*peregrinus*, 759)).

122 **content with just one man:** *Meretrices* are not normally 'one-man girls', and Thais, for all her good points, is not so in this play; indeed, the arrangement worked out at the end reinforces this view.

123 **a large part:** Unless Parmeno is exaggerating wildly here, we have evidence of the continuing cost to Phaedria of maintaining his relationship with Thais, quite apart from the expense of the Ethiopian slave girl and the eunuch (see 79-80n., 163-4n., 169n.). The whole matter may have been more evident in the Greek original; cf. Don.'s statement at 1001 that Men. explained more clearly the long-standing hostility of the old man to the *meretrix*.

125-6 **a captain ... set off for Caria:** Thraso, who is referred to here, is pictured as a mercenary fighting in one of the wars of Alexander the Great's successor generals in the late fourth and early third centuries BC. These generals were fighting for a share of Alexander's empire, and in several cases founded dynasties (cf. Thraso's talk of "the king" 397ff.). Caria, in south-west Asia Minor, was the frequent scene of such conflicts; it is one of the places where Moschion, were it not for his love for Plangon, would have chosen to serve as a soldier in Men.'s *The Girl from Samos* (628-9). Again, such details may have meant little to Ter.'s audience, apart from preserving in their eyes the authenticity of the play's Greek setting.

Thais is careful to say that Thraso fell in love with her, not she with him. Her dealings with him are business-like and practical, especially since the recovery of her 'sister' is involved.

130 *amabo:* "Please", lit. "I shall love you", often, as here, with an imperative. In Ter. the word is used exclusively by female characters (though in Plautus it is occasionally spoken by men). Of the eleven occurrences in Ter., eight are in *Eu.*, two spoken by Thais (here and at 150) and the others by Pythias (534, 537, 663, 674, 838, 915). See Martin 142.

132 **had a good figure:** Lit. "with a handsome appearance" (*forma ... honesta*). The adjective *honestus* is used to refer to physical beauty five times in Ter. - of Pamphila here and at 230, of Chaerea at 474 and 682, and of Glycerium at *An.* 123. On every occasion except *Eu.* 474 it is used with the nouns *forma* or *facies* ("appearance") in a set phrase, and at *An.* 123 and *Eu.* 682 it is coupled with another adjective, *liberalis* "gentlemanly / ladylike", which is itself sometimes used alone with the nouns (cf. *liberali facie*, 473). Both adjectives carry connotations of moral character and of status

as well as of physical appearance, and are used to describe persons who will eventually be found to be free-born. The underlying idea is that each person has an appearance corresponding to his or her (true) character and rank, and the use of this phrase to describe Pamphila here would be another pointer to the audience (cf. 110n.) of her true status.

133   **was a skilled musician:** Lit. "knew how to play the lyre (*fides*)"; cf. references to her as a "music-girl" (lit. "female lyre-player", *fidicina*), 457 and 985. Lyre-playing is a frequent accomplishment of young girls, especially slaves and 'apprentice *meretrices*', in this type of play; cf. the music-girl (*fidicina* again) loved by (another) Phaedria (*Ph.* 109) and Palaestra's attendance at a music-school (*ludus fidicinius*) (Plautus, *The Rope* 43).

134   **put her up for sale ... and sold her:** A fragment quoted from Men. by the first- / second-century AD grammarian Ammonius (but without naming the play) is tentatively suggested by Körte (II 209, fr. 658) as the possible original for these words:

ἀπεκήρυξεν αὐτὴν ἀγαγών.

"He took her and offered her for sale."

     by a stroke of luck: As always in these plots, coincidence is everything.

144   **No, nothing more:** This brief interchange adds a further important piece of information about Pamphila - that she is still a virgin. Within the context of the play, it is essential that she should be so for two reasons. Firstly, it is vital for the success of Thais' plan to restore her to her family and thereby acquire friends and a patron for herself. No self-respecting Athenian would accept a girl back into his household as a family member if she had lost her virginity, and this explains Thais' anger and frustration when she discovers that Chaerea has raped the girl (868-70: "You've turned my plans so upside down that I can't hand her back to her family"). Secondly, the girl herself must be a virgin if she is to achieve a suitable marriage at the end of the play when she is found to be free-born. (In Pamphila's case the fact that Chaerea rapes her is not an impediment to such a marriage in the way that any other earlier loss of virginity would have been, because it is the rapist himself, a free-born Athenian, who marries her; cf. the similar case of Pamphilus and Glycerium in *An.*)

149   **by doing an act of kindness:** Lit. "by a *beneficium*". The Latin word means 'an act tending to the benefit of another' (*OLD*), and this act can be thought of as being bestowed or received. Here Thais will be *bestowing* a *beneficium* on Pamphila's family by restoring her to them, and she will thus have the right to expect something - their friendship and support - in return; cf. *Ad.* 72-3: "The person you attach to yourself by a *beneficium* ... is eager to make you an equal return". Elsewhere, however, Thais talks (871) of *receiving* a *beneficium* for herself by the selfsame act of reuniting Pamphila with her family.

155-7   **"A little girl was kidnapped ... "** : Phaedria's mocking reprise of Thais' earlier words also acts as a recapitulation of the salient facts for the benefit of the audience.

162   *cedo*: This 2nd person sing. imperative is formed from the particle *ce* (the same as is used enclitically in pronouns like *hic*) and the root of *dare* "to give". Its plural, *cette*, is found in Plautus, but not in Ter. The basic meaning "give me" (cf. 776n.) is rarer in Ter. than the derivative one "tell me" (here and at 950).

163-4   **Have you ever known a time ... :** Further evidence of the financial cost to Phaedria of his relationship with Thais.

169   **twenty minae for them both:** As is his custom, Ter. retains the Greek currency units.
There were 100 drachmas to the *mina*, and 60 *minae* to the talent.

In this type of comedy only round numbers are used in these situations, and so there
is probably little to be gained in comparing prices. Thus 20 minae is the sum mentioned
for a girl in *Ad.* (191) and Plautus' *Pseudolus* (52), 30 in *Ph.* (557) and Plautus' *The
Rope* (45), and 40 in Plautus' *Epidicus* (52). However, one point may be significant -
that 20 minae for *both* the Ethiopian *and* the eunuch accordingly seems cheap, and this
fits with remarks elsewhere that they were unimpressive gifts (cf. Phaedria at 214,
where he seems to think his presents need 'talking up', and Parmeno at 231, where he
calls the eunuch "decrepit"). We should not, of course, take seriously Thraso's estimate
at 471 of just three minae for the Ethiopian alone.

A discrepancy arises later in the play, where Parmeno tells Phaedria's father that 20
minae was the cost of the eunuch, not of the eunuch *and* the Ethiopian (see 984n.).
minas: Latin tended to insert vowels (usually *i* or *u*) into words borrowed from Greek
which contained combinations of consonants which the Romans found hard to
pronounce. Hence *mina* for Greek *mnā* (μνᾱ) here; cf. *techina* for *technē* (τέχνη) 718,
drachuma for *drachmē* (δραχμή) *Hau.* 601 etc.

171   ***quid istic ... ?:*** Lit. "What (is to be said) in this matter of yours?" In this expression of
resigned acceptance *istic* is an adverb, and some such phrase as *dicendum est* is to be
supplied (*OLD, istic,* 2a).

174   **I'll do as you say:** Thais' apparent willingness to give way to Phaedria could be
regarded as genuine, but, as Parmeno sees (178), is more likely to be a ploy designed to
get him to agree to her request.

178   **He's wavering ... :** A good example of an aside delivered primarily for the benefit of
the audience. Parmeno's remark alerts them to Phaedria's imminent climb-down
(which they can then observe more closely), and is all the more pointed since the last
time he spoke (154) he was congratulating his young master on standing up to Thais at
long last.

187   **I'll go to the country:** The family's country estate or farm (*rus,* 519, 971; *villa,* 633,
641) features on a number of occasions in this type of play. It is a dramatically
convenient place to which characters can retire (as here) or be sent on a wild goose
chase to get them out of the way (as Demea, *Ad.* 400ff.). The estate, and especially its
mill, are often also the threatened places of punishment for slaves (*An.* 199, *Ph.* 249-
50).

189ff. **Parmeno, make sure ... :** This order is repeated at 207 with the addition of "as I told
you earlier" to explain the repetition. There are several unusual features in the passage
between the almost identical orders (see 191n., 203-5n., 206n.), and these, when taken
together, provide good reason for believing that Ter. may have written it himself, rather
than taken it from his Greek original. For full details, see Brothers (1969). The two
new vital pieces of information contained in the passage are Thais' affirmation of the
genuine nature of her story and of her feelings for Phaedria (199-201) and what she says
about Chremes (203-5). These are precisely the kind of thing that could have been
contained in a divine prologue which Ter. dispensed with (if, of course, such a prologue
existed in Men.'s play - see Introduction pp. 25-6).

One unusual (though by no means unparalleled) feature is that there is no indication
of when Parmeno, or for that matter Phaedria, leaves the stage. In the absence of any

implicit stage direction, it is best to assume that Parmeno leaves immediately after he has replied "Certainly" to his master's instruction. He presumably retires into Phaedria's father's house.

191 **Is there anything else you want?** This leave-taking formula is usually employed by someone who is about to, or intending to, leave the stage - rather like the gentleman's gentleman's "Will that be all, Sir?" - and that is how it is employed elsewhere in Ter. (341, 363, *Ph.* 151, 458, *Hec.* 272, *Ad.* 247, 432). On several of these occasions Don. makes such comments as "The words of someone who is leaving" (*Hec.* 272, *discedentis verbum*) or "People who are leaving customarily employ this phrase" (*Ad.* 247, *hoc uti dicto discedentes solent*). Here, however, the words are spoken by the person who is intending to remain *to* the person who is about to leave. Furthermore, that other person interprets the phrase literally and replies to it (as happens also at *Ad.* 247).

192-6 **Only that ... :** Phaedria's final unmanly lovesick entreaty before he leaves completes the picture of the 'elegiac' lover; see 46ff. n.

Phaedria must leave the stage as soon as he has finished speaking at 196 - he cannot remain to hear Thais' expression of her feelings at 199-201. Since he re-enters with Parmeno at 207, it may safely be assumed that he goes into his father's house.

In Men.'s original Phaedria may have left for the country at this point - see the introductory note to Act Two Scene One. If the remainder of the scene has been written in by Ter., then Thais, too, must have left the stage at about this point in Men.'s play, and gone back into her house, possibly after speaking a short monologue or an exit-line. The stage will thus have been left empty; see 206n.

196 **be my heart:** A striking phrase; cf. Barsby (1999a) 8-10.

197ff. **Oh, dear! ... :** Thais' speech is a good example of a monologue or soliloquy, another prominent feature of this type of comedy. Other notable examples in *Eu.* are provided by Gnatho (232-69), Chremes (507-30), Antipho (549-56), Chaerea (549-56), Dorias (615-28) and Phaedria (629-42). Sometimes, as here, it is a 'pure' monologue, but at other times it is put to further use dramatically by being commented on by another character, as Gnatho's is by Parmeno (254, 265).

198 **from the characters of other women:** A clear hint that Thais is not like those others.

199-201 **But, really ... :** Thais vouches for the truth of her story about Pamphila (and thus for the genuineness of her need to get Phaedria to give place to Thraso), and then gives voice to her real fondness for Phaedria. She is alone on stage, with nobody else present whom she needs to impress and convince; the audience are therefore assured that she is sincere on both counts, and the picture of her as a 'kindly' *meretrix*, already perhaps hinted at (81-2), is now established.

Thais reinforces her words by the use of the oath *pol* (199; lit. "by Pollux", here translated "really"). Perhaps significantly, she used the same oath earlier (96) when she was attempting to reassure Phaedria to his face about her feelings for him. It is an oath employed predominantly by women; of the 14 occasions when it is used in *Eu.*, it is only once spoken by a man - Chaerea at 606 (*pace* McGlynn II 28, who confuses the names Dorias and Dorus).

203-5 **I've got high hopes ... :** The obvious implication of these lines is that Thais' enquiries have led her to this brother (Chremes), but that she has not yet met him and has therefore arranged to see him at her house that day. But when Chremes arrives (507), it quickly becomes clear (512-30) that he has already met her on a previous occasion and is now on his way to his *second* meeting with her. The various attempts to resolve this inconsistency - such as that the word here translated "I've ... found" (*repperisse*, 204) implies "I've found *and seen*" (Knoche 252ff., Webster (1960) 72) or that the first meeting can be assumed to take place behind the scenes between 206 and 507 (Marouzeau I 259 n. 1) - are not convincing; see further Brothers (1969) 318.

It should be noted that Chremes is "of very respectable family", a good sign for Pamphila's future prospects (and for Thais too).

206 **I'll go inside ... :** An obvious exit-line. In fact, Thais does not wait for Chremes' arrival, but goes to dinner with Thraso, leaving instructions (passed on by Pythias 531-7) that he be asked to come back the next day, or failing that to await her return, or as a last resort to join her at Thraso's house (which is what in fact happens).

With Thais' departure the stage is left empty, though there will have been no pause in Ter.'s play before Phaedria and Parmeno re-enter (see Introduction p. 39). However, it could be that, if Ter. is faithfully following his original at this point (something which we have seen is at least doubtful), the first act-division and choral interlude occurred here in Men.'s *The Eunuch*. The stage is again left empty at 390/1, 538/9, 614/5, 816/7 and 922/3. It is possible that the other act-divisions / choral interludes in Men. followed 390, 614 and 816 of our play.

ACT TWO SCENE ONE

Phaedria re-enters with Parmeno from his father's house, and leaves for the country in deference to Thais' wishes, after first repeating his instructions to his slave. He is further characterized through the obsessive anxiousness of his orders, his doubts about his own ability to stay away for the required length of time, and his unconvincing attempt to steel himself to do so. A short monologue by Parmeno, which follows Phaedria's departure, highlights the great change which love has produced in his young master, and prepares the audience for the arrival of Gnatho, Thraso's odious henchman, who is bringing along Pamphila for Thais.

Barsby (1999) 120-1 makes the attractive suggestion that in Men.'s *The Eunuch* the scene consisted solely of a monologue by 'Parmeno', with 'Phaedria' having left for the country at a point equivalent to 196.

207 **As I told you earlier:** See 189ff. n. ·

209 **what a question!:** Parmeno's exasperated outburst draws attention to Phaedria's anxious fussing over his instructions.

211 **to make a loss ...** *I'm* **a total loss:** An attempt to capture in translation a punning repetition of the Latin verb *pereo*. It can mean both 'to be squandered, go to waste' and 'to pine away, die (from an emotion); to be madly in love' (*OLD, pereo*, 2 and 4).

214 **Use your eloquence ... :** Obviously, the eunuch and the Ethiopian slave girl are not good enough gifts to 'speak for themselves', and will require some smart talking by Parmeno to appear acceptable. This indication of their somewhat second-rate nature is reinforced by Parmeno's fear that he will "make a poor showing" with the "decrepit" eunuch (230-1); cf. 169n.

217-8 **Do you think ...?:** As at 50-6, Phaedria is only too aware of his own failings (cf. also his talk of his own "feeble attitude", 222). Coming so soon after his firm "I'll go to the country and stay there" (216), this sign of weakness ensures that the audience will see through his final display of resolution before he leaves ("My mind's made up", 224).

224 *to the audience's left*: See Introduction p. 10; by convention it is this exit into the 'wings' which leads to the country and / or the harbour. The exit to the audience's right conventionally leads to the centre of town, and it is from this side that Gnatho will enter at 232; he is coming from Thraso's house, which is presumed to be in the town (Athens).

225-7 **Good god!** ... : Parmeno's description of the change that has come over Phaedria illustrates the helplessness of a young man when confronted with the power of love; see Introduction p. 29. Phaedria is caught up in something he cannot control, and therefore deserves the audience's sympathy.

228 **But who's that ... ?:** The announcement of the approach of a new character, this time from the wings, is much more elaborate than the one preceding Thais' arrival from her house at 79. Gnatho is named, his role and position are specified, and the purpose of his arrival is made clear.

228-9 **Gnatho, the captain's sponger:** Since Gnatho has been imported from Men.'s *The Toady*, it follows that in Men.'s *The Eunuch* the arrival of someone else (probably the rival's henchman or slave) must have been anticipated here. Don., who makes hardly any mention of the two imported characters when they are talked of in the prologue, does comment here: "These [words] are not in Menander, in his *The Eunuch*, as he himself admitted [25], but have been transferred from *The Toady.*"

230 **What a beautiful creature!:** Lit. "with a handsome appearance" (*facie ... honesta*); see 132n.

ACT TWO SCENE TWO

Gnatho enters and, after a long monologue and some banter with Parmeno, delivers Pamphila and her maid to Thais' house and invites Thais to dinner at Thraso's. After he has left, Parmeno sees Phaedria's brother Chaerea approaching.

This scene is the first of the seven in the play to feature one or both of the characters introduced by Ter. from Men.'s *The Toady*. Like all the others, it is a lively and entertaining scene, with Gnatho's amusing monologue explaining his way of life and his 'philosophy' of sponging, and, following that, some spirited exchanges between him and Parmeno.

Most of the scene does not contribute to the development of the plot. Gnatho's monologue, which accounts for over half its length (232-64, with asides by Parmeno at 254 and 265), has nothing to do with the plot at all, and probably comes straight from *The Toady* (cf. 238n.). The 25 lines of banter which follow advance the plot in only two particulars, the delivery of Pamphila to Thais' house and the invitation to Thais to dine at Thraso's. In the corresponding scene in Men.'s *The Eunuch*, it is probable that the rival (or, more likely, his henchman or slave) delivered the girl to the *hetaira*'s house and mentioned the dinner invitation, while being observed by the Parmeno character; he may also have delivered a (much shorter) monologue and conversed with 'Parmeno'. It is quite possible that the rival was also a soldier and his henchman also a toady in the original, though, if so, both will have been less colourful and less boldly drawn characters than the ones Ter. chose to substitute from Men.'s *The Toady*. See Introduction p. 23.

Gnatho is pictured as self-satisfied (241-2), arrogant (247), rude and contemptuous of others (239) - a character the audience can cheerfully love to hate. For his character in general, see Introduction pp. 35-6. At the same time we see another side of Parmeno, who is shown to be loyal, quick-witted, and well able to hold his own against Gnatho in defence of Phaedria.

235 **had squandered:** Lit. "had licked right up", a striking phrase. The verb used, *abligurrio*, appears in its simple form, *ligurrio*, at 936, where it apparently refers to the dainty table manners of *meretrices* when they are eating out with their lovers. According to Eugr. (Don. III i 103), the addition of the prefix *ab-* implies eating up everything, presumably with rather fewer connotations of daintiness.

236 **covered in ... his years:** Lit. "overgrown with rags and years", not only a vivid metaphor and a bold zeugma, but also an effective jingle in the Latin (*pannis annisque obsitum*). A simpler version of the phrase, *pannis obsita*, is used of a scruffy servant girl at *Hau.* 294.

237 **em:** This interjection draws attention to something ("Look", "Here / there you are"), and occurs four times in *Eu.* It can be followed by an exclamatory clause (as here), by an accusative (*em alterum* 459) often with an ethic dative (*em eunuchum tibi* 472), absolutely (*em ad sinisteram* 835), or with an imperative. See McGlynn I 161-2, Luck 47-69.

238 **all my friends ... abandoned me:** Two lines preserved by the first-century AD grammarian Erotianus may provide the original of this sentence (Körte I 118, fr.5; Arnott (1996) 196-7, fr. 9):

ἀλλ' οὐδὲ γεννήτην δύναμ' εὑρεῖν οὐδένα
ὄντων τοσούτων, ἀλλ' ἀπείλημμαι μόνος.

"But I can't find a relative, when I have so many,
but I've been cut off all alone."

Erotianus actually ascribes the lines to *The Toady* of Philemon (a writer of New Comedies who lived from *c.* 361 to 262 BC). However, as Arnott says, a play of that name is nowhere else attributed to him, and Philemon may have been mistakenly put for Menander; but this is no more than a possibility.

244-5 **I can't play ... being knocked about:** Ter.'s language here recalls the words of the parasite Ergasilus in Plautus' *The Prisoners* (*Captivi*) 469-77, who is lamenting the demise of this 'old-fashioned' parasitic activity (cf. Gnatho's words at 246). Ergasilus, too, employs the word *ridiculus* (here translated "buffoon"), and, where Ter. has *plagas pati* ("stand being knocked about", lit. "suffer blows"), he uses the noun *plagipatidas* ("sons of blow-sufferers", 472) - a term sometimes also used of slaves. Cf. also *The Prisoners* 88-90 (Ergasilus again).

247 **I was the first ... :** Gnatho's boast is not true, in either a Terentian or a Menandrian context, though this irony - with its implications for Gnatho's character - may well have been lost on many in Ter.'s audience. This view of the parasite's craft is found as far back as Greek Old Comedy. Eupolis (who produced his first play in 429 BC) has a chorus of flatterers in his play of that name say: "And if the rich fellow chances to say something, I praise it exceedingly and am dumbstruck, pretending to delight in what he says. Then we go off to dinner, one of us here, one there, to someone else's food, and there the flatterer has to give voice to lots of entertaining chatter straight away, or else he's carried out through the door." For another good example of this toadying art, see

Artotrogus in the opening scene of Plautus' *The Swaggering Soldier* (*Miles Gloriosus*) (1-78).

248ff. **There's a class of people ... :** The audience is here given a hint both of Thraso's character and of the way Gnatho will deal with him; thus they will better appreciate the scenes between them which follow later in the play.

252-3 **Someone says no ... everything they say:** Quoted by Cicero (*Amic.* 93) in illustration of a man "who changes to fit in not merely with another man's feelings and wishes, but also with his expression and his nod." Cf. 391-2n.

256-7 **all the delicatessen merchants ... :** The parasite's habitual preoccupation with food is well illustrated by Gnatho's cultivation of the various market traders.

264 **Gnathonists:** The closest parallel in philosophical terms for Gnatho's pompous *Gnathonici* is *Platonici* ("Platonists").

265 **someone else's food:** Never having to feed himself is the parasite's sole objective in life; cf. 1058-9n. and the Eupolis quotation, 247n.
why don't I ... ?: Lit. "Am I hesitating to / slow to ... ?", a set phrase; cf. 996 (tr. "I must lose no time in"), *Hau.* 410, 757 etc.

267 As it stands, the line will not scan. By parallels with the Latin accusative (266, 270), dative (188, 275) and ablative (545, 956) of Thais' name, its genitive must be *Thāidis*; this violates the metre, but is in all MSS. (*Thaidis* here is the only instance of the genitive, apart from two occurences in the Summary (*Periocha*), which is not by Ter., but much later.) Don. reports what seems to be a variant reading *Thainis* (in the forms *Thaiinis*, *Thaimis*, *Thanus* and *Thais* in his MSS), and several editors, including those of the Oxford text, have accepted this, with scansion *Thāinis*. But it is most unlikely that this unique genitive form would appear here, especially with the regular accusative *Thaidem* occurring one line previously and three lines later. More likely is the suggestion that a word such as *meretricis* ("of the courtesan") originally stood here, and that *Thaidis* crept in as an explanatory gloss on this, which eventually ousted the true word from the line.

269 *hisce*: Nom. pl.; this is the only occurence of the form in Ter., though there are several examples in Plautus, e. g. *The Prisoners* 35: *hisce autem inter sese hunc confinxerunt dolum* "these men have devised this ruse between themselves".

270 **Gnatho bestows ... :** A pompously elaborate and formal greeting, delivered with heavy sarcasm.

271 **What's your position?:** This is a conventional greeting "How are you?", "How's it going?" (lit. "What is being done?"); cf. Thraso's greeting to Thais, 456. But Parmeno cheekily interprets it literally by replying "I'm standing" (lit. "It is being stood"). He is well able to hold his own against Gnatho (and later Thraso) in wit, repartee and insult.

274 **How wrong he is!:** The conventions of the aside are really being exploited here. Gnatho's previous remark was intended as an aside, but it is overheard by Parmeno, who then makes an aside of his own in response to it.

276 **everything that goes up ... :** Lit. "All things have their reversal" - perhaps a hint that Thraso, whose fortunes are riding high at the moment, will eventually come to grief.

283-7 **Anyone you'd like ... ?:** In the absence of anything like stage directions, Gnatho's movements have to be inferred from such phrases as "Still standing here, Parmeno?" (286).

It is a common convention in this type of play that events taking place off stage can be telescoped into an impossibly short time; thus in the time it takes Parmeno to speak his words in 283-5 ("Just you let ... and getting nowhere") Gnatho has had time to go into Thais' house, introduce himself, deliver Pamphila and come out again.

285   *ne*: The affirmative particle "indeed", not the negative adverb and conjunction.

    faxo: The old Latin fut. indic., formed by adding *-s-* to the root of the verb. In Plautus half the examples are parts of *faxo* (*fac-s-o*), and in Ter. there are hardly any examples apart from these. The form occurs again at 663.

289   **But I can see ... :** Another good example of the announcement of a character's approach (cf. 79n.), though the new arrival (Chaerea) is not actually named until 308. The knowledge that he is in a hurry and looking for something (291) increases the audience's anticipation.

    Don. (I 329) implies that for Ter.'s *erilem filium* ("master's son") Men. had τρόφιμον (= Körte II 69, fr. 170); he makes similar comments at *An.* 602 (I 88) and *Ph.* 39 (II 359). The word τρόφιμος ("young master") certainly occurs in Greek New Comedy, e.g. in *The Arbitration* (Ἐπιτρέποντες, *Epitrepontes*) (Körte I, 19, l. 201; Arnott (1979) 428, l. 377) and *The Rape of the Locks* (Περικειρομένη, *Perikeiromene*) (Körte I 49, l. 74; Arnott (1996) 386, l. 264).

290   **Piraeus:** The port of Athens; the name may have been familiar to many of Ter.'s audience.

    public guard duty: Chaerea is clearly an *ephebus* (ἐφηβός); the term "in 4th cent. BC Athens ... came to have a special paramilitary sense, boys who in their eighteenth year had entered a two-year period of military training. In the first year they underwent, in barracks in Piraeus, training by *paidotribai* (physical trainers) and technical weaponry training ... In the second year they served at the frontier posts of Attica ..." (*OCD³*, 527). Ter. does not use the technical term *ephebus* here, though he does use it twice elsewhere (824, *An.* 51) purely to denote age - as does Plautus (*The Merchant* (*Mercator*) 40, 61).

291   *from the audience's right*: Since Parmeno has said (290) that Chaerea is currently on duty at the Piraeus, it would be natural to envisage him entering from the audience's left (cf. Introduction p. 10 and 224n.). But until he was waylaid (302), he was closely following Pamphila (328), who had entered with Gnatho from the right (cf. 224n.). He, too, must therefore come on from the right; perhaps we are to imagine that the arrangements he was making for the dinner party with his friends (539-41, 607-8) had taken him into town.

ACT TWO SCENE THREE

Chaerea enters and tells how he has fallen in love with Pamphila at first sight, but has lost track of her when he was delayed; he asks Parmeno for help in getting to her. Parmeno explains where she has gone, and then jokingly suggests that Chaerea change places with the eunuch Phaedria is about to give Thais, and thus get into Thais' house. Chaerea takes the idea seriously and, despite Parmeno's protests, they both go inside to put the ruse into operation.

This whole 'Chaerea element' of the plot comes as a complete surprise - though it may have been mentioned in the prologue to Men.'s original, if there was one. The younger brother's existence has not even been hinted at until Parmeno's announcement at 289; but, when Chaerea explains his plight, the audience realize that there is going to be much more to the play than the straightforward triangle of Phaedria, Thais and Thraso. Moreover, by the end of the scene, when Chaerea takes up Parmeno's jocular suggestion about the eunuch, the significance of the play's title becomes clear to them. By contrast, the 'Phaedria element' now drops very much into the background, virtually until the closing scenes of the play, while attention is focussed on Chaerea's swiftly unfolding adventures. See further Introduction pp. 27-8.

Chaerea himself is totally different, both in his character and in his approach to love, from his brother, and this contrast, beautifully highlighted by Ter., provides one of the chief points of interest in the play. The closing lines of the scene (377-90) further characterize Parmeno. The audience get their first clear indication that he is not going to turn out to be the usual ever-enthusiastic schemer and successful operator. Instead he is appalled by Chaerea's eagerness to act on his joking suggestion about the eunuch, and only agrees to go along with it (388-9) under orders and after receiving assurances that he will not be blamed if things go wrong. See Introduction pp. 32-3.

292ff. **Damn!:** Chaerea's opening monologue quickly puts the bare bones of the new development before the audience, just as Parmeno's aside which follows (297-301) provides a thumb-nail sketch of the new arrival for the audience's benefit.
occidi: This one-word line is extrametrical; there is only one other such example in Ter. (*Ph.* 485).

293   **The girl's ... I'm lost too:** Lit. "The girl is nowhere and neither am I."

299   **Unlucky old master!:** Because Chaerea's love-affair will involve his father in more expense.

302   **that old fellow:** Archidemides (327). Ter.'s use of the rare word *senius* here, instead of the more usual *senex*, seems to stress his senility and dotage.

307   *hem!*: Luck 13 calls this common exclamation of surprise "the expression of a person who has not heard correctly or who acts as if he has not heard correctly"; he argues that the word has an interrogative force and regularly prints *hem?*. However, R. H. Martin, in his commentary on *Ad.* (Cambridge (1976) 139) says that "What!" is often a more appropriate translation than "What?", and that the word "most commonly expresses astonishment at the unexpected, whether pleasant or unpleasant". Cf. 636, 647 etc.

308ff. **you often used to promise me ... :** An interesting picture of life within the household, and of the young Chaerea's relations with his *paedagogus* (cf. 57n.).

310   **your room:** The diminutive *cellula* ("small room", "cell"), which Ter. uses here, is also used of a slave's accommodation at Sen. *Con.* 7. 6. 8.

311   *sis*: *si vis* ("please", lit. "if you will"); cf.756, 799.

313ff. **whose mothers ... :** An instructive picture of the criteria for female beauty, probably taken over by Ter. from Men. But at least some of the following description applied to Roman women too (cf. 314n.).

314   **flat chests:** Lit. "with their chests bound". There are several references in Latin literature to the binding of the breasts with a band (*fascia*), e.g. Prop. 4. 9. 49, Mart. 11. 104. 7, Tac. *Ann.* 15. 57.

315   **too much on the chubby side:** The comparative adjective used here, *habitior*, refers to what we should call an 'ample' figure; it recalls Gnatho's use of the related noun *habitudo* ("sleekness") of his own well-nourished frame (242).

316 **a good figure:** The Latin phrase (*bona...natura*) refers here not to character or temperament, but to 'the physical characteristics, size, shape, structure, etc., of a person or thing; (esp. as determined by natural causes)' (*OLD, natura*, 8).

318 **a natural colour ... juicy figure:** Presumably Pamphila is healthily tanned and not artificially pale from being kept indoors and from the use of make-up.

sixteen: Phanium in *Ph.* is even younger, since it is said there that Chremes seduced her mother "about fifteen years ago" (1017). Such young ages would not have seemed so strange to ancient audiences as they do to us, since girls normally married in their mid-teens; Ischomachus' young wife in Xenophon's *Oeconomicus* was "not yet fifteen years old" (7. 5) when he married her.

At this point Chaerea can only be guessing at Pamphila's age, but sixteen is later confirmed by Chremes (526).

320 **mea nil refert:** In the impersonal verb *refert*, the precise origin of which is disputed, *re-* came to be regarded as the abl. sing. of *res*, and can be constructed with the fem. abl. sing. of the personal pronoun, here *mea*, "it is of importance to me" (*OLD, refert*, 1b). *nil* is an internal acc. used with adverbial force "not at all" (*OLD, nihil*, 11).

324 **as I came along:** 292ff.

334 **some ghastly stroke of fate:** Lit. "like a *monstrum*". A *monstrum* is 'an unnatural thing or event regarded as a portent', 'an awful or monstrous thing, event, etc. (here)', 'a monstrous or horrible creature', 'a person of extreme wickedness' (696), or 'a monstrous act, horror, atrocity' (656) (*OLD*).

340 **one of my supporters:** The word used, *advocatus*, does not have the legal significance of our word 'advocate', but denotes a friend called in to give support and advice to someone faced with legal proceedings. It can also refer to witnesses to a formal contract (as when Micio pretends that he has been asked to witness the marriage contract between a friend of his and Sostrata's daughter Pamphila, *Ad.* 646, 677), or to supporters of a more informal kind in a rather more violent confrontation (such as those whom Chremes is eager to enlist against Thraso, 764).

341 **an hour went by:** Exaggeration by the over-excited Chaerea, as is "from miles away" (335) and the description of Archidemides (336); cf. "while they're getting things on the move, while they're trying to get going, a year's gone by" (*Hau.* 240). But some delay is necessary in order for the events of the previous scene to be completed before Chaerea's arrival.

347 **and a servant-girl:** The only indication that a maid accompanied Pamphila to Thais' house (cf. the stage direction in the translation at the end of Act Two Scene One). If she is Pamphila's own maid, Pamphila herself is of some wealth and status; and, as a new arrival, the maid will presumably be numbered among the "few new ones" left behind by Thais when she goes to dinner with Thraso (581-2). Alternatively she may not be Pamphila's, but one of Thais' maids, sent to escort Pamphila on the way.

353 **Thraso:** The first time Phaedria's rival is named.

354 **a tough role:** The same metaphor from the theatre (*duras ... partis*) is used by Ter. at *Hau.* 402; *partis* ("role") also appears elsewhere in its literal theatrical sense (*Hau.* 1, 10; *Ph.* 27).

356-7 **that wretched-looking fellow he bought yesterday:** It is strange that Chaerea, who is meant to be away on guard duty (290), not only knows about this purchase, made only the day before, but has also evidently seen the eunuch already, since he knows what he looks like. It seems that Ter. (or Men.) has slipped up here - though the audience would hardly have time to notice the inconsistency.

359 **I didn't know ... :** This again seems odd, though Parmeno's statement that Thais has not been living next door for very long, and Chaerea's supposed absence in Piraeus, help to explain his ignorance. In fact, occupants of adjacent houses being fairly new neighbours is a not uncommon situation, cf. Chremes and Menedemus (*Hau.* 53ff.), and Micio and Sostrata (*Ad.* 649).

360 **Hey, though, tell me ... :** Even at the time when he is raving about Pamphila, Chaerea, with his great interest in female beauty, can find time to ask about Thais' good looks.

363 **Will that be all?:** Cf. 191n. At this juncture Parmeno clearly does not intend to deal with Chaerea's problem immediately; but his innocent reply to Chaerea's ensuing question soon changes that.

369 **What if *you* ... ?:** In view of his later protest (378) that he was only joking, Parmeno's remark here is a mere flight of fancy, or at the very least a suggestion made on the spur of the moment without any thought for the consequences.

374 **none of the women there know you:** This fact is crucial to the execution of the plan, as is the fact that Chaerea has never met Thais (360). These points, together with Thais' only recent arrival next door and Chaerea's guard duty, are all part of a carefully established set of circumstances which make it plausible that Chaerea can carry out his ruse successfully.

376 **Excellent idea!:** Lit. "You have spoken beautifully." All MSS except for the second hand in D give the syncopated form of the word for "you have spoken", *dixti*. But this would make the line an isolated trochaic septenarius in the middle of a long sequence of iambic octonarii (367-90). It is preferable to follow Umpfenbach's acceptance of D², which has the unsyncopated form *dixisti*. This has the effect of making the line an iambic octonarius like the others. Cf. 1017, and confusion in the MSS between the syncopated and unsyncopated forms of other verbs at 322 (*amisisti / amisti*) and 328 (*novistin / nostin*).

377 **Come on ... :** The string of imperatives in this line well illustrates Chaerea's youthful impetuosity.

378 **Oh, damn!:** The 'bungling' side to Parmeno's character immediately becomes apparent; see the introductory note to the scene.

381 **this will be a rod for my back:** Lit. "this bean will be threshed on me", presumably a proverbial expression. The Elder Pliny uses the same verb (*cudere*) of threshing beans in a literal sense (*Nat.* 18. 257).

382-7 **Is it wrong ... ?** Chaerea demonstrates his quick thinking by the speed with which he can produce arguments to counter Parmeno's worries - as he does later to reassure Thais (872-5).

383 **harridans:** Lit. "crosses", the instruments of execution. This striking application of the word to people occurs elsewhere (Plautus, *The Pot of Gold* (*Aulularia*) 522; *The Persian* 795).

386 **bamboozle my father:** To those of the audience who knew their plays, this remark would raise a smile, since the deception of fathers by their sons is a frequent motif in this type of play; see Introduction p. 4.

390 **I'll never shirk ... :** All MSS agree in ascribing the words "I'll never shirk the responsibility. Follow me." to Parmeno and "Heaven grant success!" to Chaerea; but

editors are equally agreed that this is wrong. The error, which must have occurred very early in the MS tradition, presumably arose from the assumption that Parmeno must be the 'cunning' slave who normally takes responsibility for plans, tricks and escapades, while his young master weakly follows behind hoping and praying for success. But, as has been seen, in this play the roles are virtually reversed, with Chaerea eager to adopt a very reluctant Parmeno's light-hearted suggestion.

At the end of this scene the stage is left empty. It is probable that the second choral interlude occurred at this place in Men.'s *The Eunuch* (but with the action resuming at a point corresponding to 454, not 391 - see the introductory note to the next scene.

ACT THREE SCENE ONE

Thraso arrives, accompanied by Gnatho, to take Thais to his house for dinner. Parmeno comes out again, and listens to and comments on their conversation.

This second scene involving characters from Men.'s *The Toady* (this time both of them) does not advance the plot at all. The central section (395-433, over half its length) has, apart from two asides by Parmeno (418-9, 431), nothing to do with *The Eunuch* at all. It almost certainly comes straight from *The Toady*, since two fragments of that play exist which seem either to come from it (420ff. n.) or to refer to it (498n.). Moreover, this central section shows Gnatho practising on Thraso the 'new' toady's art which he expounded in 232-64, and we have seen that 232-64 also came from *The Toady* (see the introductory note to Act Two Scene Two).

The *Toady* section of this scene is tied into the plot of *The Eunuch* by the first five and the last twenty lines. At the start (391-5) Thraso asks Gnatho what reception his gifts for Thais have received, and Parmeno comes out of his master's house to see if the time is right to take Chaerea (dressed as the eunuch) and the Ethiopian slave girl to Thais' house (see 394n.). In the final twenty lines (434-53) Gnatho advises Thraso on how to pursue his relationship with Thais in the light of the existence of Phaedria as a rival - and it is significant that Gnatho's role and attitude are here markedly different from what they have been in the central *Toady* section (see 434ff. n.).

It is likely that no corresponding scene existed in Men.'s *The Eunuch*. The departure of 'Chaerea' and 'Parmeno' will have been followed immediately by the entrance of the rival (probably without his henchman / slave) to see what reception his gifts have had and to take Thais to supper at his house - see the introductory note to Act Three Scene Two.

Thraso, the only example of the 'swaggering soldier' (*miles gloriosus*) in Ter., is in some ways not typical of his type as seen, for example, in Plautus. For his character in general, see Introduction pp. 34-5.

391-2 **Is Thais ... ?:** A good example of two characters entering part-way through a conversation - see the introductory note to Act One Scene One.

Cicero (*Amic.* 98; cf. 252-3n.) quotes this exchange to illustrate the "toadyism of parasites in comedies" (*parasitorum in comoediis assentatio*). He points out that for *ingentis* (here translated "enormously") it would have been enough to answer *magnas* ("greatly"), but that the flatterer always exaggerates.

394 **I'm coming out ... :** Parmeno's re-emergence so early in the scene leaves him awkwardly standing about listening to Thraso and Gnatho, and later Thais, for the

whole of this scene and the start of the next - 66 lines in all - until he approaches Thais at 461. During this time his sole contribution is four asides (418-9, 431, 457-8, 459-60). *hoc*: The archaic spelling of the adverb *huc* "to this place"; cf. 501.

397 **the king:** One of Alexander the Great's successor Hellenistic monarchs; cf. 125-6n. Another such king is mentioned at *Hau.* 117.

401-2 **regarded you ... as the apple of his eye:** Lit. "carried you in his eyes" (*in oculis gestare*), a proverbial expression in which the verb *ferre* seems to have been commoner than *gestare* used here. Cf. Cic. *Q. fr.* 3. 1. 9: *Balbum... in oculis fero*, lit. "I carry Balbus in my eyes".

405 **as if ... you know?:** Marouzeau (I 251-2) suggests that Thraso is here embarking on a quotation, but cannot complete it without Gnatho's help.

406 **get rid of all the troubles from his mind:** The Latin, *exspueret miseriam ex animo*, seems poetic, and could well be a quotation. The wording is recalled by Lucretius (2. 1041) *exspuere rationem ex animo* "to get rid of reason from the mind" (cf. 6. 68).

408 **a very particular king!:** Gnatho's sarcasm is, as always, completely lost on Thraso. For *elegantem* "particular", "choosy", cf. 566, *Hau.* 1063.

413 **Indian elephants:** The Greeks first encountered war-elephants when Darius III of Persia used them in his army during his defeat by Alexander the Great at the battle of Gaugamela in 331 BC. Alexander himself never used them, but his successor Hellenistic monarchs did. The Romans first encountered them when King Pyrrhus of Epirus used Indian elephants in his invasion of Italy - to particularly good effect at the battles of Heraclea (280 BC) and Ausculum (279). Romans were further familiarized with the creatures by the Carthaginians' use of (African) elephants in the First and Second Punic Wars, and first used them themselves in the second Macedonian War against Philip V of Macedon, particularly at the concluding battle, Cynoscephalae, in 197 BC. See Scullard, H. H. (1974), *The Elephant in the Greek and Roman World* (London).

This is the only mention of elephants in Ter.; but in Plautus' *The Swaggering Soldier* 25ff. the soldier Pyrgopolynices, egged on by his sponger Artotrogus, boasts of how he attacked an elephant with his fist, and in his *Curculio* 424 the banker Lyco describes the seal on a letter as showing a soldier with a shield splitting an elephant in half with his sword.

415 **are you so fierce ... ?:** It may be that the adjective used here, *ferox*, through its connection with *ferus* (also "fierce", "wild") and its feminine *fera* ("wild animal", "beast"), might conceal some subtle joke. But it is better to take Thraso's quip as a fairly pathetic attempt at a joke - but one which is nevertheless extravagantly praised by Gnatho.

418 **Good god!:** Parmeno's aside, like his other one in this scene (431) and his two early in the next (457-8, 499-60), serves to highlight the unattractiveness of the characters of Thraso and Gnatho and the awfulness of Gnatho's toadying art.

420ff. **the Rhodian at a banquet:** It seems that in Men.'s *The Toady* the young man was a Cypriot, not a Rhodian. A line of that play, preserved by Plutarch (*Mor.* 57A = *How to tell a Flatterer from a Friend* 13), is obviously the original of *Eu.* 498 where Gnatho recalls this joke ("that story about the chap from Rhodes, whenever it comes to mind"). But Men.'s line (Körte I 118, fr. 3; Arnott (1997) 188-91, fr. 3) is about a Cypriot:

γελῶ τὸ πρὸς τὸν Κύπριον ἐννοούμενος.
"I'm laughing when I think of that joke against
the Cypriot."

The reason for the change is unclear.

424 a tart: The Latin word, *scortum*, is a coarse one. It occurs only twice in Ter. (here and at *Ad.* 965), but over 40 times in Plautus.

426 You're on the menu yourself ... : Lit. "You're a hare, and you're seeking the hors d' oeuvres?" The joke, like the origin of its victim, has been changed. Another fragment from *The Toady* (Körte I 119, fr. 8; Arnott (1997) 192-3, fr. 6) consists of the two words "Cypriot bullock" (βοῦς Κύπριος). The source of the words - the second-century AD paroemiographer Zenobius (2. 82), in a collection of proverbs known as the *Corpus Paroemiographorum* - says this is a Greek proverb equivalent to "you're a shit-eater", because Cypriot bullocks were said to eat dung. Thus in Men. the young Cypriot has his place of origin turned against him in a vulgar joke.

Ter.'s version (425-6) is still vulgar, but in a different - and to a Roman more intelligible - way. A *pulpamentum* is 'a small piece of meat, etc., used to start a meal' (*OLD*), and hare would often feature as a dish at table. The point is that the young Rhodian who is pursuing Thraso's lady-friend is sexually desirable himself. As Don. puts it (I 364): *quod in te habes, quaeris in altero* "you are seeking in another what you have in yourself". See Barsby (1999) 163-4.

For the homosexuality implicit here, cf. Thraso's observation about Chaerea when he appears in the eunuch's clothes (479): "Even if I was sober, I know what I could do to that eunuch, if I was pushed!"

428 I thought it was an old one: The saying seems to have been proverbial. The author of the *Historia Augusta* (*Lives of Carus, Carinus and Numerian* 13. 5) says: "In point of fact, comic writers often introduce soldiers in such a way that they make them repeatedly employ old sayings, for 'You're a hare and you're seeking the hors d' oeuvres?' is a saying of Livius Andronicus." The writer not only describes Thraso's insult here as a frequent motif, but ascribes the saying to Livius (Rome's first dramatist; see Introduction p. 6), not Ter. If the expression had been coined as long ago as Livius' time, it would add more point to the joke of Thraso claiming it as his own (and the audience would probably have been aware of its age and thus appreciated the joke better). But, on the other hand, it is unlikely that Ter. would have used exactly the same words as Livius, whose language was in any case more 'archaic' than Ter.'s; it is more probable that the *Historia Augusta* writer is mistaken in ascribing the words to Livius instead of Ter. However that may be, Ter. has substituted a Roman joke for a Greek one, and Thraso is trying to pass off a proverb as his own invention ("Well, it's mine", 429).

434ff. But listen ... : The closing lines of the scene return to the story of *The Eunuch*. The change in subject matter is accompanied by a marked change in Gnatho's role. He stops his toadying and becomes a serious adviser to Thraso in his pursuit of Thais - a *parasitus* of the 'fixer' sub-type, like Phormio in *Ph.* (see Introduction p. 36 and n. 170). Cf. Chaireas advising Sostratos on how to plan his quest for the hand of Knemon's daughter in Men.'s *The Bad-Tempered Man* (Δύσκολος, *Dyskolos*) 50ff., esp. 57-68.

435 her suspicions: Already voiced by Thais at 142-3.

440-1 immediately mention Pamphila's: The first time the girl has been named.

442-3 **call on Pamphila to sing:** According to Dorias' account of what happened at Thraso's dinner party (615ff.), he followed Gnatho's advice - though giving his orders ("Hey, boy, fetch Pamphila to entertain us here", 624-5) in response to the arrival of Chremes, not Phaedria.

442 *commissatum:* Supine of purpose with a verb of motion, like *cantatum* in 443. Cf. also 589, 600, 752, 860, 892.

446 **If she really loved me:** The pathetic tone of Thraso's words reveals the insecurity that underlies his bombast in the main part of the scene, and highlights the intensity of his feelings for Thais. These aspects of his character reappear in the closing scenes of the play (1026, 1053-5).

452-3 **Nonsense! ... :** Gnatho 'reverts to type' with this final piece of flattery.

ACT THREE SCENE TWO

Thais comes out of her house to be greeted by Thraso. Parmeno comes forward and gives Chaerea (disguised as the eunuch) and the Ethiopian slave girl to Thais. Gnatho is sent ahead to check on the preparations for the dinner party, and Thais takes her presents indoors. She then comes out again and sets off with Thraso, leaving instructions with Pythias, one of her maids, about what is to be done if Chremes should arrive in her absence.

This is the first of five scenes in the play which involve more than three speaking actors. Therefore, on the assumption (see Introduction p. 3) that Men. never wrote scenes with more than three such actors (except possibly for very small parts played by supernumeraries), we must suspect Terentian 'thickening' here. One obvious candidate for being added by Ter. (or for being a supernumerary or silent character in Men.) is Thais' maid Pythias, who only speaks two words (504), assenting to her mistress' instructions. The other addition is almost certainly Gnatho; his contributions to the scene are few (459, 472, 487-8, 497-9, 500) and for the most part short, and can be removed without difficulty (cf. 459n.). Moreover, the greater part of one of his two longer contributions (497-8) comes from Men.'s *The Toady*.

The equivalent scene in Men.'s *The Eunuch* probably showed the rival entering alone (or accompanied by a non-speaking slave or henchman), coming to the house of the *hetaira* to enquire about his gifts and to take her to dinner at his house. The two of them were interrupted by the arrival of the Phaedria character's slave bringing *his* presents, and, as Thais left for the rival's dinner, she gave her instructions either by addressing a maid standing silently by or by calling back into her house. To this original scene Ter. has added from Men.'s *The Toady* both the 'Gnatho' figure and details, based on the soldier there, to alter the characterization of the rival he found in *The Eunuch*.

457 **that music-girl:** See 133n.

457-8 **How beautifully put ... :** Since it is most likely that in Men.'s *The Eunuch* the slave did not enter until a point equivalent to 461 (where see n.), this aside by Parmeno, and his next one at 459-60, will have been written in by Ter.

Parmeno is disgusted by Thraso's lack of subtlety in immediately enquiring about his gifts after only the briefest of greetings.

459 **let's go off to supper:** Like a true sponger, Gnatho is eager to get to his free meal as soon as possible.

This comment, like most of the others made by Gnatho in this scene (472, 487-8 with Parmeno's reply 489-91, 497-8), can easily be detached without affecting its essentials in any way.

460 **You'd hardly say ... :** Lit. "Would you say he was born of man?"

461 **... and pretend I've just come out:** This must be the point at which the slave emerged in Men.'s *The Eunuch*. But in Ter.'s version he has been on stage since 394, and this line provides a bridge between the two different dramatic situations.

463 **You have been kind:** Don. I 371 is worried about what kindness Parmeno has done; but Thais' words are perhaps not meant to make too much sense. She is embarrassed and surprised to find Parmeno coming out when she is about to go off with Phaedria's rival (hence Ter.'s use of *ehem*, cf. 86n.). The situation in which she suddenly finds herself will please neither Thraso (cf. his remarks at 465), nor, when he finds out about it, Phaedria. In these awkward circumstances she has recourse to this hasty and ill-defined expression of gratitude.

469 **Time will tell:** Lit. "The situation will speak for itself".

471 **Worth three minae!:** Thraso's estimate is not to be taken seriously; cf. 169n.

472 **Dorus, where are you?:** The (real) eunuch's name is introduced casually and naturally.

473 **What gentlemanly looks:** For the Latin *liberali facie*, see 132n. The use of the adjective *liberalis* has a particular irony here, because the diguised Chaerea not only *looks* gentlemanly, but *is* a (free-born) gentleman (*liber*). Cf. "everything a young gentleman (*liberum ... adulescentulum*) should know" (477-8), where the irony is repeated.

474 **What do you say, Gnatho?:** Parmeno's remark to Gnatho must have been added by Ter. In Men.'s original the slave probably addressed the rival only.

476-7 **literature, gymnastics, music:** These are the traditional components in the education of young Athenians (not Romans). The phrase translated "athletics" is literally "on the wrestling ground" (*in palaestra*), where the exercises consisted of athletics, field events and gymnastics. The *palaestra* (παλαίστρα, *palaistra*) later became familiar to Romans as the open-air exercise area attached to Roman bathing complexes.

479 **Even if I was sober ... :** For Thraso's crude sentiments here, see 426n.

482-3 **talk of his battles and show you his scars:** In fact, Thraso is not a boastful soldier of this traditional type, like Pyrgopolynices in Plautus' *The Swaggering Soldier* (cf. Introduction pp. 34-5). Is the characterization given here an indication that the rival in Men.'s *The Eunuch* was a soldier in the traditional mould?

487-91 **Yes, I'm sure ... :** Cf. 459n.

491 **snatch the offerings from a funeral pyre:** Lit. "take food from the flames", which Don. I 379 says is a proverbial expression. The allusion is to the removal of offerings of food from a funeral pyre, obviously a most despicable act. Cf. the literal meaning of the word *bustirapus* ("snatcher-from-a-pyre"), which Plautus uses as a term of abuse (*Pseudolus* 361), and Catullus 59. 2-5: "Menenius' wife, whom you've often seen in cemeteries snatching food from the actual funeral pyre, when, chasing after a loaf that's fallen from the fire, she gets beaten up by an unshaven corpse burner."

494-5 **It isn't right ... :** A good illustration of Parmeno's ability to give as good as he gets. There is no indication in the text of when the slave leaves the stage, but it would be natural to assume that he does so immediately after delivering this parting shot. There is no indication, either, of where he goes. He can hardly go into Phaedria's father's house, because when he comes back on stage (923), he has no idea Phaedria has returned from the country and extracted the truth about Chaerea's escapade from the real eunuch Dorus (who was still in the house). He must use one of the 'wing' exits, and, whichever one he uses, he must, of course, come on again from the same side at 923.

497 **What are you laughing at?:** Gnatho's laughter has been prompted by Parmeno's parting remark (and thus is a clear sign of what the sponger really thinks of Thraso). But, when challenged by Thraso, he pretends he has been amused by the latter's rather pedestrian rejoinder ("What you said just now"); then, probably realizing that that does not sound too convincing, he claims to be laughing at the memory of the joke about the Rhodian, told by Thraso over 70 lines earlier.

498 **and that story ... :** For the Greek original of this line, from Men.'s *The Toady*, see 426n.

500 **Very well:** An obvious 'exit-formula'.

500-1 **Make very sure, Pythias ... :** Thais' instruction must be delivered as an aside. She would not want Thraso to hear plans which involved Chremes turning up at his house, for fear the jealous soldier would regard him as a rival - which he in due course does (623).

505 **look after that young girl ... :** The audience, knowing that it was Chaerea who had been taken into Thais' house and guessing something might happen, would see the irony here.

ACT THREE   SCENE THREE

Chremes, who has conveniently just been named (501), enters from the left (i.e. from the 'country' exit - he has a country estate (519)), and delivers a monologue before approaching Thais' house. Pythias greets him, and eventually persuades him to go with Dorias, another of Thais' maids, to meet Thais at Thraso's house.

In Men.'s original the Pythias character probably came out of the house in answer to Chremes' knock at a point equivalent to 531. But in Ter., since Pythias has been written in to the previous scene, she presumably stays on stage eavesdropping on what Chremes has to say and interrupts him as he goes to knock at the door. But there is no indication of her movements in the text, and another possibility is that she goes back into Thais' house at the end of 506, to re-emerge at 531.

Don. I 382 says of Chremes: "In Menander this character is that of a rustic young man." Certainly Chremes lacks the sophistication of young men-about-town like Phaedria and Chaerea, and Barsby (1999) 178 comments that his language in this scene is "brusque to the point of rudeness". Don. implies that this characterization was even more obvious in Men.'s original, and he comments further on Chremes' 'rustic' characterization in Ter. at 531 (I 385), 745 (I 428) and 803 (I 444).

507ff. **Really, the more I think of it ... :** Chremes' speech is a fine example of a monologue. It performs several functions: to characterize the speaker as wary and suspicious; to explain the state of his negotiations with Thais; and to add further certainty to the hints already given to the audience about Pamphila's identity.

512 **When I arrived:** Chremes is talking of an earlier meeting with Thais, and is now on his way to see her for a second time; cf. 528 "She's sent again now" and 530 "I won't be coming a third time". This situation contradicts Thais' words at 203-5 (where see n.), and all attempts to reconcile the two passages are unconvincing. It is better just to accept the fact of Ter.'s inconsistency.

515 **placed herself beside me:** Lit. "lay down with me". Greeks and Romans reclined on couches while eating, and Chremes here uses one of the regular Latin words for this practice, *accumbere*. Later (728) he uses a similar word with identical meaning, *accubare*.

518ff. **had recourse to asking:** Thais here lists all the 'ingredients' necessary for the traditional recognition scene - parentage, place of birth, loss, recognition tokens, and the existence of people able to confirm the identity.

519 **an estate at Sunium ... how far ... from the sea:** The audience, recalling that Pamphila was "kidnapped from Sunium" (115), would see another piece of the jigsaw falling into place. The same thing would happen when they heard Chremes confirming (524) the kidnap and (526) Chaerea's guess at the girl's age in 318.

524-5 **unless her plan is ... :** Chremes' suspicious nature comes across clearly here (cf. "Already at that stage I suspected", 514). Instead of assuming that Thais might have some news of his sister, he immediately jumps to the conclusion that she wants to pass herself off as the missing girl.

531 **Oh, my dear young Sir!:** Pythias' language is extremely fulsome (lit. "Oh, you nicest dear young person!"); cf. "has asked you most particularly" (532-3) and "please" (534, 536). She knows she has a difficult customer to deal with; but her words only serve to put Chremes on his guard even more (532).

536 **go to hell:** A violent outburst, lit. "will you go from here to destruction?"

538 **Off you go, Dorias:** Thais has specifically told Pythias (500-3) to bring Chremes to Thraso's house herself, but here Pythias tells Dorias to do it. This anomaly is the consequence of Ter. writing in the character of Dorias to take over part of the role of the Pythias character of Men.'s *The Eunuch* (see Introduction pp. 24-5). It follows that this line is Terentian, and that in Men.'s original it was 'Pythias' who took Chremes to Thais at Thraso's house.

In Ter. there is no indication of where Pythias goes at the end of this scene. But, since she cannot be on stage to hear Chaerea's account of his rape of Pamphila, she must be assumed to return into Thais' house. This is awkward. How does she manage to avoid bumping into Chaerea (who emerges from the house at 545)? And why does it take her so long to find out about the rape (she comes out, having discovered it, at 643)? In Men. things were arranged better, because 'Pythias' was away at Thraso's until a point equivalent to Dorias' return at 615.

ACT THREE SCENE FOUR

A new character, Antipho, enters in search of his friend Chaerea; on seeing him emerge from Thais' house, he decides to find out what has been going on.

We have Don.'s testimony (I 387) that Antipho is a Terentian addition to his original: *bene inventa persona est, cui narret Chaerea, ne unus diu loquatur, ut apud Menandrum* "The character to whom Chaerea can tell his story is well devised, to prevent one man giving a long monologue, as in Menander." Thus in Men.'s *The Eunuch* this scene did not exist, and Act Three Scene Five will have followed immediately in the form of a monologue by Chaerea telling of his escapade.

539   **met up at Piraeus:** Antipho is another *ephebus* on duty in Piraeus (cf. 290n.). He accordingly comes on from the left, and is coming to Athens in search of Chaerea.

540   **to arrange our contributions:** Lit. "in order to eat from contributions". The practice is Greek (referred to also in *An.* 88-9 and several times in Plautus), as is the word Ter. uses for "contribution" (*symbola*, Gr. συμβολή); it means 'a sum contributed towards the expenses of a common meal by each participant' (*OLD*).

541   **pledges:** Lit. "rings", given as surety for their attendance in accordance with the agreement.

542   **the place we fixed:** Presumably in Piraeus; but, since Chaerea is not there, the only thing Antipho can think is that he has come to his father's house in Athens (545).

545   **who's that coming out of Thais' place?:** There is a possible inconsistency here. It is at least odd that, while Chaerea did not know that Thais was his father's next-door neighbour (359), Antipho is well aware of where she lives. Cf. 563n.

548   **from back here:** A sure indication in the text that Antipho is going to eavesdrop.

ACT THREE SCENE FIVE

Chaerea emerges from Thais' house and gives an account of his rape of Pamphila. His elation at what he has just done, and his eagerness to tell others about it, are features that commentators have found hard to come to terms with - see Introduction pp. 30-1 and esp. n. 150. It is, of course, dramatic licence that Chaerea, who is afraid his brother and father might be at home (610-11) and who might anyway expect to be pursued by the slaves remaining in Thais' house, nevertheless has the time to tell his adventures to his friend in some detail.

For Ter.'s alteration of a monologue by Chaerea into a dialogue with Antipho, see the introductory note to the previous scene.

549ff.   **Anyone about? ... :** Chaerea's opening monologue is skilfully constructed to depict his wild excitement: two short questions, each followed by a short answer (549); a longer question and an oath (550); an extravagant statement of his joy ("I could honestly put up with death", 551-2); an exclamatory accusative and infinitive construction ("To think that there's no nosey-parker...", 553-4), which ends with no fewer that seven indirect questions which the nosey-parker might ask (555-6).

551-2   **now's the time I could honestly ... :** A somewhat similar sentiment is found in *An.* 959-61: "I think the life of the gods is everlasting because their pleasures are their own for ever; for I've won everlasting life, if no misery gets in the way of this joy of mine". Don. comments on the passage (I 258): "He [Ter.] has transferred this entire sentence from Menander's *The Eunuch.*" Don.'s standard of criticism is not high, but he seems very certain about this; if he is correct, Ter., when writing *The Girl from Andros* (and presumably long before he decided to adapt Men.'s *The Eunuch*), inserted a passage from the latter play into the former. Further support may be given to the idea from similarities to *Eu.* 553ff. in the next line in *An.* (962): "But who should I like most of all to cross my path, so that I might tell him this news now?"

552   **spoiling:** The verb used, *contaminet*, has great importance for the study of Ter. because of its use twice in the prologues (*An.* 16, *Hau.* 17) in a so-called 'specialist literary'

sense; see Introduction pp. 18-19. Here we have its only other occurrence in Ter., in a 'normal' sense outside the prologues.

558-9 **what's the reason ... ?:** Four of Antipho's seven questions deliberately pick up four of the seven Chaerea envisaged the nosey-parker asking in 555-6.

560 **Why don't you ... hullo:** The line as given in the MSS does not scan, and it is not clear what metrical form any emended version should have, since the opening lines of the scene (549-61) are in a variety of metres. The phrase translated "Oh, happy day" (*o festus dies hominis*, lit. "Oh festival day of a man") is striking, though there is a partial parallel in Plautus (*Casina* 137) where someone is called *meus festus dies* ("my festival day") as a term of endearment.

563 **you mean Thais, I presume?:** This need not necessarily mean that Antipho, as well as already knowing where Thais lived (cf. 545n.), also knew of her relationship with Phaedria. A gesture from Chaerea to accompany his words "you know this woman ... ?" would have been enough for Antipho to make the deduction.

566 **fastidious observer of the female form:** Chaerea not only prides himself on his abilities as a connoisseur of feminine beauty, but makes sure all his friends are aware of them too.

568 **I fell in love:** For the dramatic brevity, cf. Chaerea's equally dramatic "I'm in love" to Parmeno (307).

570 **came up with a suggestion:** Chaerea naturally does not go on to explain that Parmeno very quickly made clear his suggestion had only been a joke.

574 **I could see, hear and be with ... :** Chaerea's words echo his own at 367 and, less closely, Parmeno's at 373. At this point in his escapade he was only thinking of such relatively innocent pleasures. The fact that they are set before the audience three times serves to stress that the rape itself was not premeditated.

578 **no man:** The Latin for man, *vir*, is deliberately chosen; it is occasionally used 'contrasted w. a eunuch or sim., as implying sexual potency' (*OLD, uir*, 1c).

579 **in the inner rooms:** In Men. the reference was presumably to the specifically women's quarters of a Greek house (γυναικεῖον, *gynaikeion*) which were normally separate and often in its inner part away from the main door. Such an arrangement did not exist in a Roman house. The Latinized version of the Greek word (*gynaeceum*) is used once by Ter. (*Ph.* 862) and several times by Plautus.

582 **to have a bath:** See below, 592n.

584 **at a picture:** An interesting light on the interior decoration of a Greek or Roman house.

584ff. **the painting in it:** St Augustine (*C.D.* 2. 7) uses Chaerea's description of his actions to illustrate his contention that men are more inclined to follow the examples of the gods than the arguments of philosophers, and he quotes 584-5 and 590-1: "For all the worshippers of such gods prefer to contemplate what Jupiter did than what Plato taught or Cato thought. Hence in Terence the scandalous young man looks at a picture painted on a wall, 'the picture in it ... into Danae's lap', and from such a great authority as this he furnishes a defence for his base conduct when he boasts that in that conduct he is imitating the god. 'And what a god,' he says, 'He who with his thunder ... just what I did and gladly.' "

584-5 **Jupiter sent a shower ... :** Danae was the daughter of King Acrisius of Argos, who had been told by an oracle that he would be killed by Danae's son. Therefore, to prevent her becoming pregnant, he shut her up in a tower of bronze (in the most well-known version of the Greek myth; in other forms of prison in other versions). But Jupiter (Zeus) visited Danae in the form of a shower of golden rain, and she gave birth to Perseus (who eventually accidentally killed his grandfather with a discus).

588 **a god had turned himself into a man:** In the myth Jupiter took the form of the shower of gold, but did not come himself in human shape. Don. was puzzled by the seeming difficulty (I 397): "Is it because Jupiter was pictured in human shape sending the shower of gold, not gold instead of Jupiter?" Barsby ((1999) 197) draws attention to wall-paintings found at Pompeii which "show both the shower of gold and Jupiter in the form of a young man".

589 **down through the skylight:** Ter.'s word, *impluvium*, refers to the rectangular opening in the centre of the roof in the main room (*atrium*) of the Italic house, down to which the roof sloped on all four sides. Rainwater drained off the roof through this into a rectangular pool (*compluvium*) directly below, eventually to be stored in a cistern below floor level. This method of water collection, and the *atrium*-house itself, are specifically Italian, so Ter. has altered his original to describe a situation better known to his Roman audience (rather as has been done with "skylight", to suit modern readers). Cf. *Ph.* 707, where a snake falling down from the tiles through the *impluvium* is included in a list of supposed portents, and Plautus, *Amphitryo* 1108, where two great snakes came down into the house through the *impluvium*, to be strangled by the baby Hercules at his birth.

590 **He who with his thunder ... :** Don. I 397 explains that "with his thunder shakes" is a parody of Ennius (for whom, see Introduction p. 8), presumably from one of his tragedies; and he adds that "the highest realms of heaven" is deliberate tragic diction. Indeed, the whole line (an iambic senarius) may be taken from Ennius. See Jocelyn, H. D. (1967), *The Tragedies of Ennius* (Cambridge) 137.

591 **mere mortal:** The Lat. *homuncio* is a derogatory diminutive, = *homullus* 'a human being, mere man (opposed to superior beings or forces)' (*OLD*).

592 **was summoned to go for her bath:** Don. I 397-8 notes that the Latin word for "was summoned" (*accersitur*) is appropriate for the summoning of a bride for her wedding. He drew parallels between Pamphila's bath and a bride's ritual bath at 581 (I 394-5), and goes on to stress the wedding connotations of "laid her on a couch" at 593 (I 398). Philippides comments at length on these passages and Don.'s comments on them; she sees Ter. as deliberately introducing the elements of the marriage ritual, which, she says (279), "minimize to a considerable degree the violation as well as the detestable feelings about it, since the rape takes place within the marriage frame".

593 **She went off, had it and came back:** The inessential details are passed over even more quickly in the Latin by just three words, *iit, lavit, rediit.*

601 *limis***:** Masc. abl. pl. of the adjective *limus* ('transverse, oblique') with *oculis* understood: 'giving a sidelong glance' (*OLD*).

602 **like this:** One imagines exaggerated, self-mocking mimicry by Chaerea here.

604 **I suppose so:** Ter. skilfully and naturally avoids giving the unpleasant details of the rape.

606 **really:** Chaerea uses the oath *pol* (lit. "by Pollux"; see 199-201n.

607 **about the dinner party:** Lit. "about the contributions"; see 540n.

610 **I've got to keep away from:** Lit: "I am an exile from".

610-1 **I'm afraid my brother:** Chaerea does not know that Phaedria has retired to the country. The reference to his father perhaps returning "back from the country by now" is a hint to the audience about his eventual arrival (971); they would know that fathers in this type of play have a habit of turning up at inopportune moments.

612 **Let's go to my house:** Since Antipho is a Terentian addition, his house would not have been available to 'Chaerea' in Men. But the Chaerea figure must have debated with himself where to change, and gone off somewhere in order to do so.

614 **I want your advice:** Chaerea must be thinking of a Phaedria / Thais type of relationship for himself and Pamphila, since he has no idea that she may be free-born and thus a suitable bride. But at least he is here proving that he is not planning to forget her after his rape.

The stage is left empty, and it is possible that the third choral interlude occurred at the corresponding point in Men.'s original. Antipho's (parents') house is presumably in Athens, so the pair will go off to the audience's right. In Men. it would not have mattered that 'Dorias' (or rather 'Pythias'; cf. 538n.) would shortly enter from the same side, since the choral interlude would have removed any possibility of the three bumping into one another; but in Ter. the situation is rather more awkward.

The dramatic reason for his presence being over, Antipho does not reappear in the play. But his name and his house are mentioned again (840-4) to explain why on his return Chaerea is still wearing the eunuch's clothes.

ACT FOUR SCENE ONE

Dorias returns from Thraso's house carrying Thais' jewels, and gives an account of what went on at the dinner party. Her racy narrative displays all the customary devices employed in Latin to make the story vivid and memorable: the vivid 'historic' present tense (618, 622, 627), the 'historic' infinitive (618, 619, 623, 626), asyndeton, and short sentences (some with no verb expressed (622, 625, 626)).

Since Dorias has been created by Ter. out of part of the role of Pythias, it follows that 'Pythias' would have delivered this monologue in Men.'s *The Eunuch*.

617 **the girl's brother:** Dorias is jumping the gun here, since it is not *firmly* established that Chremes is Pamphila's brother until the arrival of Pamphila's old nurse at 912. Presumably she overheard her mistress' conversation with Chremes, and drew the obvious (though, strictly speaking, at this stage premature) conclusion. Cf. also her reference to "his sister" (621).

618 ***ill':*** *ille*; a rarer example of dropping of final *-e* (cf. 86n.), occuring twelve times in Ter. (e.g. *Hau.* 197, 515).

623 **thought a rival had been brought in:** Clear evidence of Thraso's suspicious jealousy; cf. 500-1n.

625 **fetch Pamphila:** Thraso is following Gnatho's earlier advice; see 442-3n.
Not for all the world: Thais' reaction stresses her concern for Pamphila and highlights the chaste way she has been brought up (cf. 748n.). Respectable girls did not go to dinner-parties, and, as Barsby (1999) 204 says, Thais would not want her to be seen by Chremes in such company.

627 **took off her jewelry:** It is not clear why Thais did this. Don. I 403-4 suggests that she was afraid Thraso might take it off her in compensation for his loss of Pamphila, or that

she wanted to be unencumbered by it in case she either had to make a quick getaway or
got involved in fisticuffs with Thraso.

628   There is no pointer in the text to show what happens to Dorias at the end of the scene. It
might seem natural for her to go into Thais' house before Phaedria's arrival - she
certainly does not 'announce' him, as characters often do when someone is about to
come on stage (cf. 79n.). But in fact she must stay on stage, since she has a brief part to
play in Act Four Scenes Three and Four (though not Two), and is told by Pythias to take
Thais' jewelry indoors at 726. In Men.'s original the Pythias character would have gone
inside with the jewels at this point, and discovered the rape during Phaedria's
monologue.

ACT FOUR SCENE TWO

Phaedria returns early from the country, explaining his reasons in a monologue. He has been
absent for over 400 lines, and the audience will think that his return marks a switch of
attention from Chaerea's story back to his. But the emergence of Pythias at the end of the
monologue (642) ensures that Chaerea's escapade remains the focus of the action.

    Dorias' presence during Phaedria's words (which she gives no sign of hearing and to
which she does not react) is awkward.

634   **our farm:** See 187n.

636   **for two days:** Even though Phaedria had boasted (223) that he could do without Thais
for three days, he had actually only agreed (181-6) to be away for two.

640-1 **To love from the side lines:** Lit. "to love from the furthest line" (*extrema linea
amare*). The phrase is possibly a metaphor drawn from the stadium. It recurs much
later in a commentary on Statius (*Theb.* 3. 283) attributed to Lactantius Placidus:
"Loving a girl from the furthest line of love (*extrema amoris linea*), he satisfies his heart
by only looking at her".

ACT FOUR SCENE THREE

Pythias rushes out of Thais' house, having found out about the rape. Thinking the real eunuch
to be somehow responsible, she accuses Phaedria, who goes into his house to see if the
supposed rapist has returned there.

    In Ter. we have the odd situation that it has taken Pythias over 100 lines to discover the
rape (see 538n.). But in Men.'s *The Eunuch* 'Pythias' will only have entered the house at a
point corresponding to 628 (where see n.) and so made her discovery much more quickly (as,
we feel, in real life she would have done). Dorias is on stage throughout the scene, but speaks
just two lines (656, 664); these can be detached without affecting the rest of the scene in any
way, and will have been written in by Ter.

    As the scene progresses, it becomes clear that Pythias' role is much more than that of a
conventional female slave with just the odd word or two to say. She is forceful, emotional
and authoritative, and more than capable of holding her own against the free-born Phaedria.
She has a personality of her own, which will be further developed as the play goes on.

646   **tore the poor thing's clothes and pulled out her hair:** These details have upset
modern commentators. In Men.'s *The Arbitration* (488-91) a girl is described as tearing
her own hair in her distress at having been raped, and as having her cloak torn to shreds

(presumably during the rape itself). But Pythias is quite clear here that Chaerea committed both outrages on his victim himself, and *after* the rape, not in the height of passion during it. Moreover, the detail of the torn clothes, though not of the hair, is confirmed by Thais at 820 (though admittedly without any mention of when they were torn).

It is tempting to see Pythias' remark as one exaggerated or distorted by her state of extreme agitation (cf. her suspicion that Chaerea may have stolen something from the house as he fled (660-1), about which nothing further is heard). But these details are not mentioned as suspicions but as facts, and there is no attempt to gainsay them later in the play. We have to accept Chaerea's actions, with all their unpleasant implications, as they stand.

651 **You can go to hell:** Lit. "Are you going from here to where you deserve to be?", a question equivalent to a command. For a very similar phrase, cf. *Hau.* 813.

in': *isne*; for the dropping of the final *-e*, see 86n., 99n., and cf. *emin* for *emine* (691).

655 **You must be drunk:** When faced with the suggestion that a eunuch has committed rape, Phaedria's reaction is a natural one - that the author of the suggestion must be either drunk or mad (cf. "You're off your head", 657).

656 **But, please, Pythias my dear ... :** For Dorias' comment, and her one other contribution to this scene (664), see the introductory note to the scene.

au: An exclamation spoken only by women (cf. 680, 899). Here, as often, it is used in close conjunction with *obsecro* "please".

mea Pythias: Don. (I 410) calls the use of *mea* here, like *mea tu* (664, also addressed by Dorias to Pythias) and *amabo* (cf. 130n.) "blandishments suited to women" (*muliebribus apta ... blandimenta*); cf. Pythias' *mi Chremes*, 535. Martin (144-5) contrasts Dorias' fulsome address to Pythias here and at 664 with the latter's unadorned *Dorias* to the former at 538 and 720; he interprets the difference as indicating that "though Pythias is younger than Dorias, she ranks above her in Thais' domestic hierarchy".

660 **that fine fellow of yours:** Philippides (284) points out that in the Latin Chaerea is for the first time termed *vir* ("man") rather than *adulescentulus* ("youth"), and that the same thing happens at 850. Noting that both these instances occur after the rape, she sees significance in the use of *vir* to indicate Chaerea's transition to manhood and to eventual marriage.

661 **he stole something:** See 646n.

662 **that wretched specimen:** Phaedria is, of course, thinking of the real eunuch Dorus, and is here acknowledging that he is not a very impressive present for Thais (cf. 214n.).

ACT FOUR SCENE FOUR

Phaedria comes out of his father's house with Dorus and, when Pythias fails to identify the latter as the eunuch who had been brought across, questions him and discovers the truth. After he and Dorus have gone inside again, Pythias, who is beginning to suspect that Parmeno is behind the whole affair, agrees with Dorias to keep quiet about what they know, and sends Dorias into Thais' house with her mistress' jewelry.

The scene involves four speaking characters, and it is clear from what has been said already that Dorias is the extra character who has been written in by Ter.

A different side to Phaedria now appears. The new developments take his mind off his own troubles and, thus unencumbered, he shows vigour, determination and a certain amount of cunning in his treatment of Dorus; see Introduction p. 30. Dorus himself makes his only appearance in the play, and his character is hardly developed at all.

Pythias' prominent role in the scene, her scornful reaction to the suggestion that Dorus is the rapist, and her insistence on the correctness of her story, all serve to reinforce the audience's opinion of her as a major character in the play. By contrast, Dorias makes only one insignificant contribution (675) until her brief conversation with Pythias in the closing lines, and she does not reappear after she goes into Thais' house at the end.

669   **you runaway ... a bad buy:** Both these terms (*fugitivus, male conciliatus*) are part of the stock vocabulary of abuse hurled at slaves, but in this context they have a more literal application. Dorus is wearing Chaerea's clothes, and Phaedria draws the natural conclusion that he has changed into them in order to escape (cf. 671, 673); and any slave who tries to escape must be a "bad buy".

674   **Of course I have:** The way in which Phaedria and Pythias are talking at cross purposes, and the gradual uncovering of the rapist's true identity, provide good theatre.

682   **handsome, gentlemanly looks:** See 473n.

688   **wrinkled, ancient, spent:** The Latin words used (*vietus, vetus, veternosus*) are rich in alliteration and assonance.

689   **with the colour of a weasel:** Don. I 416-17 explains that Ter. has erred in his adaptation at this point, and in so doing he provides a fragment of Men.'s *The Eunuch*: "COLORE MUSTELLINO [*sic*]: Terence has made a mistake through failure to understand Menander's phrase αὐτός ἐστιν γαλεώτης γέρων ["he himself is a spotted lizard of an old man"]. [Menander] mentions the spotted lizard (*stellio*), which is a creature not unlike a lizard (*lacerta*) with a freckled skin. For the fact is that the appearance of eunuchs' bodies is likened to that species, because most of them are freckly. So our author has made a mistake, because it is a γαλῆ which is called a weasel (*mustella*) and a γαλεώτης which is called a spotted lizard (*stellio*)."

The Suda, a tenth-century AD lexicon / historical encyclopedia, quotes the same Men. phrase in the slightly different form οὑτοσὶ δὲ γαλεώτης γέρων ("this one here is a spotted lizard of an old man"). Körte (II 67, fr. 163) prefers the Suda version on the ground that οὑτοσί is more appropriate than αὐτός when the eunuch is actually on stage.

We are again left wondering about the standard of / criteria for Don.'s criticism. If he feels it worth commenting on this small point of detail, why does he have so little to say on other, more important deviations from Men.'s original?

691-2   **Tell him to answer me ... :** Pythias has the forcefulness and authority to interrupt Phaedria's questions with one of her own.

693   **sixteen-year-old:** Chaerea must actually be at least eighteen, because he is an *ephebus* (cf. 290n.), a fact of which Pythias herself seems aware when she calls him an *ephebus* at 824 - if she is using the term technically and not loosely there. Barsby (1999) 216 suggests that Pythias may be exaggerating Chaerea's youth to emphasise the contrast with Dorus. Is it significant that Pamphila too is sixteen (318)?

696ff. Chaerea arrived: The answers to Phaedria's quick-fire cross-questioning are at this stage spoken in Pythias' hearing; they are what lead her to suspect (718) that "this is a trick of Parmeno's".

704-5 Come on now ... : Phaedria is becoming convinced of the truth of what Dorus has told him, and these words constitute a desperate ploy to avoid acknowledging it in public.

706 Come over here a bit ... : By moving Dorus away from Pythias, Phaedria ensures that, though she can still hear what he says aloud to the eunuch (cf. her reaction at 709-10), she cannot hear the asides he delivers in 712 and 715.

709 the bare-faced scoundrel: Chaerea, about whose guilt Phaedria is now completely certain. The alternative is to suppose that the remark is spoken aloud and refers to Dorus, who Phaedria is in desperation trying to make out is a liar.

714 telling the truth without a flogging: In both Greece and Rome the evidence of slaves was admissible only if it had been extracted under torture, and Phaedria is transferring the practice to the domestic sphere. But we need not suppose that the innocent Dorus will actually be flogged; the threat is part of a 'put-up job' between Phaedria and the eunuch, designed to get them both back into the house.

716 get out of this honourably: Phaedria is probably not so much concerned with personal honour as with the effect that Chaerea's action might have on his own relationship with Thais.

719 a way to pay him back: This threat prepares the audience for Parmeno's discomfiture in Act Five Scenes Four, Five and Six.

720 What do you think we should do now?: It seems odd for the dominant Pythias to be asking a lesser maid for advice. This slight inconsistency in characterization is caused by Ter.'s alteration of what was most probably a monologue by 'Pythias' in Men. (in which she stated her intention to keep quiet about the rape) into a conversation with Dorias.

721 *utrum taceamne an praedicam*: The MSS are divided between *praedicam* from *praedīcere* ("say first") and *praedīcem* from *praedīcare* ("make known", "declare"), as well as about the position of *-ne*. All agree on the order of the two verbs. *utrum ...-ne an ...* is the correct form for the indirect disjunctive question (*OLD, utrum*, 2b), and Pythias is anxious to 'get in first' and give her side of the story before Thais can have her say.

722 you'll know nothing of what you know: Almost identical advice is given by Syrus to his fellow-slave Dromo at *Hau.* 748.

724 But is that Chremes ... ?: The customary announcement formula is here combined with 'pre-announcement' of the return of Thais at the end of the following scene (even though she is announced there too (738)).

726 take these jewels indoors: Ter.'s creation of Dorias out of the role of Pythias has meant that she has been on stage holding her mistress' jewelry for over 100 lines. See 628n. and Introduction pp. 24-5.

ACT FOUR SCENE FIVE

Chremes returns from Thraso's, rather drunk, and wonders why Thais, who left before him, has not yet returned.

Several considerations, when taken together, indicate that the whole of this scene may have been written in by Ter.: the peculiarity that Chremes left Thraso's house after Thais but, even when drunk, reached Thais' house before her, which is never explained; the fact that in the following scene Chremes does not seem at all drunk; and the announcement of Chremes and 'pre-announcement' of Thais by Dorias at the end of the previous scene (see 724n.), which may conceal announcement of both of them by 'Pythias' in Men. Thus in the original Chremes and Thais will have arrived together immediately after the end of Act Four Scene Four; see also 795n.

It is impossible to tell whether Ter. wrote the scene out of his own head or borrowed a similar scene from another Greek original. In either case, he must have thought that a scene involving a drunk would add another amusing ingredient to his play.

728 **while I was still at the table:** Cf. 515n.

732 **No food and drink ... :** Lit. "Without Ceres and Liber, Venus is frozen." Ceres, Roman goddess of growth and corn equated with the Greek Demeter, and Liber, god of the vine equated with Bacchus / Dionysus, are used to represent bread and wine, as Cicero saw (*N. D.* 2. 60, where he quotes Ter.'s words). Venus is the goddess of love, equated with Aphrodite. For the sentiment, cf. Euripides' *Bacchae* 773: "When there is no longer any wine, there is no Cyprian [Aphrodite]."

ACT FOUR SCENE SIX

Thais arrives and tells Chremes that Pamphila is staying in her house. Chremes, alarmed at the approach of Thraso, Gnatho and a bunch of slaves to remove Pamphila by force, has to be encouraged by Thais to stay and face the new arrivals. Thais produces a box which contains Pamphila's keepsakes.

In Men. Thais and Chremes will have arrived together (cf. the introducory note to the previous scene), and prepared to face the rival who was coming to claim back the girl.

739ff. **I expect he'll be here ... :** Thais' entrance monologue not only prepares the audience for the arrival of Thraso and his party, but also shows her tough and determined attitude, in contrast to Chremes' timidity later in the scene. Her mention of Thraso's "stupidity" and "pompous talk" (741) shows her true feelings towards him, almost for the first time.

743 **I've been here for ages:** An exaggeration, of course, like most of Chremes' judgements about time (cf. 734).
the very person I've been expecting: An odd expression when Chremes has arrived before her.

745 **your sister:** Thais now seems convinced of Pamphila's identity, even before any formal recognition has occurred.

748 **a credit to you and to her:** This important point about Pamphila's virtuous upbringing has already been stressed (116-17); Thais' purpose here is to reassure Chremes that the girl can safely be taken back into his family (though, of course, Thais does not yet know about the rape).

749 **not asking for any payment:** Thais may not want money, but she certainly hopes (cf. 144n.) that Chremes will in gratitude become her patron.

753 **the little box with her keepsakes:** It is a regular feature of these plays that the girl (often, as in Pamphila's case, kidnapped, but sometimes exposed or sold) conveniently possesses some means of identification, which ultimately establishes her parentage. In *Hau.* (614-7, 649-57) it is a ring, but the most common item is a box (*cistella*) containing small items of jewelry ('trinkets') which function as 'recognition tokens'. In

Men.'s *The Arbitration* the central arbitration scene revolves around the ownership of a pouch containing various trinkets (including a ring), Plautus' *Casket Comedy* (*Cistellaria*) takes its name from the box itself, and in his *The Rope* (1143-65) a box is produced and the girl (Palaestra) proves her identity by being able to describe its contents without seeing them.

754 **You're so annoyingly slow:** Pythias must goes into Thais' house immediately after receiving this rebuke from her mistress.

755 **what a huge army:** Lit. "what great forces". As the audience, over the next few lines, come to recognize Chremes' timidity, they will realize, even before the 'army' arrives, that it is probably not going to turn out to be all that large and fearsome. They have already seen Chremes' tendency to exaggerate (743n.).

Since it is most likely that the siege in the following scene was not in Men.'s *The Eunuch* (see the introductory note to Act Four Scene Seven), it follows that Ter. has altered his original here to suit the changed nature of what is to come.

760 **a foreigner, with less influence than you:** Chremes, as a citizen, has more rights, as well as more standing, than Thraso.

764 **supporters:** See 340n.

766ff. **Just tell him ... :** None of these facts about Pamphila are yet established. But it is in Thais' and Chremes' interests to pretend to Thraso that they are.

767 **Show him the tokens:** Pythias has presumably come back on stage just before Thais speaks these words. She must return into Thais' house immediately after Thais tells Chremes to take the tokens; there is no hint that she is present during the 'siege' in the following scene, and her presence as a silent bystander during it would be awkward - as well as untypical of the bold and ebullient Pythias.

769 **Get ready for action:** Lit. "Hitch up your cloak" (*attolle pallium*), to prepare for battle (not, as Don. I 433 believes, because Chremes through naivety or drunkenness has let his cloak trail on the ground!). The *pallium* is the long *Greek* cloak which gives its name to the *fabula palliata* (see Introduction p. 5).

ACT FOUR SCENE SEVEN

Thraso, accompanied by Gnatho and a motley group of servants, arrives to take Pamphila back from Thais. After making elaborate plans to lay siege to Thais' house, he decides to talk matters over with her first, but is completely deflated by Chremes' statement that Pamphila is a free-born Athenian and his sister. Chremes goes off with the box of Pamphila's keepsakes to find the girl's nurse, Thais shuts herself up in her house, and Thraso and his party, acting on some specious advice from Gnatho, withdraw.

Once again, the characters from Men.'s *The Toady* are prominent, and it is from there that Ter. must have taken the details of the siege. The siege itself is only to the fore for the first 17 lines of the scene (771-87, until Thraso sees Thais and decides to talk to her) and at the very end (814-16, when Thais' departure leaves Thraso high and dry); in these sections Thais and Chremes take no part except for a brief exchange at 783-6. Moreover, the very abrupt way in which the siege is called off invites suspicion, though Ter. manages this episode cleverly so as to characterize Thraso and Gnatho further.

The scene has five speaking characters, and it is obvious that Sanga, the one member of the slave 'army' who has anything to say (776, 778-9, 816), has been written in as a speaking character by Ter. as part of his policy of 'thickening up' the play. The other character added is probably Gnatho; apart from the siege sections, his contributions to the scene are mostly abusive reiteration of what Thraso says, and these can be removed without in any way upsetting the rest of the dialogue.

Thus in Men.'s *The Eunuch* the rival will have arrived, perhaps with a non-speaking slave or henchman, to claim back the girl he had given to the *hetaira*. A discussion, perhaps heated, ensued, with the Chremes character's claim that the girl was his sister proving enough to see the rival off.

The resultant scene, with Thraso's sham militarism and Gnatho's time-serving and abuse, is very lively and amusing. Marouzeau I 284 comments: "The scene deserves to be presented as a good argument in defence of *contaminatio*."

772 **Syriscus:** A diminutive of the common slave name *Syrus* ("Syrian"). At *Ad.* 763 the slave Syrus uses the form ("dear little Syrus") when addressing himself.

773-4 **Good ... Excellent! ... Splendid!:** Gnatho is practising the philosophy he outlined at 251ff. Here he enthusiastically praises Thraso's eagerness for the fight, but when the captain changes his mind and decides to talk to Thais first, he praises that too (790-1).

774-5 **the centre of the line ... the left wing ... the right:** The humour of this motley rabble being drawn up like a true army speaks for itself.

776 **centurion Sanga and his band of thieves:** Sanga is evidently chief slave in Thraso's kitchen (cf. "my mind's been on my cooking-pots for ages now", 816), and his "band of thieves" are an unspecified number of non-speaking extras, additional to Simalio, Donax and Syriscus.

cedo: Here used in its literal meaning "give me"; cf. 162n.

777 **a sponge:** According to the second-century AD scholar Festus (pp. 231L, 260-1L), the Latin word used here, *peniculus*, denoted either a loofah-like sponge or a hair whisk, used in kitchens etc. to wipe down tables. In Plautus' *The Brothers Menaechmus* (77-8) the sponger Peniculus says he has been given his name "because when I eat I sweep the table clean".

780 *qui*: "How (do you mean) ... ?"; cf. 36n.

malum: Used 'as an oath, added parenth[etically] to emphasise a question' (*OLD*, *malum*, 8). Barsby (1999) 233 compares the English "how the hell?", "what the devil?".

781 **behind the front rank:** Modern readers will inevitably think of Gilbert and Sullivan's Duke of Plaza-Toro, who "led his regiment from behind - he found it less exciting".

783 **Pyrrhus:** This reference to the famous King of Epirus (319-272 BC) is certainly Terentian and was not in Men. Pyrrhus reigned as a minor from 307/6 to 303/2, but was then ousted, only becoming king again (jointly with Neoptolemus) in 297. His war with Demetrius I of Macedon had hardly begun when Men. died *c.* 291 BC. On the other hand, Pyrrhus would have been well known to Romans from his championing of Tarentum against them in the 280s (cf. 413n.).

784 **It's obviously the right plan ... :** These words need not imply that Chremes and Thais are already in the house; Chremes is merely again advocating the plan he first suggested at 763.

787 **your concealed position:** There would have been little opportunity for actual concealment in the theatres of Ter.'s time, though the width of the stage would have made a pretence of concealment possible (as well as explaining how Thraso does not see Thais until 788).

789　**It's right for the wise man ... :** These words form the transition from the situation in Men.'s *The Toady* (the siege) to that in *The Eunuch* (the discussion). See the introductory note to the scene.

793　**these next few days:** It is nowhere specifically stated that Thais has made this promise to Thraso, but since "these next few days" are precisely the amount of time for which she asked Phaedria to give place to his rival (151), it can safely be assumed that she did.

794　**your lover:** Cf. Dorias at 623: "The captain obviously thought a rival had been brought in."

795　**and slipped away with him:** Here it seems that Thais and Chremes *did* leave Thraso's dinner together. Is this further evidence for the Terentian origin of Act Four Scene Five (where see the introductory note)?

801　**I'll make sure you remember ... :** An almost identical line occurs at Plautus' *The Prisoners* 800. W. M. Lindsay in his 1900 edition of that play (300) baldly states: "This line is stolen by Terence."

806　**free-born ... of Attic citizen stock ... my sister:** See 766ff. n.

807-8　**I'm going to find the nurse:** At 767 Thais had advised Chremes to show the tokens to Thraso, but here Chremes decides to find the nurse and show them to her. This is clearly the better course, as the nurse would recognize the tokens whereas there is no reason why Thraso should; but it is also the safer course, since it gives the timid Chremes an excuse to leave at a time when violence might still erupt.

811　**Why don't we go home?:** Gnatho gives Thraso the excuse he wants to call off his 'troops'.

815　**hearth and home:** The regular things for soldiers or exiles to think of when away from home (cf. Cicero, *S. Rosc.* 23). But the cook Sanga takes "hearth" literally and thinks of his pots and pans in the kitchen.

816　**Follow me this way:** The stage is left empty, and it is probable that the fourth and last choral interlude occurred at this point in Men.'s original. In Men. the interlude would have helped mask the period of time it took for Thais (who only left the stage at 810) to find out about the rape and begin her cross-questioning of Pythias.

ACT FIVE　SCENE ONE

Thais and Pythias enter from Thais' house; Thais has discovered the rape and is questioning her maid about it. Almost as soon as Pythias has told her mistress that Chaerea was responsible, Chaerea himself is seen approaching.

817　**You worthless creature:** Thais' discovery of the rape has rendered useless Dorias' advice to Pythias (722) to keep quiet about it.

820　**her clothes are all torn:** See 646n.

824　**That young brother:** The word translated "young" is *ephebus*; see 290n., 693n.

827　**I suppose he'd fallen in love:** A surprising admission for Pythias, considering her otherwise outright opposition to Chaerea. But the statement reminds the audience of Chaerea's motives and paves the way for the resolution of his problem.
　　　　I'm sunk: The reason for Thais' despair is more fully explained at 867-71. See also 144n.

831　**just as you ordered:** Cf. Chaerea's account at 578-9.

834 **Quiet, madam ... :** When she sees Chaerea approaching, Pythias, who has been uncharacteristically subdued before her mistress' anger, immediately recovers her spirits.

835 **over there to the left:** This must be to the speaker's left (i.e. the audience's right, the direction in which Chaerea had departed at 614). A gesture by Pythias will in any case have made the matter clear.

837 **What will we do with him then ... ?** Thais is well aware that, as a foreigner living in Athens, her chances of redress against a citizen would be small. Cf. Chaerea's attitude at 849.

ACT FIVE SCENE TWO

Chaerea enters, having had no opportunity to change out of the eunuch's clothes. Still pretending to be Dorus, he attempts to brave out the situation, but when Thais makes it clear she knows who he is, he pleads his love, and Thais, despite Pythias' protestations, forgives him. When Chremes is seen returning, Chaerea goes into Thais' house to change.

In the early part of the scene, Chaerea's attempts to lie his way out of a difficult situation do him no credit, but his change of tone when it becomes clear he has been unmasked shows him in a better-light. Thais displays cunning in stringing him along, authority and firmness in dealing with Pythias' objections, and her essential humanity in her final treatment of Chaerea. Pythias remains true to character - bold in her willingness to stand up to her mistress and determined in her opposition to Chaerea.

In this scene the first (and most difficult) step is taken towards the resolution of Chaerea's problem - his reconciliation with Thais. There remains the need to establish Pamphila's free-born status (which the audience will know by now is a virtual certainty) and to secure Chaerea's father's agreement to marriage.

840 **Antipho's mother and father ... :** Since the character of Antipho is a Terentian addition to his original, Chaerea's words here involve Terentian rewriting; in Men. he must have gone somewhere else to change (see 612n.). Nothing is said of what became of Antipho, who left with Chaerea at 614.

845 **an empty alley:** As at *Ad.* 576, 578, the alley (*angiportum*) is a minor lane or side-street, as opposed to a more major road (*platea*, 344, 1064, or *via*, 906), such as that on to which the houses of the stage 'set' face. Sometimes an *angiportum* is thought of as just off stage, providing a place for a character to hide (*Ph.* 891), but it has no such specific reference here. For the problems posed by the *angiportum* as an adjunct of the stage set, see Beare 256-63.

849 **what does it matter?** Chaerea's readiness to 'tough it out' does nothing to improve the audience's opinion of him.
quid mea: sc. *refert*; see 320n.

850 **Dorus, my fine fellow:** Thais is testing Chaerea by calling him Dorus, since she already knows (824) who he really is.

851 **Yes, madam:** Since Chaerea and Thais have never met (cf. 360), he thinks that she really believes he is Dorus, and attempts to feed her delusion. This pretence, continued in "Forgive this one offence" (852-3) and "another slave, like me" (lit. "a fellow-slave", 858), compounds the poor opinion of him formed at 849.

856 **Something small:** This comment of Chaerea's is perhaps the hardest of all to excuse, based as it is on the assumption that raping a fellow-slave (858) is a matter of little importance. In his eagerness to maintain the pretence that he is Dorus, he is merely digging a bigger hole for himself.

'Small', you shameless idiot: Pythias' fury (seen also at 859-60, 861-3) contributes greatly to the scene and provides much of its humour.

861 **You go back indoors:** Lit. "are you going away from here?"; cf. 651n.

Why should I do that?: Pythias, who only a short while ago (817ff.) was so cowed before Thais' questions, is now so angry that she even dares to disobey her mistress.

864-6 **Chaerea, what you did ... :** Thais drops the pretence of believing that Chaerea is Dorus. Now very serious, she lectures him on the concepts of "worthy" (*dignum* 864, *digna* 865) and "unworthy" (*indignus* 866). By conceding the possibility that she herself might be in a high degree "worthy" of such insulting treatment, and contrasting that with the "unworthiness" of Chaerea's behaviour, she highlights the different standards expected of a *meretrix* and a citizen. The audience have already formed a favourable opinion of Thais, and the contrast between her behaviour and Chaerea's brings into sharp relief the enormity of the latter's action. Then, having had her say, Thais does not dwell on the matter, but turns to the practical consequences of Chaerea's actions for herself and for her hopes for Pamphila.

868-71 **You've turned all my plans so upside down ... :** A good illustration of how Thais' plans for Pamphila are not wholly altruistic, but combined with self-interest. Granted, she knew it was "right" to restore the girl to her family and was "keen" to do so, but her purpose was "to produce some lasting benefit to myself"; see further Introduction p. 32. For the "benefit" (*beneficium*) - in this case the acquisition of Chremes as a patron - see 149n.

872ff. **My hope is ... :** The change in Chaerea is marked, as often when a brash and over-confident youngster is brought down to earth by a sharp rebuke. His talk of "a permanent friendship" (872) and "close ties" (874) contains the first hint that Thais' salvation may not lie with Chremes after all, but with Chaerea's family.

875 **some god or other:** Don. I 458 says that Chaerea means the god Love; but it is worth noting that Chaerea includes Fortune (also a deity) among those he should praise (1046) and prays to Jupiter (1048) that his family's happiness should last.

877 **to insult you:** Lit. "for the sake of insult (*contumelia*)". Chaerea uses the same word Thais had used at 865 ("insulting treatment").

880 **My character's not that inhuman ... :** Thais' essential humanity shines through, but her elevated sentiment is somewhat undercut by her reference to her "experience" - she has known many men and so seen the many aspects of love's power.

883 **Then, my goodness ... :** Pythias remains implacably hostile to Chaerea and thoroughly disapproves of her mistress' reconciliation with him. Her protestations in the rest of the scene (884, 896, 897-8, 898-9, 900, 901-2, 903-4, 908) inject a lighter note into the serious discussion between the other two.

886-7 **I'm entrusting myself ... as my protector:** It is ironical that the free-born Chaerea wants a foreign woman (and a *meretrix* at that) as his patron, when it should be the other way round. This is the second time that the person who would naturally be the patron wants or needs one himself; at 770 Thais had commented that Chremes, whom she was hoping would be her defender, himself needed a protector.

The word for "I'm entrusting" (*commendo*) is the regular one in such contexts. Chaerea uses it again (1039) when describing how Thais "has entrusted" (*commendavit*) herself to his father as her patron.

888 **I'll die if I can't have her as my wife:** It is important to note (a) the intensity of Chaerea's feelings and (b) that for the first time he talks of marriage. He has heard from Pythias that Pamphila is free-born (858, though this has yet to be confirmed) and so there is no more talk of entering into a Phaedria / Thais type of relationship with her as there was at 613-14.

889 **Oh, he'll be willing ... :** In these plays fathers (whose consent is always needed for their sons to marry, just as it was in real life) often oppose marriages where the intended bride is socially unsuitable or has an insufficient dowry. But since Pamphila is free-born, Chaerea can be reasonably confident of obtaining his father's agreement. As Barsby (1999) 250 says: "Apart from this [the question of the bride's status and her dowry], fathers are generally happy to see their sons married, if only to end the squandering of the family's wealth on courtesans."

891 **the girl's brother ... :** Chremes' imminent return is anticipated for the audience's benefit.

894-5 **Would you like us to wait inside ... ?:** At first sight the purpose of Thais' words is to provide the means to get Chaerea off stage at the end of the scene; but his own words at 905-7 provide perfectly adequate motivation closer to his point of departure. The more important reason for Thais' words is that her invitation to Chaerea to return into the very house where he committed his outrage allows Pythias to object, and gives rise to the amusing exchanges which follow.

903 **you can keep an eye on me:** Chaerea's reconciliation with Thais has restored his customary cheerfulness, so he makes fun of Pythias by 'winding her up'. He succeeds, because she reacts to his offer as if it were serious.

907 **Not because you feel ashamed?:** Thais is now sufficiently fond of Chaerea to indulge in a little gentle leg-pulling.

ACT FIVE SCENE THREE

Pythias just has sufficient time to say that she is thinking of a way to get even with Parmeno when Chremes enters with the nurse Sophrona. She learns from Chremes that the nurse has recognized Pamphila's tokens, and ushers them both into Thais' house. She then sees Parmeno approaching and, after saying that she has thought of a plan for him, she goes into her mistress' house to get definite news of the recognition, promising to return to put her plan into action.

The scene sets the seal on what has gone before by confirming Pamphila's identity. But, unlike in, for example, Plautus' *The Rope*, the actual recognition scene does not take place on stage. Chremes' assurances to Pythias tell the audience that it will happen, but confirmation that it has is only given by Pythias at 952 and Chaerea at 1036. Thus the recognition is very low-key - even more so than in *Hau.* 614-7, where at least the nurse is seen identifying the vital ring.

The other purpose of the scene is to look forward to Pythias' revenge on Parmeno, which occupies the next three scenes (Act Five Scenes Four to Six). This revenge has already been threatened by Pythias at 718-19, but here she refers to it no fewer than three times in thirteen lines.

The nurse speaks only one word; even this may have been written in by Ter., with the nurse a non-speaking character in Men. Chremes' brief appearance with her is the last we see of him in the play; since the recognition is assured, and since Chaerea's desire to marry Pamphila lays the way open for his father to become Thais' patron, his role in the play is over.

911   **that wicked monster:** Parmeno, to whom Pythias transfers her attention in accordance with her threat (couched in similar language) at 718-19. She realizes that there is no point in pursuing her enmity with Chaerea now that Thais has befriended him, and she is not to know that Parmeno was actually aghast when Chaerea took his suggestion about the eunuch seriously.

912-13   **get a move on ... I *am* getting a move on ... you're not making much progress:** There is a play on words in the Latin between *moveo* ("move") (Chremes' first remark and Sophrona's reply) and *promoveo* ("move forward") (Chremes' second comment) .

917   **for quite a while:** Pythias is getting impatient; Thais has in fact been inside for less than ten lines.

921-2   **I'll go in ... :** Pythias gives precise information about her movements for the benefit of the audience.

922   The stage is left empty, but only momentarily, as Parmeno's arrival has already been announced. The announcement makes it unlikely that there would have been a choral interlude at this point in the Greek original. On the other occasions where the stage is empty (after 206, 390, 614, 816), there is no such announcement, and those are therefore more likely places for the choral interludes in Men.

ACT FIVE   SCENE FOUR

Parmeno enters, gloating over the (presumed) success of Chaerea's escapade and gleefully anticipating the praise he will earn, and the benefits to Chaerea, as a result. Pythias comes out of Thais' house and sets her trap for him. She pretends that Chremes, having heard of the rape, is preparing to punish Chaerea as an adulterer. Parmeno first thinks of trying to prevent this, but, on seeing Chaerea's father approaching, decides to tell him what is supposedly going on in Thais' house.

Parmeno is seen clearly as the 'bungling' slave; his swift descent from smug gloating to abject terror recalls the equally swift change from jocularity to horror when Chaerea took up his suggestion about the eunuch in Act Two Scene Three, and thus confirms the audience's earlier impression. But, to his credit, he also clearly demonstrates his loyalty to his young master; when he realizes that he would be powerless to prevent Chaerea's punishment if he went into Thais' house himself, he quickly decides he must tell Chaerea's father what he thinks is happening, even if it means getting punished afterwards.

Pythias is in her element. Having come up with a scheme amazingly quickly, she puts it into operation with verve and enthusiasm, and lays on a convincing display of histrionics to deceive her victim. After the scenes with Thais, she is now back in control, and she is enjoying herself hugely. There is virtual role-reversal here: Pythias shows all the inventiveness, quick thinking and ability to play-act and deceive which is normally the preserve of the 'cunning' slave in these plays, and she practises them on a slave of quite different type.

The whole revenge sub-plot is worked skilfully into the play. Earlier indications of Parmeno's 'bungling' role have prepared the audience for his reactions here, and Pythias has already been seen as spirited enough to work her plan successfully. Moreover, the revenge is not just an isolated incident; Parmeno's decision to 'spill the beans' to Chaerea's father leads directly to the father's agreement to his son's marriage, and to his willingness to become Thais' patron, which in turn helps resolve the problems which his other son Phaedria is having in *his* relationship.

923 **I'm just popping back:** Parmeno has been off stage for some 430 lines, so knows nothing of how Chaerea's escapade went.

There is nothing in the text to indicate from what side the slave enters, but he must come on from the side by which he left at 495; see 494-5n.

925 **what a mighty harvest of real praise:** Parmeno is thinking first and foremost of himself, and takes the credit for Chaerea's escapade - having conveniently forgotten how appalled he was when his young master took his idea seriously.

927 **a grasping madam:** The slave still sees Thais as a typical greedy *meretrix*; see 79-80n.

929 **there's this second point:** This piece of far-fetched moral justification, coupled with his earlier gloating, ensures that the audience will not feel too sorry for Parmeno when he gets his 'comeuppance'.

930 **master-stroke:** The Latin word, *palmarium*, derives from *palma*, the palm branch 'placed in the hands of the victor in a contest' (*OLD, palma*, 4d).

936 **show off their dainty table manners:** See 235n.

937-9 **But to see ... yesterday's broth:** There has been no hint that Thais' household is in any way like this; indeed, Chaerea's description of her house (580ff.), with its talk of baths and pictures on the walls, implies much the opposite, and serves to show just how wrong Parmeno's 'traditional' view is.

941 **these words of yours:** It is clear that Pythias has come out of the house in time to hear at least some of Parmeno's monologue, but there is no pointer in the text to show precisely when that was.

943 **In heaven's name:** The γ MSS indicate a new scene here, but there is no precedent in Ter. for a scene change without a change of speaker. Here there is only an (admittedly startling) change of metre; Pythias' first two lines, spoken as an aside, continue the spoken iambic senarii of Parmeno's monologue, but when she begins to act her role as the distraught bearer of dreadful news from inside the house, the metre changes to the more excited recitative trochaic septenarii.

944 **that wicked Parmeno:** Pythias, aware of course that she will be overheard, takes care to mention Parmeno's name early on, to ensure that he pays close attention.

946 **punishment:** The Latin *exemplum* (lit. "example") can mean ('warning example, deterrent' (cf. 1022) and then 'an exemplary punishment' (*OLD, exemplum*, 3a and b).

949 **poor young lad:** Pythias deliberately employs the diminutive of *adulescens*, *adulescentulus*. She had previously used the diminutive form (686) to stress Chaerea's youth.

952 **a free-born Athenian:** Now that the recognition has taken place, Pythias can speak with conviction.

953 **I ... really don't know:** Parmeno had been present at the conversation between Phaedria and Thais at 110-13 about whether Pamphila was free-born. He probably

dismissed the possibility there (see 110n.), but his guarded response here may mean that he recalls what was said.

956   **while Thais was begging him not to do it:** A nice piece of embellishment by Pythias.

957   **what's usually done to adulterers:** In Athens, a husband who caught an adulterer in the act could deal with him in whatever way he wished (cf. Lysias 1. 49). He could kill him, or he "could inflict on the adulterer various bodily humiliations" (Harrison, A. R. W. (1968), *The Law of Athens, Part I: The Family and Property* (Oxford) 33). According to Aristophanes (*Clouds* 1083) these humiliations included the insertion of a large radish into the adulterer's anus, plucking out his pubic hair and piling on hot ashes. But generally in comedy the punishment was castration. In Plautus' *The Little Carthaginian* (*Poenulus*) 862-3 the slave Syncerastus says: "I'm doing something which adulterers caught in the act usually don't do...I'm taking home my equipment intact", and at the end of *The Swaggering Soldier* (1394ff.) the soldier Pyrgopolynices is threatened with castration but eventually gets away *salvis testibus* ("with balls intact", 1420). See also Hor. *S.* 1. 2. 44-6.

Of course, Chremes is not the husband, he has not caught Chaerea in the act, and Pamphila is not married (though the charge of adultery does seem to have embraced unmarried girls). But Pythias is making up a good story for effect, and is anyway no legal expert. Note her feigned reluctance to specify what the terrible punishment is.

Ter. uses the Greek word for adulterer, *moechus* (μοιχός, *moichos*) here and at 960, 992 (and *An.* 316).

960   **in the house of that sort of woman:** Lit. "in the house of a *meretrix*". Parmeno has a point here, inasmuch as sex with a *meretrix* / *hetaira* was not adultery. But it is the end result that counts, and Chaerea, albeit unknowingly, raped a free-born girl.

961   **I ... really don't know:** Pythias mockingly repeats Parmeno's response at 953.

962   **I solemnly tell you:** The Latin has the formal air of legal language, in the form of a dicolon crescendo with asyndeton, *dico edico* ("I state, I proclaim"). Parmeno is putting all the solemn force he can behind his words.

962-3 **What! Really?:** Pythias' feigned astonishment gives the opportunity for some splendid over-acting.

965   **do no good to him, and come to grief yourself:** As a slave, Parmeno could not expect his word to be taken seriously, and he could well get a good hiding for his pains.

967   **from the country:** Hence he will enter from the audience's left.

970   **you tell him everything:** The father's return is an unexpected bonus for Pythias, which she cannot have anticipated when she formed her plan. But she has the quick wit to encourage Parmeno to tell him the false story, since by 'going public' the slave will be made to look doubly foolish, and her triumph will be all the greater.

ACT FIVE SCENE FIVE

The father enters and, when Parmeno repeats Pythias' story to him, rushes into Thais' house to stop Chaerea's supposed punishment.

The old man (*senex*) has only a cameo role to play in this play, in contrast to his prominent place in other plays such as *Hau*. But even though he is on stage for only a short time, he exhibits several of the chief characteristics of his type - horror at his sons' activities

(986 etc.), worry over what effect they will have on his finances (984-5, 994-6), and threats to punish his slave (989-90).

Don. I 472 says: "It should be noted that this old man's name does not appear in Terence; in Menander he is called Simon." In the scene headings in the MSS, A calls him Demea and the Σ MSS call him Laches - both of them names borrowed from old men in other plays by Ter. See the note to the list of characters.

971 **my estate:** See 187n.

976 **I'm glad you've got back safely:** A conventional formula for a slave when greeting his returning master; cf. *Ph.* 286.

977 **I'm in such a panic ... :** Throughout this scene Parmeno reinforces the image of himself as a 'bungling' slave.

980 **whatever's happened:** Parmeno is again thinking of himself first (cf. 925n.), but this time in order to save his own skin.

984 **Twenty minae:** At 169 (where see n.), twenty minae was said by Phaedria to be the cost of *both* the eunuch *and* the Ethiopian slave-girl. The inconsistency is best explained by supposing that Parmeno has either simply mis-remembered or got mixed up in his present state of panic. In any event Phaedria will be the one more likely to have the facts correct.

985 **a music-girl:** See 133n.; Parmeno implies that Pamphila is a *meretrix*. He fails to mention the fact that she has been found to be free-born.
Has he come into town?: His father thinks that Chaerea is on duty in Piraeus; see 290n. Ter. uses the Greek word *astu* (ἄστυ), regularly used by Athenians to denote Athens (often as opposed to Piraeus).

988 **he didn't do it at my instigation:** As at 980, Parmeno is now quick to deny any responsibility for the escapade for which he was so recently (925) eager to claim the credit.

992 **they arrested him ... and tied him up:** Parmeno is again altering the story Pythias fed him. She had said (955) that Chremes tied Chaerea up, but Parmeno's use of the plural implies that Thais and her household did it. His purpose, as at 985, is to shift the blame on to the *meretrices* (cf. "See how shamelessly these women carry on", 994) and to avoid the awkward subject of the involvement of a citizen and his free-born sister.

996 **I must lose no time ... :** See 265n.

997ff. **There's no doubt ... :** Parmeno's short monologue masks the time it takes for Pythias to witness the father's discovery of the true facts before she emerges to confront the slave - though, by a common stage convention, the events off-stage would in real life take much longer than the five-line monologue allows; see 283-7n.

999 **trouble coming to this lot too:** Parmeno seems to be trying desperately to salvage some comfort in his misery. His hostility to Thais continues to the end.

1001 **to do something drastic to them:** Don. I 477 says: "Menander explains more clearly that the old man, for a long time hostile to the *meretrix* because Phaedria has been corrupted by her, will, now that he has found an opportunity, at last get his revenge." This implies that the father had a more prominent role in the original. It need not necessarily mean that he appeared on stage more, merely that his attitude was explained more fully by Phaedria and / or Parmeno and / or Thais.

ACT FIVE SCENE SIX

Pythias comes out of Thais' house, laughing at the success of her ruse, and explains to Parmeno how she has duped him. When Parmeno feebly threatens to get his own back, she points out that for the moment it is he who is going to be punished, and returns into the house.

The scene brings the revenge sub-plot to its conclusion - the triumph of Pythias and the downfall of Parmeno.

1002 **Really, there's nothing that's happened ... :** Pythias' monologue is a genuine one, not one spoken so that Parmeno will overhear it. Nevertheless the slave does overhear it, and sees what is coming to him.

1011 **a cunning, clever fellow:** The Latin for "cunning" is *callidus*, the customary epithet for the 'cunning slave' in this type of comedy. By using it here, Pythias stresses how far Parmeno has fallen short of that ideal.

1015 **dressed up in those clothes:** Chaerea has still not had time to change.

1019 **I'll pay you back:** In his present state, Parmeno's threats carry little conviction.

1021 **it's you who'll be strung up:** Lit. "you will hang." Slaves are regularly pictured as "hung up" to be flogged; their hands were tied to a cross-beam and weights were attached to their feet (Plautus, *Comedy of Asses* (*Asinaria*) 303-5). Cf. *Ph.* 220 ("I'll be strung up and flogged"), Plautus, *Casina* 1003, *The Brothers Menaechmus* 951 etc.

1023 **I'm off:** This is the last we see of Pythias. With the revenge sub-plot ended and her victory won, she has no more place in the play.

1024 **like a mouse by its squeaking:** The Latin word used, *sorex*, apparently means a shrew-mouse, as opposed to the ordinary mouse (*mus*). Don. I 480 says that this is a proverbial saying referring to "those who give themselves away, because a *sorex* is not easily caught unless it squeaks at night". He also says: "It is a characteristic of shrew-mice that they either squeak more clearly or make more noise than mice when they gnaw at their little bits of food."

ACT FIVE SCENE SEVEN

Thraso returns with Gnatho, explaining that he has come to surrender himself to Thais' wishes. Chaerea bursts out of his father's house.

Although his name is absent from the scene headings in all MSS, Parmeno is present during this scene (cf. Dorias in Act Four Scene Two). He was given no 'exit line' at the end of the previous scene, and must be on stage right at the start of the next one to hear Chaerea's words at 1031ff.

The characters from Men.'s *The Toady* return after an absence of over 200 lines, and are present for the final three scenes of the play. In these scenes, Thraso replaces the rival of Men.'s *The Eunuch*, but Gnatho has been added by Ter. from *The Toady*, either completely or to replace the rival's non-speaking slave / henchman (see further the introductory notes to the next two scenes).

Thus in Men. the rival will have returned, either alone or accompanied by a non-speaking actor, and stated his intention to surrender to Thais in a brief monologue.

1026 **to surrender myself to Thais:** Thraso's intentions go totally against the advice given him by Gnatho at 811-3 (that he go home and wait for Thais to come to him), which is why Gnatho is asking him what it is he is going to do.

1027 **as Hercules was Omphale's:** Hercules was told by the Delphic oracle that he could
only be cured of the madness brought on by his killing of Iphitus, son of King Eurytus
of Oechalia, if he was sold into slavery for three years and his price given to the boy's
father as blood-money. Hermes arranged the sale, Queen Omphale of Lydia was the
buyer, and Hercules performed a number of labours for her, including the capture of the
Cercopes and the killing of Syleus. In some versions of the myth, Omphale became his
wife and bore Lamus to him; more familiar is the version where she made him wear
women's clothes and perform women's work.

1028 **beaten to a pulp with her slipper:** Cf. Lucian 9. 10: "[Herakles] beaten by Omphale
with her slipper." Ter. keeps the Greek word (σανδάλιον, *sandalion*) which is rarely
found elsewhere in Latin. It occurs twice in the fragments of the writer of *palliatae*
Turpilius (see Introduction p. 8).

1029 **There's a noise at her door:** Lit. "Her doors have made a noise." By convention, in
both Greek and Roman comedy, the doors of the stage 'set' made a noise when they
were being opened from inside, and an actor could draw attention to this and alert the
audience to the emergence of a character from one of the houses. In practice, ancient
doors were noisy affairs, so this convention would appear fairly natural - though there is
no need to expect it to reflect real life exactly. For the difficulties which this matter has
caused, see Beare 285-94, Duckworth 116-17.

1030 **I've never seen this fellow before:** Thraso does not recognize Chaerea because he has
changed out of the eunuch's costume he was wearing when Thraso saw him at 472.
Chaerea must have changed - presumably into borrowed clothes - on his father's orders
(cf. Pythias' words at 1015-16). Don. I 482 has a less plausible explanation: "Chaerea
bursts out in the eunuch's costume but with virile confidence, and terrifies the soldier as
if by the appearance of a rival."

ACT FIVE SCENE EIGHT

Chaerea expresses his joy that Pamphila has been found to be free-born, that he is to marry
her and that Thais has found her patron in his father - thus ensuring a happy outcome for his
brother too.

Chaerea's problems are now over, and his relationship reaches its anticipated happy
ending. It seems, too, that Phaedria's troubles are set to reach a happy ending with the
complete ousting of the rival (1040, 1041) - which makes the unexpected solution actually
reached in the final scene all the more surprising (see the introductory note there).

The scene has four speaking characters. Gnatho makes only two small contributions
(1037, 1044), and is added by Ter.; see the introductory notes to the preceding and following
scenes. Thraso, too, makes only a small contribution (1043), but he takes the place of the
rival in Men.'s *The Eunuch*, who must have been on stage there to hear Chaerea's news.

In Men.'s *The Eunuch* the conversation between the Chaerea character and the slave
will thus have been overheard, and perhaps commented on, by the rival.

1031 **My fellow-countrymen:** Such an address to the public at large is also given by the
pimp Sannio appealing for help at *Ad.* 155, and is found in Plautus (e.g. *The Pot of Gold*
406, *The Rope* 615).

The reading of DELp, Don. and Eugr. (*me vivit hodie*) makes the line an iambic
octonarius like all the other lines in the scene. *me hodie vivit*, read by APCF (and

adopted by Kauer-Lindsay), makes it a trochaic septenarius, the metre of the previous scene.

1035 **deviser, initiator and perfecter:** The Latin words (*inventor, inceptor, perfector*) contain the assonance of which Chaerea appears so fond; cf. *cotidianarum harum formarum* 297, *mi ostentam, tantam, tam brevem, tam optatam, tam insperatam* 605.

1036 **So I've heard:** From Pythias (952).

she's engaged to me: Both Chaerea's father and Chremes would need to consent to the marriage. This consent is assumed rather than, as the author of the summary (*periocha*) implies (11-12), shown on stage.

1037 **Do you hear what he's saying?:** Gnatho's question produces no response from Thraso; it can be removed without affecting the rest of the scene in any way.

1039 **under our guardianship and protection:** The Latin words used here (*clientela* and *fides*) reflect specifically Roman juridical terminology; cf. Cic. *S. Rosc.* 93: "ask under whose protection and guardianship they are" (*quaere in cuius fide sint et tutela*); but this does not necessarily mean that something corresponding to this idea did not appear in the original - only the wording need be Roman. The Greek idea of a *prostates* (προστάτης) was essentially similar to that of a *patronus* at Rome, and the idea could well have appeared in that form in Men.

1040 **She's all your brother's then?:** The affirmative reply to this question, and "the captain's being kicked out" (1041), implying as they do total victory for Phaedria, are at variance with what happens in the final scene.

1041 **the captain's being kicked out:** The verb is in the present tense (*pellitur*) in A, G and L. This seems more in keeping with the present tenses in 1038 ("we're all one household now") and 1040 ("She's all your brother's then") than the future tense (*pelletur*) in D, P, C, F and E, which is favoured by Kauer-Lindsay.

1042 **wherever he is:** Chaerea was absent when Phaedria returned from the country and questioned Dorus, and so knows nothing of his whereabouts.

I'll go and see if he's at home: Parmeno does not reappear after he goes into the father's house. His part in the play thus ends on a low note, as befits his less-than-successful role. But we can assume that the punishment threatened by the father (989-90) will not be meted out.

1043-4 **There's no doubt ... no doubt at all ... :** As Gnatho has been added to this scene by Ter., Thraso's question and the toady's reply may replace a simple comment by the rival in Men.'s original.

1047 **into just one day:** These words stress the so-called 'unity of time' whereby the events of a play are concluded in a single day; cf. the young man Sostratos in Men.'s *The Bad-Tempered Man* 864-5: "In one single day I've achieved a marriage that nobody would ever have thought possible." This unity was not always observed; the action in *Hau.* (Brothers (1998) 192) and in Plautus' *The Prisoners* certainly extends over more than one day, and this was possibly also the case in Men.'s *The Arbitration* (Gomme and Sandbach 325-6).

1049 The scene ends part-way through a line, something which occurs elsewhere in Ter. only at *An.* 580, *Hau.* 954, *Ph.* 795, *Hec.* 767, and *Ad.* 81, 635, 958. In most of these instances, as here, some MSS do not mark a new scene, and this is an indication of the haphazard nature of such scene-divisions.

ACT FIVE SCENE NINE

Phaedria comes out of his father's house to congratulate his brother on his new-found good fortune. Thraso asks Gnatho for help so that he can retain some place in Thais' affections, but when Phaedria sees him he is firmly rebuffed. Gnatho, however, negotiates an arrangement whereby Thraso and Phaedria share Thais and he himself is admitted into Phaedria's circle.

The solution arrived at in this final scene is not what we have been led to expect from Chaerea's remarks in the preceding one (see 1040n.). It had seemed there that Thraso was "being kicked out" (1041), but instead we find him included in the arrangements by being allowed continued access to Thais. When we try to relate this ending to what may have happened in Men.'s *The Eunuch* and *The Toady*, the situation is, of course, complicated by the fact that we do not know how either of Men.'s plays ended. But there is evidence that an unexpected ending, a 'sting in the tail', was at least sometimes favoured by Men. In *The Bad-Tempered Man*, when the name-character has made his dispositions and we expect him to be left in peace, he is forced, in a rollicking final scene, to join in the celebrations against his wishes and despite his protests; and in the original of Ter.'s *Ad.* (if Ter. has been faithful to it), the Micio character finds the tables unexpectedly turned on him.

Thus the ending of Men.'s *The Eunuch*, involving the Phaedria and Chaerea characters and the rival, may have shown some sort of unexpected deal between the two lovers of the *hetaira* (which may or may not have been the one pictured in Ter.). But the substitution of the Thraso character from *The Toady*, and the importation from the same source of 'Gnatho' (again the obvious fourth speaking actor added by Ter.), may have introduced further unexpected elements. Certainly Thraso seems at first sight to get more than he deserves. He has been portrayed as an unsympathetic character to whom no concessions need be made (even at the end of a comedy), but he gets at least some of what he wants by being allowed a share in Thais' company. On the other hand, his grovelling request to Gnatho (1054-5) to secure this by any means is a great humiliation for him, and his role in the arrangement will cost him dear, since he will not only have to support Thais' expenses (1073-82), but also continue to provide open house for Gnatho (1058-60); so perhaps he gets his just deserts after all. But it seems, to modern eyes at least, more difficult to justify Gnatho's share in the arrangement. He has been shown to be even more unpleasant than Thraso, yet the play ends on a note of victory for him, since he not only secures the open-ended invitation to Thraso's table already mentioned, but is also granted admission to Phaedria's circle (1084-5).

There is a strange aspect, too, to the solution as it affects Phaedria. It seems out of character for someone who all along has been portrayed as a jealous and possessive lover, unwilling to share Thais' favours, to be so quickly persuaded to share her with Thraso. It is very tempting to see this inconsistent characterization as due to the transfer of the solution worked out for the young man of *The Toady* to the ending of Ter.'s play. If we seek to explain the outcome for the Phaedria of Ter.'s play, we can argue that his over-romantic approach to love may not have struck too sympathetic a note with a Roman audience, and perhaps it is fair that he does not get things all his own way. Yet, on the credit side, he is relieved of the burden of financing Thais himself and must be aware that, as Gnatho points out (1080), Thais does not love Thraso and that he himself can get rid of the captain whenever it suits him.

A final oddity is that Thais, who has been shown to be quite capable of managing her own affairs, has her future arranged for her in her absence and behind her back. But we must not get over-sentimental about her (see Barsby (1999) 281). She has acquired her patron, and she is, after all, a *meretrix*, and *meretrices* are not one-man girls. Will she really be so upset that, when she has got the impecunious Phaedria, she will also have access to Thraso's money to indulge her more expensive tastes?

So two characters (Thraso and Gnatho) get more than they deserve, while one (Phaedria) gets less than he wants. Does the play perhaps show the somewhat negative view that love in all its forms (and several forms have been depicted) is in the end not simply a matter of the heart, but partly also a deal, a matter of making suitable compromises and concessions?

1049 **Heavens, what an incredible tale ... :** This is the first occasion in the play where the two brothers meet.

1050 **Parmeno's just told me:** When the slave went in at 1042.

1054-5 **By begging and bribes:** The Latin employs a dicolon with asyndeton and alliteration: *precibus pretio.*

1058-9 **I demand that you keep open house for me:** Gnatho's price is the toady's greatest desire, an open invitation to eat at Thraso's table even when the latter is not at home.

1063 **I solemnly say to you ... :** This may indicate that in Men's *The Eunuch* the rival was sent packing, in which case Gnatho's "that's no way to behave" (1065) switches the plot to the ending of *The Toady*. But it has been seen (cf. the introductory note to the scene) that the ending of Men.'s *The Eunuch* need not have been so straightforward.

The whole of Phaedria's speech in 1063-5 ("You know what ... you've had it") is ascribed to Chaerea in A; but it must be Phaedria, not his brother, who rejects the rival. This is the first of several occasions in this scene (1066, 1068, 1086, 1094) where the MSS disagree about who speaks certain words.

1068 **Let's hear him:** While the Σ MSS ascribe these words to Phaedria, A is surely right in giving them to Chaerea. It is better that Chaerea has to urge his brother to give Gnatho a hearing, rather than that Phaedria should give way at once, so soon after showing his hostility to Thraso.

Go over there a bit: A clear instance of use of the wide stage, to ensure that Thraso appears out of earshot.

1070 **with my own interests in mind:** Gnatho's self-centred view of life in a nutshell.

1075 **she, perforce, must be given a lot:** Gnatho either pictures Thais as a typically greedy *meretrix*, or is simply telling the truth about the size of her household; in either case, it is in his interests to do so in order to get Phaedria to agree to the deal.

1079 **he's silly, stupid and slow:** The toady openly states what he really thinks of Thraso for the first time - though a number of his asides earlier in the play have made his views clear.

1080 **You needn't be afraid ... :** Gnatho has correctly judged Thais' opinion of Thraso (cf. her references to his "stupidity" and "pompous talk" at 741). His remarks are aimed at reassuring Phaedria (and the audience) about where her real affections lie.

1081 **What do we do?:** Most editors (including those of the Oxford Text) agree with Bentley in giving these words to Chaerea, but it is preferable to follow the MSS, which ascribe them to Phaedria. Phaedria is wavering and asks his brother for advice, which Chaerea gives in 1083.

1084 **I've got one more thing to ask:** Gnatho's request seems to contradict his earlier one (1058-60) to be allowed permanent free access to the hospitality of Thraso (of whom he now says he has had enough). Perhaps he now sees that he is on to a better thing with Phaedria, or perhaps his never-ending appetite requires two men's tables to be satisfied. Either way Gnatho is further characterized.

1085 **pushing this particular stone uphill:** Gnatho likens his present life of toadying to Thraso to the punishment of Sisyphus in the Underworld. Sisyphus was forced to push a huge rock up to the top of a hill, but, every time it nearly reached the top, it rolled back down to the bottom and he had to start again. In Plautus' *The Swaggering Soldier* 1024 the soldier Pyrgopolynices is compared to a stone (*saxum* as here): "No stone is more stupid than this fellow."

We accept you: It is strange to find Phaedria (backed up by Chaerea, 1086) accepting Gnatho without a murmur; this is all part of the particular awkwardness of the ending as it affects the toady. But we are presumably meant to assume that the brothers agree in gratitude for Gnatho's securing Thraso's wealth for Thais (and, in a way, for them).

1086 **Phaedria and you, too, Chaerea:** The double naming has a legal solemnity about it, as befits the clinching of a deal.

1087 **I give you Thraso:** Spoken in the context of proposing a toast; cf. "Ladies and gentlemen, I give you the Queen."

1089 **These fellows didn't know you:** A final piece of monstrous flattery (and falsehood) from Gnatho.

1092 **I've never been anywhere ... :** To the end Thraso remains firmly fixed in his own world of self-delusion.

1093 **Attic polish:** The Athenians were proverbial for their sophistication. Thraso himself was not native Athenian (759).

1094 **Come this way:** The players retire into one of the houses, though there is no indication in the text of which one. It must be Thais' house, because she herself and the brothers' father are already there.

Farewell, and give us your applause: All Ter.'s plays end with a direct appeal to the audience, though in *An., Hec.* and *Ad.* it is reduced to "Give us your applause". In Plautus (e.g. *The Comedy of Asses (Asinaria)* 942-7, *The Prisoners* 1029-36, *The Tale of a Trunk* 782-7) it is sometimes considerably more elaborate. Since there was no curtain in the theatres of Ter.'s day (see Introduction p. 10), some such indication is required to signal that the performance is at an end. These addresses to the spectators reflect the endings of the plays of Greek New Comedy appealing for applause and for success in the dramatic competitions at which the plays were originally staged; cf. Men.'s *The Bad-Tempered Man* 965-9, *The Girl from Samos* 733-7.

In our MSS of Ter. the words of the appeal are prefixed by the symbol ω. Bentley (on *An.* 981) thought this was a corruption of **CA.**, the abbreviation for the Latin *cantor* "singer", and compared Hor. *Ars* 154-5: "if you want an approving listener, who waits for the curtain [such as was used in later Roman theatres] and who will remain seated until the singer says 'Give me your applause'." In Plautus the appeal is spoken by the whole troupe of players or by a single actor, and the same may well have applied in the case of Ter. I have followed the traditional view about the *cantor*, but doubt must remain.

Index

Numbers in plain type refer to pages; numbers in bold type refer to line numbers in the commentary.

PUBLISHED VOLUMES IN THE SERIES

full details including printing status and lists of contents are obtainable from Aris & Phillips website:

www.arisandphillips.com

AESCHYLUS
THE EUMENIDES ed. A.J. Podlecki
THE PERSIANS ed. E. Hall

APPIAN
THE WARS OF THE ROMANS IN IBERIA ed. J.S. Richardson

ARISTOPHANES ed. A.H. Sommerstein
ACHARNIANS
BIRDS
CLOUDS
KNIGHTS
LYSISTRATA
PEACE
WASPS
THESMOPHORIAZUSAE
FROGS
ECCLESIAZUSAE

ARISTOTLE
ON THE HEAVENS I & II ed. S. Leggatt
ON SLEEP AND DREAMS ed. D. Gallop

AUGUSTINE
SOLILOQUIES *and* IMMORTALITY OF THE SOUL ed. G. Watson

CAESAR
CIVIL WAR Books I & II ed. J.M. Carter
CIVIL WAR III ed. J.M. Carter

CASSIUS DIO
ROMAN HISTORY Books 53.1-55.9 ed. J.W. Rich

CATULLUS
SHORTER POEMS ed J. Godwin
POEMS 61-68 ed. J. Godwin

CICERO
TUSCULAN DISPUTATIONS I ed. A.E. Douglas
TUSCULAN DISPUTATIONS II & V ed. A.E. Douglas
ON FATE with **BOETHIUS** CONSOLATION V ed. R.W. Sharples
PHILIPPICS II ed. W.K. Lacey
VERRINES II.1 ed. T.N. Mitchell
ON STOIC GOOD AND EVIL ed. M.R. Wright
LAELIUS ON FRIENDSHIP and THE DREAM OF SCIPIO ed. J.G.F. Powell
LETTERS OF JANUARY TO APRIL 43 B.C. ed. M.M. Willcock

EURIPIDES
ALCESTIS ed. D. Conacher
ANDROMACHE ed. M. Lloyd
BACCHAE ed. R. Seaford
ELECTRA ed. M.J. Cropp
HECUBA ed. C. Collard
HERACLES ed. S. Barlow
HIPPOLYTUS ed M.R. Halleran
ION ed K.H. Lee
IPHIGENIA IN TAURIS ed. M.J. Cropp
ORESTES ed. M.L. West
PHOENICIAN WOMEN ed. E. Craik
SELECTED FRAGMENTARY PLAYS I ed. C. Collard, M.J Cropp, K.H. Lee
TROJAN WOMEN ed. S. Barlow

GREEK ORATORS
I   ANTIPHON, LYSIAS, ed. M. Edwards, S. Usher
II   DINARCHUS I, HYPERIDES 5 & 6 ed. I. Worthington
III ISOCRATES Panegyricus and To Nicocles, ed. S. Usher
IV   ANDOCIDES ed. M. Edwards
V   DEMOSTHENES On the Crown, ed. S. Usher
VI   APOLLODORUS against Neaira, ed. C. Carey

HELLENICA OXYRHYNCHIA ed. P.R. McKechnie & S.J. Kern

HOMER
ODYSSEY I & II ed. P.V. Jones
ILIAD VIII & IX ed. C. Wilson

HORACE
SATIRES I ed. P.M. Brown
SATIRES II ed. F. Muecke

JOSEPH OF EXETER
THE TROJAN WAR I-III ed. A.K. Bate

LIVY ed. P.G. Walsh
XXXVI
XXXVII
XXXVIII
XXXIX
XL

LUCAN
CIVIL WAR VIII ed. R. Mayer

LUCIAN
A SELECTION ed. M.D. Macleod

LUCRETIUS
DE RERUM NATURA III ed. P.M. Brown

DE RERUM NATURA IV ed. J. Godwin
DE RERUM NATURA VI ed. J. Godwin

MARTIAL
EPIGRAMS V ed. P. Howell

MENANDER
SAMIA ed. D.M. Bain
THE BAD-TEMPERED MAN ed. S. Ireland

OVID
AMORES II ed. J. Booth
METAMORPHOSES I-IV ed. D.E. Hill
METAMORPHOSES V-VIII ed. D.E. Hill
METAMORPHOSES IX-XII ed. D.E. Hill
METAMORPHOSES XIII-XV ed. D.E. Hill

PERSIUS
THE SATIRES ed. J.R. Jenkinson

PINDAR
SELECTED ODES ed. S. Instone

PLATO
APOLOGY ed. M.C. Stokes
MENO ed. R.W. Sharples
PHAEDRUS ed. C.J. Rowe
REPUBLIC V ed. S. Halliwell
REPUBLIC X ed. S. Halliwell
STATESMAN ed.C.J. Rowe
SYMPOSIUM ed. C.J. Rowe

PLAUTUS
BACCHIDES ed. J.A. Barsby

PLINY
CORRESPONDENCE WITH TRAJAN FROM BITHYNIA ed. W. William

PLUTARCH
LIVES OF ARISTEIDES AND CATO ed. D. Sansone
LIFE OF CICERO ed. J.L. Moles
MALICE OF HERODOTUS ed. A.J. Bowen
LIFE OF THEMISTOCLES ed. J.L. Marr

THE RUODLIEB ed. C.W. Grocock

SENECA
FOUR DIALOGUES ed. C.D.N. Costa
LETTERS: a selection ed. C.D.N. Costa
MEDEA ed. H.M. Hine

SOPHOCLES
AJAX ed. A.F. Garvie

ANTIGONE ed. A.L. Brown
PHILOCTETES ed. R.G. Ussher

SUETONIUS
LIVES OF GALBA, OTHO AND VITELLIUS ed. D.C.A. Shotter

TACITUS
ANNALS IV ed. D.C.A. Shotter
ANNALS V & VI ed. R. Martin
GERMANY ed. H.W. Benario

TERENCE
THE BROTHERS ed. A.S. Gratwick
THE EUNUCH ed. A.J. Brothers
THE MOTHER-IN-LAW ed. S. Ireland
THE SELF-TORMENTOR ed. A.J. Brothers

THUCYDIDES
HISTORY II ed. P.J. Rhodes
HISTORY III, ed. P.J. Rhodes
HISTORY IV–V.24. ed. P.J. Rhodes
PYLOS 425 BC: IV.2-41 ed. J. Wilson

WILLIAM OF NEWBURGH
THE HISTORY OF ENGLISH AFFAIRS I ed. P.G. Walsh, M. Kennedy

XENOPHON
HELLENIKA I-II.3.10 ed. P. Krentz
HELLENIKA II.3.11-IV.2.8 ed. P. Krentz
SYMPOSIUM, ed. A.J. Bowen
ON HUNTING with **ARRIAN** ON HUNTING ed. A.A. Phillips, M.M. Willcock